Charles Jencks was born in 1939 in the USA and now lives in London. He studied English Literature and Architecture at Harvard, and has a Ph.D. in Architecture from London University, where he studied under Reyner Banham. His publications include *Meaning in Architecture* (edited with George Baird, 1969), *Architecture 2000 – Predictions and Methods* (1971), *Adhocism* (with Nathan Silver, 1972), and *Le Corbusier and the Tragic View of Architecture* (to be published later in 1973), and he has contributed to various architectural journals.

CHARLES JENCKS

MODERN MOVEMENTS IN ARCHITECTURE

Penguin Books

Penguin Books Ltd, Harmondsworth, Middlesex, England
Penguin Books Inc., 7110 Ambassador Road, Baltimore, Maryland 21207, U.S.A.
Penguin Books Australia Ltd, Ringwood, Victoria, Australia

First published 1973
Copyright © Charles Jencks, 1973

Filmset by Oliver Burridge Filmsetting Ltd
and printed in Great Britain
at the University Press, Oxford
by Vivian Ridler
Printer to the University

Designed by Gerald Cinamon and Paul McAlinden

ACKNOWLEDGEMENTS

In a historical study such as this, one builds up enormous debts, of very different kinds, which should be acknowledged, if not adequately paid back. Perhaps the most important debt is to those whose ideas have shaped the book: Hannah Arendt's ideas on politics and revolution, I. A. Richards's and Coleridge's ideas on the imagination, and E. H. Gombrich's ideas on the way art, or here architecture, can communicate meaning. The reader will find detailed acknowledgement of these ideas in the notes, but I must emphasize here my utmost gratitude to these people. Without their writings, and example, this book would never have developed. I feel a similar kind of gratitude to the architects Le Corbusier, James Stirling and Aldo van Eyck whose work and presence have also sustained my interest in the whole project.

There is a different kind of creditor, to whom I am indebted for personal aid, discussion, gossip, first hand information and just acquaintance: the students of the Architectural Association where I have been teaching, the architects Peter Cook, Joseph Zalewski and Alan Colquhoun, the historians Thomas Stevens and Eduard Sekler and a constant friend, the architectural theorist George Baird. Without these people, and the ever present stimulus of *Architectural Design*, this book would have been out of date and architecturally irrelevant. The last named magazine has been especially important in keeping my thoughts on edge and information diverse. Even when I disagree with its policy and trenchant comments, I am aware that its choice of subject is unique and its eye for architectural relevance the most acute.

Finally a word of thanks to my two critics – Reyner Banham who supervised this book in an earlier form when it was a thesis and my editor Nikos Stangos who suggested alterations and cuts. Just to invert convention, I would like to say that if any omissions, errors or infelicities remain, they are solely the fault of my two critics, but I am acutely conscious that the reverse is true. They have been tough, vigilant and creative in their close readings – ideal readers in a sense – and I alone remain, alas, responsible for any faults which still exist.

Charles Jencks
London, July 1971

MODERN MOVEMENTS
IN ARCHITECTURE

INTRODUCTION: THE PLURALITY OF APPROACHES

Every critical opinion is an ellipsis; a conditional assertion, with the conditional part omitted. (I. A. RICHARDS)

There is a conventional view among historians and the general public that some unified theory and practice called 'Modern Architecture' really exists. Perhaps, from time to time, this capital-lettered concept has enjoyed a wide understanding and informed consensus, so that it does make sense to call this area of agreement Modern Architecture. But more often than not its use is generally informed by ignorance. Those who use it are either unaware of the plurality of live architectural traditions, or else they hope to coalesce this plurality into some integrated movement. For instance, when one hears a historian say 'The Modern Movement', one knows what to expect next: some all-embracing theory, one or two lines of architectural development, something called 'the true style of our century', and a single melodrama with heroes and villains who perform their expected roles according to the historian's loaded script. Dazzled by this display of a consistent plot and inexorable development, the reader forgets to ask about all the missing actors and their various feats – all that which ends up on the scrap heap of the historian's rejection pile. In part this selection and omission of data is desirable, since it creates some conceptual order out of the overwhelming complexity of detail. But unfortunately it often serves to reinforce one ideology – one tradition of development – at the expense of a live plurality.

This can be shown with one characteristic example. Nikolaus Pevsner, in his *Pioneers of Modern Design*,[1] gives a very clear account of certain developments that led, as his sub-title explains, 'From William Morris to Walter Gropius'. Looking back after thirty years at his book, he said in 1966:

> To me what had been achieved in 1914 was *the* style of the century. It never occurred to me to look beyond. Here was the one and only style which fitted all those aspects which mattered, aspects of economics and sociology, of materials and function.[2]

This candid admission is very interesting for what it helps explain about Pevsner's and other historians' work. Like so many of his generation, Pevsner believes that there is a deterministic relation between certain content and form, or 'those aspects' which he mentions and '*the* style' – instead of adopting the more flexible notion that the relation between style and content is 'unmotivated'.[3] Furthermore, Pevsner's statement is a frank avowal of his own selective values. And this obviously explains why he originally left out two such important architects as Gaudi and Sant'Elia – whom he called 'freaks' and 'fantasts' until, as he suggests, the swing of opinion forced him to insert them into the main body of the text.

There are many such 'ideological' omissions in Pevsner's book, as in all histories of modern architecture,[4] and we could justify them as the historian's 'interpretative licence' if their effect were not so profound. For what has been the historian's actual effect on architectural history? Conservative, élitist and prophetic. This has been as much as anything because architectural theory has become itself historicist, or motivated by arguments which contend that there is one inevitable line of development. In one of the key theoretical formulations, *Vers une architecture* (1923), Le Corbusier tried to persuade his listeners that 'industry [is] overwhelming us like a flood which rolls on toward its destined ends'. Perhaps his ideals were positive and the effect salutary, but the method of argument was as dangerous as any determinism, which contends that one should follow the general trend of realistic events wherever they lead.

The historian of recent architecture has, for the most part, followed the same line of argument by implicitly becoming either an apologist for a single tradition, say the International Style, or the prophet of inevitable development, say technology and structural determinism. Practising architects and the public are naturally persuaded by these convincing arguments and so the amount of live traditions or alternatives to the future is radically limited. Because of such suppression two architectural movements, Futurism and Expressionism, were surgically removed from our memory for thirty years. However, this kind of omission may be due as much to the historian's methodology as to his ideology. Trained to look for links between architects, he assumes they always exist. As the very basis of his work, he looks for links between contemporaries or across time as if there were either one all-pervasive world tradition which everyone was in touch with, or only one possible moral and logical development.

Opposed to both the *Zeitgeist* theory and the single strand theory, this study of recent architecture postulates a *series of discontinuous movements* and treats this pluralism with different methods, in different chapters. This is not to say, however, that I will or even could avoid omitting certain architects and keep from using selective concepts. As the reader will soon discover, I have made use of various ideas such as multivalence, Camp, and the 'six' traditions' which are just as restrictive as other concepts. The use of concepts is as inevitable in historical writing as in science, a point which is amusingly made by E. H. Gombrich in his discussion of 'Classification and its Discontents'.[5] The crucial questions are whether the concepts illuminate their objects, have great explanatory power, are relevant in themselves and as plural as the developments.

At a certain level of abstraction, there are basically two kinds of historically relevant material: the influential (or that which is interesting because of its importance as a link in a significant chain) and the perfected (or that which has value in itself, as a small, internally relevant world). The first kind of event is part of a movement; literally a development within a tradition or problem situation. Such is the development of the communal house in Russia, or the Pop movement in England, to take two widely different and discontinuous examples discussed in later chapters. The relevance of this kind of developing tradition is best brought out by historical narrative, whereas the second kind of event or building is best analysed critically for its internal relations. For instance the *multivalent* work of Le Corbusier, James Stirling and Aldo van Eyck is so significant in itself that historical narrative has to stop – and analysis of internal relations take over.

Since we are all the time making qualitative judgements about buildings and in particular since a selective history is based on judgement above all, I think it is necessary to devote some space to explaining the criterion for selection adopted here. Certain buildings have a richness and density of meaning which make them more enjoyable to inhabit, view and visit than others. These are the buildings which are reinterpreted anew by every generation. We return to them again and again, not necessarily because of any particular meaning which they may convey, but more because of the exciting and deep way in which the meanings are interrelated or fused together into a powerful pattern. For this quality I have adopted the general term multivalence because it points to the presence of multi-valued levels of meaning.[6] To be more precise, multi-valence consists of four distinct qualities: imaginative *creation*, or the putting together of parts in a new way, the *amount* of parts so transformed, the *linkage* between the parts which is the cause of this creation and which allows the parts to *modify* each other. By far the most concrete way of demonstrating the theory of multivalence is to apply it to two works which differ in quality – one by Le Corbusier which shows imaginative fusion and the other by Frederick Gibberd which shows an aggregation of parts that is univalent.

UNITÉ D'HABITATION AND LIVERPOOL CATHEDRAL

The *Unité d'Habitation* by Le Corbusier [1] is probably, within architectural circles at any rate, one of the most famous post-war buildings in the world. It has received much attention in the Press, not all of it favourable, and it remains a prime object of architectural pilgrimage whether by students or practising architects – most of whom are trying to work out the advantages and mistakes of a megastructure and the social ideals of the *Ville Radieuse* which inspired it. In fact the ideals which inspired it go back much further than this and rest ultimately on a series of diverse traditions which Le Corbusier has turned upside-down and synthesized in a creative way.

GARDERIE D'ENFANTS
RAMPE (SERVICE SANTÉ, 17e ETAGE SUD)
TOUR D'ASCENSEURS
CHEMINÉE DE VENTILATION
MUR BRISE-VENT (THÉÂTRE)
GYMNASE
VESTIAIRES ET TERRASSE SUPÉRIEURE
RUES INTÉRIEURES
SERVICES COMMUNS DE RAVITAILLEMENT
LOGGIAS BRISE-SOLEIL
ESCALIER DE SECOURS
TERRAIN ARTIFICIEL (MACHINERIES)
LES PILOTIS

NORD

1. Le Corbusier: Unité d'Habitation, Marseilles, France, 1947–52, explanatory section and elevation. Called by Le Corbusier 'A Habitational Unit of Appropriate Size', this 'home' for 1,600 people contains twenty-six different kinds of communal facilities; the *amount* of elements is a criterion of multivalence.

For instance, he took the idea of an autonomous living unity from Fourier's *Phalanstère* – a nineteenth-century commune of manageable size which would determine its own collective destiny – and envisioned a city made up of them. To see the inversion of the traditional idea, one has only to recall the recurrent Utopian theme of a small, isolated community set off from the unmanageable city. Both the traditional monastery and the Utopian communities of, say, Robert Owen follow this pattern. And yet although Le Corbusier was directly inspired by the Monastery of Ema and Fourier's Utopian socialism,[7] he really intended his *Unité* as part of larger city schemes – either the *Ville Radieuse* or his replanning projects for St Die and Marseilles, etc. Thus the autonomy and self-sufficiency which is evident in the *Unité* should be seen as only partly intended. What Le Corbusier really wanted was to house the four million French families which were made homeless in the war in a series of related *Unités* which would spread all across France and, most importantly, keep the landscape free from suburban sprawl.

In addition to this inversion of traditional Utopias, his major, social intention was something of a paradox – although a paradox which was shared by most modern architects. This is that family life, the domestic everyday life of the home, is elevated to the level of a public monument. Here is the closest modern equivalent to the Greek Temple [2]; and yet to the Greeks those people who were given over to private, domestic matters were called 'idiots' because they had not entered the public realm where they could become educated and gain their political rights. As if this inversion of classical values were not enough, Le Corbusier has also made other unusual combinations of past traditions: the columns taper downwards

15

instead of up, the landscape and garden are on the roof instead of the ground, the streets are in the air and internal instead of being external and on the ground, and the shopping centre is on the seventh floor instead of being connected with the commercial life of Marseilles.

All of these inversions were enough to cause difficulty to the inhabitants and to outrage the popular and professional Press. For instance, Jane Jacobs condemned the shopping centre for being unrealistically removed from the city, Lewis Mumford criticized the long, narrow apartment units for being too thin, Sigfried Giedion faulted the internal streets for being dark corridors, and the popular Press attacked the whole idea of housing 1,600 people in a vast, anonymous, inhuman beehive. But all of these faults and affronts to traditional usage could be, and in fact were, defended as positive creations: the autonomous shopping centre gives both identity and convenience to the inhabitants; the long apartments cut down the strong Mediterranean sun, give cross-ventilation and provide a variety of new spatial experiences; the small interior corridors save money and provide a contrast to the brilliant views from within the apartments; and the housing of 340 families in a unit avoids the suburban sprawl and gives the inhabitants the mixture of anonymity and social intercourse one finds on a ship or in a resort hotel. Indeed one could say that if the Provençal farmer would feel lonely and out of place here, at least the urbanite professor and monastic bachelor would find it most suitable (as they have in fact done). On the whole, then, one finds in the *Unité* a balance of positive goals with negative

2. Le Corbusier: Unité d'Habitation, east façade. The columnar order carries a gigantic entablature of domestic accommodation divided up by the circulation core and shopping centre.

consequences which is not uncommon in any multivalent architecture. If a work has multiple determinants it will allow different plausible interpretations, some of which although opposite are equally valid. Such is the case with those four criticisms cited above.

Returning to the primary inversion of public and private domains, one finds this idea carried through right to the interior. The kitchen, the place where the housewife conducts the family affairs with all her mechanical appliances, is the centre of each apartment [3]. Le Corbusier under-

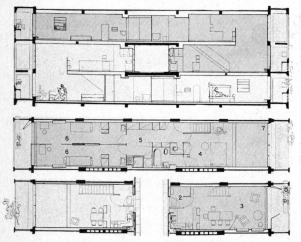

3. Le Corbusier: Unité d'Habitation, section and plan. Apartments interlock around a central corridor; the kitchen and bathroom cores are located above and below it, while the parents' and children's bedrooms are placed furthest apart.

lined her role as custodian by accentuating her place in the 'new hearth' of the home. In fact, the exaggerated symbolic importance given to every element of family life was an old idea of Le Corbusier's, going back to the twenties when he formulated the house as the central problem of contemporary architecture. He proposed that the major social disruptions caused by industrialization – uprootedness, chaos – would be answered primarily by re-establishing the harmony of daily life and the home. That many critics see the *Unité* as an archetypal image of the uprooted life – the ship, the hotel or monastery – once again just underlines the paradoxical nature of Le Corbusier's creation. But he obviously saw it as re-establishing the cosmic harmony of man with nature that had been destroyed by rapid urbanization. Hence his pronouncements on introducing all the activities of the twenty-four-hour life cycle into one unity and placing men into a direct and unmediated relation to the natural landscape.

Exploring his intentions further, we find a commitment to a multitude of positive qualities which is almost without parallel. He provides: (a) twenty-three different apartment types to comprehend the variety of family sizes; (b) all made absolutely private through sound insulation and placement within a frame; (c) all placed apart from

4. Le Corbusier: Unité d'Habitation, roofscape with heroic foul-air stack, running track, ramp to the nursery school, etc. An example of compaction composition; see also [93].

the usual urban vices of traffic fumes and noise; (d) integrated with twenty-six different kinds of communal facilities [4], such as a nursery-school and gymnasium on the roof; (e) the whole unified behind a Purist aesthetic which is, at the same time, a technical form of mass-production. For instance, if one investigates the pre-cast system on the exterior or the repetitive wall units on the interior, one finds that a small number of similar elements have been used in a variety of different positions. This has the effect of making what appears to be a purely gratuitous formal gesture into an economic and technical rationale. Since both interpretations are equally valid, one can enjoy seeing the objects become modified as they slip from one level of interpretation to another. Since this *modification* is another criterion of multivalence, it would be well to look at another small example of it in detail: the window seat [5]. Actually this L-shaped form is not so specifically a seat as it is also a table, a structural stabilizer, an outdoor storage container, a place for children to hide under, and a part of the modular order which merges with several other visual contexts. From within the apartment it becomes part of the view over the trees and landscape, while from the side the L-shape merges with the other geometric elements in a white, rhythmic drama sharpened by the strong sun. In short there are eight immediate contexts for this single form to work in, or, put another way, there are at least eight links to different contexts. If each one of

5. **Le Corbusier: Unité d'Habitation,** window-seat-table-etc.

6 (*opposite*). **Frederick Gibberd: Liverpool Cathedral, 1960-67.** The exterior divides into three major planes, all of which are comparatively unrelated in form, colour and material (sheet aluminium, concrete, and stone).

these links modifies the way the form is seen and used, it also modifies the surrounding area, making it richer in meaning.

Turning now to the Liverpool Cathedral [6], we can see how poor univalent form is in linkage. To begin with the exterior, it is apparent that each part of the design is abstracted from a previous context: the crown of thorns and structure is reminiscent of Niemeyer's work in Brazil; the use of stained glass recalls Perret's church in Le Havre; the symbolic door and bell tower remind one more of

Breuer's work than they invite original contemplation; the concrete intaglio is similar to Wright's and the pinnacles and finials are clearly pseudo-Gothic.

The fact that these motifs are borrowed is not so disturbing as the fact that nothing original is done with their interrelation by way of either contrast or integration. Each element is just slammed into the next as if it didn't exist. The structural pylons remain mere technical necessities unmodified by their relation to other elements: they break through the artificial ground level without any acknowledgement and then go on to bash through three more horizontal bands in a ham-fisted way as if the architect had wished to create the soaring gesture of Niemeyer's cathedral and then lost conviction at each state of the heavenward flight. If somehow this loss of faith were

acknowledged instead of being denied behind the neat, polished surfaces, then at least the architect could have made an ironic contrast to his primary intention – a contrast which Le Corbusier often uses to his advantage, as we will see. Instead, through constrained rectitude in detailing, Gibberd has kept up the pretence that he meant the forms to be exactly as they appear. Thus taken on their face value the protruding chapels have to be taken literally: as half-hearted polygonal constructions tacked on to a circular ground plan – a compromise between technical necessities and formal requirements. They are scaleless, clumsy, inert masses of stone whose primitive gesture is again denied by their precise finish – an example of ambiguity which is not sustained because the intentional poles are too far apart: i.e. there are not enough mediating elements which are also ambiguous.

On the interior, the same univalent literalism is apparent throughout. The 'crown of thorns' which, as one would guess, 'symbolizes the kingship of Christ' on the outside, also, as one would predict, crowns the high altar on the inside [7]. There is simply no discovery, or surprise,

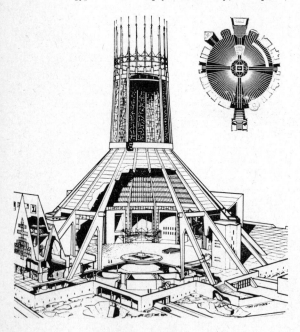

7. **Frederick Gibberd: Liverpool Cathedral,** cutaway perspective and ground plan showing sixteen concrete pylons around the circular nave and slightly raised high altar.

8 (*opposite*). **Frederick Gibberd: Liverpool Cathedral,** aluminium baldachin holds acoustic and mechanical equipment without acknowledgement; behind this the choir floats in space and the 'Chapel of the Blessed Sacrament' sits on axis.

or sense of mystery on the inside – just one large, central space that is taken in at a glance and fixed with its univalent meaning. This central space is designed like a 'theatre in the round' to bring the congregation into a closer relation to the elaborate Roman Catholic ritual – more particularly the celebration of High Mass. Everything is done to re-inforce this centrality from the radial floor pattern to the lantern above. The only problem is that, again, each element sticks out of its context so literally that it shouts down the contending voices: item, one raised-marble altar; item, one aluminium baldachin; item, one religious-stained-glass-window with, item, sun-bursts of yellow symbolizing, item, truth, etc. [8]. The method is the result of dispassionate aggregation and, since none of the items are linked in any special way and thus fail to modify each other, it would not much matter if there were more or less of them. It could have been that the isolated elements would relate by violent and bizarre opposition as in a Surrealist collage, but again the possible intrinsic contrast is suppressed and so the latent irony is dissipated. Finally, if one looks at the pattern-making in the stained glass or on

the façade of the bell-porch, the same univocal literalism can be found [9]. The patterns are mostly random and, besides signifying their single meaning of crucifixion or divine light, without formal meaning. Hence their arbitrary and gratuitous shape.

One of the simplest ways of finding out if a work is weak in internal linkage is to probe it from an ironic and unsympathetic position with different metaphors to see if it can withstand this attack by offering counter-meanings. We have already seen how hostile critics of the *Unité* can be answered because its multivalent form allows opposite interpretation and thus diffuses univalent criticism. The same is not true of the Liverpool Cathedral. Thus 'the

9. **Frederick Gibberd:**
Liverpool Cathedral,
entrance and bell-porch.
The loss of faith in
Christian iconography is
reflected in the slick pattern-
making (three crosses and
three crowns).

10 (*opposite*). **Le**
Corbusier: Unité
d'Habitation, west façade.
Strong, pure colours – red,
green, yellow – are used on
the sides of the building.

crown of thorns' symbolizing 'the Kingship of Christ' has been dubbed by the Liverpool wits as 'a cooling tower – the Mersey funnel' and although this quip may contain an affectionate element, it succeeds in undermining the single-minded pretence to Royal Piety, because it is one of the plausible meanings latent in the form. The other ones of 'Indian wigwam' or 'space capsule' are equally possible and equally subversive to the intended idea of divinity. If only the architect had acknowledged other meanings and recognized obvious mistakes, such as the half-hearted gesture, then he would have provided the necessary linkage and contained the ironic objections. As it is, the elements remain apart for our bleak contemplation.

Le Corbusier attains a converse involvement on our part by turning his contradictions, hardships and even mistakes to his purpose. For instance, the use of colour on the reveals [10] was conceived as a result of a mistake

in the mullion design when Le Corbusier was away from his office. The coloured sides were created to take one's eye away from the monotony of the window pattern, but they also serve other incidental functions, one of which is to reduce the scale of the gigantic project. Or the use of a material everyone had previously thought objectionable – raw concrete, *beton brut* – was first conceived as a result of a steel shortage and then seen as a possible, noble material when transformed by the pattern of wooden formwork. Indeed, the brutal concrete as well as the mistakes in construction were all turned to advantage through contrast with precisions:

> The defects shout at one from all parts of the structure . . . exposed concrete . . . to those who have a little imagination they add a certain richness . . . But in men and women do you not see the wrinkles and birthmarks . . . I have decided to make beauty by contrast. I will find its complement and establish a play between crudity and finesse, between the dull and intense, between precision and accident.[8]

This fusion of opposites within an ironic unity produces a larger order which can delineate opposite points of view: the crudity can be seen as sophisticated refinement, or vice versa, and instead of this ambiguity working to congeal the experience, it seems to make it of greater intensity.

The more one analyses this work, the more one finds link after link between the different levels of experience and the more the experience becomes self-validating as one discovers not only Le Corbusier's intentions, but more possible meanings which are latent within the architecture. It is this power of the multivalent work to engage the perceiver's powers of creation which is significant here. Not only does this allow the architecture to become alive in different ways to each generation and thus result in a lasting architecture, but it also stimulates each generation to reach beyond its familiar abstractions. Multivalent architecture acts as a catalyst on the mind, provoking wholly new interpretations which, in however small a way, affect the individual. The range, delicacy and complexity of meanings which exist in a multivalent work have an analogous effect on the mind that interacts with them. Ultimately, we are transformed by what we experience,[9] and the quality of a work is transferred, even if indirectly, into organizational states of the mind.

As already mentioned, multivalence is only one criterion for selecting buildings to discuss in this book; the other one is historical relevance within a tradition. In fact the concept of multivalence will slip into the background and be assumed throughout, only emerging explicitly in extreme cases. For the most part, explicit architectural issues will be discussed. The first chapter is devoted to a synoptic view of the six main movements which have developed during the last fifty years. After treating these traditions, I will analyse in more detail the recent work of the pioneers. Chapters 2 and 3 re-value the contributions of Mies van der Rohe, Walter Gropius and Frank Lloyd Wright, finding their late work for the most part univalent. By contrast, Chapters 4 and 5 are more conventional in their verdicts, although new interpretations are attempted: Le Corbusier as a tragic dualist and Alvar Aalto's work as a complexly coded set of messages. The last three chapters attempt to extract fairly new interpretations from familiar material: the underlying Camp attitude which colours much of American architecture, the Pop Movement in England, and some new ideas on 'place' and the concept of the open society which have developed around the world.

Thus this history is a series of discontinuous narratives and extended probes. It looks two ways at once and it focuses at different depths, but I hope for all this that the reader still doesn't become confused. The live architectural traditions are rich and complex in their profusion and any attempt to reduce them to some simplistic notion of 'modern' or 'the true style' would be myopic and destructive. It is the historian's obligation to search for the plurality of creative movements and individuals where he can find them, and elucidate their creativity. To attempt this, I have quoted architects at a length which is unusual in a book of this nature and I have given, where possible, a series of views – often a photo-strip – rather than a single, conventional view. But, having emphasized an inclusive approach, I am rather conscious of all the architects I have finally left out of the discussion.[10]

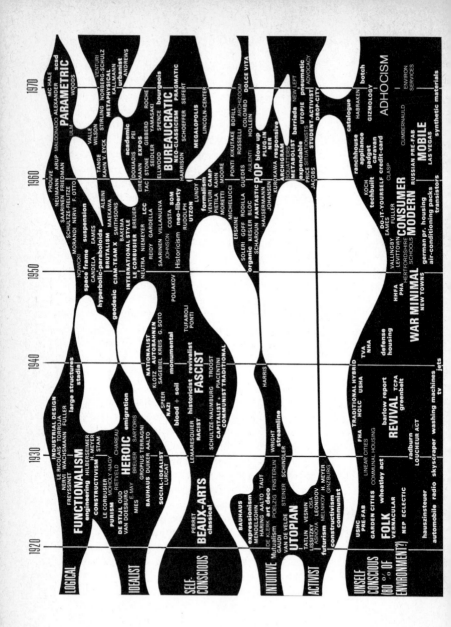

28

1. THE SIX TRADITIONS - POLITICS AND ARCHITECTURE

Both Jefferson's plan and the French *sociétés révolution-naires* anticipated with an almost weird precision those councils, *soviets* and *Räte*, which were to make their appearance in every genuine revolution throughout the nineteenth and twentieth centuries . . . [as Jefferson said] 'The wit of man cannot devise a more solid basis for a free, durable, and well-administered republic'. (HANNAH ARENDT, *On Revolution*)

11. **Evolutionary Tree, 1920-70.** The method for determining the six major traditions, classified at far left of diagram, is based on a structuralist analysis as outlined by Claude Lévi-Strauss.[1] The reader may find it helpful to refer back to this diagram at the beginning of each sub-section in this chapter.

In the period between 1920 and 1970, one can distinguish six main traditions or movements in architecture. These traditions, classified at the far left of the diagram or 'evolutionary tree' [11], represent in a metaphorical sense the major architectural species. The comparison of architectural movements with the evolution of biological species has its advantages and, of course, limitations. Like animal species, the architectural traditions wax and wane in relation to each other, and when one triumphs - the Fascist School of the thirties with its revivalist monumentality - another might succumb in 'the struggle for existence' - the Heroic Period of the idealist tradition. However, unlike animal species, architectural movements never become altogether extinct. There is always the chance of a revival of forms and ideas even if they are renewed somewhat differently. And furthermore, opposed to natural evolution, architects tend to jump from one species to another, inter-breeding with whatever they like and producing fertile offspring. In fact, as one would guess, the best architects are the least classifiable, the ones that fit into all six traditions, the ones that produce a fusion of multivalent interests and forms. Nonetheless, even with this richness and complexity, there is a certain coherence of development which tends to keep an architect within a range of overlapping ideas and forms. For instance, in the logical tradition, the architect will have to learn the related disciplines of mathematics, geometry and engineering, while he will tend to support the traditional values of the engineer: self-effacement, service-orientation, efficiency, openness to change, quantifiability, etc. The cumulative disciplines and the psychological coherence of values tend to keep each tradition distinct from and ideologically opposed to the others. Thus the architectural species evolve remaining fairly autonomous, and thus we may treat them with a biological metaphor and evolutionary analogy as long as we keep in mind the very important limits of this comparison.

In the outline of the six traditions which follows, I have concentrated on the political ideas that form the background of each movement, since these are of the utmost importance to architecture. An architect invariably postulates a society for his buildings and if he is to build anything at all, he will necessarily come up against actual political problems. Thus, not surprisingly, the major architects have defined their ideal political positions and become involved, through practice, in everyday political decisions – whether by compromise with existing society or in defiance or deflection of it. There are basically three different kinds of cause for this situation. The architect today more than ever is dependent on collective patronage, whether this is by the state, local government, or a committee of businessmen. He has to make what amounts to a political decision when accepting any commission from such a group. The choice of whether to build houses or munitions is above all political. Secondly, in a very *loose* way architecture influences the lives of those who inhabit or use it. This is not to say that architecture can by itself change society – a now discredited idea called 'architectural determinism' – but rather that it has a small, but significant, effect on people. Perhaps the most one can claim here is that the more impoverished and limited the cultural milieu, the greater the effect of architecture. A prison or space capsule largely determines the life of the inhabitants, whereas an affluent group of creative scientists or artists can prosper in almost any environment as long as it is minimally serviced. Thirdly, architecture is a political art because it crystallizes the public realm, shared social values, and long-term cultural goals. It is hence very much more involved with explicit social content than the other arts. Whereas music or painting can be relatively apolitical and unconnected with the milieu in which they are produced, architecture is utterly implicated in the public realm. This entails its taking on a responsibility towards communication and even rhetoric. It must by nature help explain and dramatize certain social meanings. This means, in turn, that today, when the whole public realm and politics are in doubt, architecture also must lack credibility, a point made in the last chapter.

Finally, a political bias is adopted here because the other major facets of recent architecture have been treated at length and are well known: the development of the 'machine aesthetic', International Style and the 'space-time' conception; the arguments for a new morality, a 'truth to materials' and social responsibility; the effects of new techniques, glass, steel, pneumatic structures and air conditioning, etc.[2] All of these key developments are important and will not be disregarded here, but they will be augmented by the informing political acts and motives of the architects.

THE IDEALIST TRADITION

Perhaps the centre of what is known popularly as 'modern architecture' is the idealist tradition. The architects Le Corbusier, Mies van der Rohe and Walter Gropius clearly defined a common position based loosely around certain social ideals – humanitarian liberalism, reformist pluralism and a vague social Utopianism – and the more recent architects such as Aldo van Eyck, Louis Kahn and James Stirling continue to proffer such ideals which spring from this mainstream tradition. If any particular goal may differ, the commitment to a general idealism remains. Thus these architects see it as an obligation to propose alternative visions to the existing social order. Opposed to the Marxist materialists, they do not concentrate on historical agencies for change (the working class and vanguard parties), and like the Platonic idealists they tend to carry through their buildings to perfection as if they represented some under-lying cosmic order.

Beginning in October 1920 and for the following two years, Le Corbusier wrote in the magazine *L'Esprit nouveau* a series of articles which were disseminated throughout Europe and which had an enormous impact in the major capitals such as Berlin and Moscow. The idealist, incantatory tone set the general background atmosphere for all further discussions of 'the New Architecture' and its 'Heroic Period'.

A great epoch has begun . . .
There is a new spirit: it is a spirit of construction and of synthesis guided by a clear conception . . .

With the emphasis always on such idealist entities as the 'new spirit', 'a clear conception' and the *Zeitgeist* – 'a great epoch' – Le Corbusier managed to subsume and crystallize all the fresh hopes that were current in the early twenties and give them seminal expression. In Russia this reference to 'construction' found an immediate and explicit echo in the newly formed movement of 'Constructivism' [43].

The fact that this idealism was an international affair can be seen in the diffusion of slogans which cut across national borders and even professional boundaries. The French writer Paul Valéry, like so many others, could see the spirituality and mental discipline underlying the machine: 'a book is a machine for reading'. Ozenfant called a painting 'a machine for moving us'; Le Corbusier termed the house 'a machine for living in' (the only formulation which people found outrageous and hence remembered); the English critic I. A. Richards opened his *Principles of Literary Criticism* with the remark 'a book is a machine to think with'; the great Russian film director Eisenstein said 'the theatre is a machine for acting'; and Marcel Duchamp took the whole idealist metaphor to a logical extreme in his aphorism – 'the idea is the machine for making art'.

Actually, to indicate how Platonic all this could become, the Dutch painter polemicist (and sometime architect) Van Doesburg claimed that the machine was the creator of a new spirituality.

Every machine is a spiritualization of an organism . . . The machine is, *par excellence*, a phenomenon of spiritual discipline . . . The new spiritual artistic sensibility of the twentieth century has not only felt the beauty of the machine, but has also taken cognisance of its unlimited expressive possibilities for the arts.[3]

The expressive possibilities which Van Doesburg elucidated in his painting and architecture were an abstract, anti-natural 'elementarism' based on straight lines, primary forms and colours, flat planes and rectangles [12].

12. Theo van Doesburg: L'Aubette Cafe, Strasbourg, 1927. This area for dancing, drinking and cinema was made up of orthogonal and diagonal geometrics, primary colours and industrial objects (radiators, lighting, etc.), treated as impersonal, abstract 'elements'. A 'universal, collective style', De Stijl.

He connected this formalism, natural to machine production, with the liberating aspects of the machine and contrasted all this with the tendency of handicraft production to reduce men to the level of automata:

Under the supremacy of materialism, handicraft reduced men to the level of machines; the proper tendency for the machine (in the sense of cultural development) is as the unique medium of the very opposite; social liberation.[4]

In political terms, the social liberation Van Doesburg refers to is not just the labour-saving aspect of the machine, but also its universalizing, abstract quality. Because it is impersonal, it forces a certain equality between men and it leads the evolution of art 'towards the abstract and universal . . . the realization, by a common effort and a common conception, of a collective style'.[5]

This summary of modern directions by Van Doesburg is particularly significant because it was shared by so

33

many of the European *avant-garde* at the time and it shows how they could see the machine in political terms: as the destroyer of class and national boundaries and creator of a democratic, collective brotherhood.

Furthermore, this diffusion of the machine metaphor indicated much more than the fact of international communication, or the world-village situation. It indicated a general European community of intellectuals committed to working out revolutionary artistic forms for a new social order to come. The number of creative movements in the early twenties which shared this view in one form or another was truly staggering: De Stijl in Holland, Purism in Paris, Constructivism in Russia and Hungary, Expressionism and Utopianism in Germany, Dada and Surrealism in various large cities including New York, the New Criticism and poetry in England and the States, formalism in Czechoslavakia, etc. Between 1917 and 1925 more actively creative movements sprang to life than at any other comparable time in this century. It was an explosive fission of the European spirit; a critical mass had been reached and there was an intellectual chain-reaction that makes other periods look dull by comparison. 'I felt very clearly that events were pressing. 1922–25, how fast everything moved,' Le Corbusier remarked of this fruitful time. He worked out almost all the principles for his 'Contemporary City for Three Million Inhabitants'

13. Le Corbusier: A Contemporary City of 3 Million, City Centre, 1922. Glass curtain wall skyscrapers in a park, interspersed with advanced technical inventions such as the aeroplane, became a common idealistic image by the end of the twenties.

[13] in the summer months of 1922 – principles which were to remain the stock-in-trade of planners for the next thirty years: the separation of the major functions and circulation systems, the city in the park, the interlocking

section and internal street of the apartment block [3], etc. Politically, however, the result was an amalgam of opposing ideologies and hence was heavily criticized from all sides. For instance, the French Communists termed it a Fascist plan because it implied a strong central government, because it was to be run by an élite *corps* of businessmen and because there was a built-in class distinction between managers and workers. The ambivalent political nature of Le Corbusier's proposals can be seen in his 'Freehold Maisonette Scheme' of 1922 – part social Utopian and Communist, part capitalist with its reference to servants, and part pragmatic with its ingenious economies of scale [14].

A communal service provides for all necessities and provides the solution to the servant question (which is only just beginning and is an inevitable social fact). Modern achievement, applied to so important an enterprise, replaces human labour by the machine and by good organization; constant hot water, central heating, refrigerators, vacuum cleaners, pure water, etc. Servants are no longer of necessity tied to the house; they come here as they would to a factory, and do their eight hours . . . From a vast kitchen the food is supplied . . . Each maisonette has its own gymnasium and sports room, but on the roof there is a communal hall for sports and a 300 yards track . . . By the system of rent purchase the bad old property systems no longer exist. No actual rent is paid; the tenants take shares in the enterprise . . . mass production . . . *low cost* . . .[6]

14. Le Corbusier: Freehold Maisonettes, 1922. A hundred and twenty individual apartments, each with its own garden suspended in the air and integrated with communal facilities. Russian designers used this as a prototype; see [45].

This project, along with its functional programme and aesthetic, was immediately taken up by the Russian Constructivists and developed into the Communal House [45]. For this and other reasons, Le Corbusier was quickly

35

pigeon-holed by reactionary elements as a Communist. In fact, in 1927 the major attack on him was written (in an attempt to stop him from winning the League of Nations competition) – 'The Trojan Horse of Bolshevism'.[7] He was viciously maligned as a secret agent of Lenin's who was converting the French citizenry surreptitiously to Communism through a combination of flat roofs, reinforced concrete, 'machines for living in' and the 'international Jewish conspiracy' – CIAM, the official organ of modern architecture. This attack was later mass-produced by the Nazis when they started to suppress the *avant-garde*. Throughout his life Le Corbusier was continuously misunderstood to be a Communist. One of the reasons was that he ended the last chapter of his epochal *Towards a New Architecture* (1923) with an ambiguous chapter called 'Architecture or Revolution':

> The primordial instinct of every human being is to assure himself of a shelter. The various classes of workers in society today *no longer have dwellings adapted to their needs; neither the artisan nor the intellectual.* It is a question of building which is at the root of the social unrest of today; architecture or revolution.[8]

But as one could guess it was precisely this passage which also infuriated the orthodox Marxists because it implied that the social problem could be solved by architectural means and without a class revolution – a typical position of the idealist architects of the time. When pressed on this political issue, Le Corbusier would acknowledge an apolitical pragmatism and fall back on technocratic justifications – neutrality and efficiency. He ended his next major book, *The City of Tomorrow* (1926), with these disclaimers:

> Since the Russian Revolution it has become the charming prerogative of both our own and the Bolshevist revolutionaries to keep the title of revolutionary to themselves alone . . . the rest [of my scheme of 1922] was severely criticized [by the Communist *L'Humanité*, etc.] because I had not labelled the first buildings on my plan 'People's Hall', 'Soviet' or 'Syndicalist Hall' and so on; and because I did not crown my plan with the slogan 'nationalization of all property'. I have been careful not to depart from the technical side of my problem. I am an architect; no one is going to make a politician of me . . .

> Things are not revolutionized by making revolutions. The real Revolution lies in the solution of existing problems.[9]

However much this may sound disingenuous or evasive, it was nevertheless a fair and typical statement of Le Corbusier's real position. He would always try to defuse any political debate with pragmatic solutions. Thus the 'rent purchase' scheme already quoted was a very real means of overcoming 'the bad old property systems', as so many cooperative apartments and housing associations have later testified. Yet these solutions were piecemeal palliatives which did not go to the heart of the social problem and which represented a compromise typical of the idealists, typical of the liberal, reformist organization of 'Modern Architecture', CIAM (*Congrès Internationaux d'Architecture Moderne*). Started in 1928, in the Swiss château of a patroness, Hélène de Mandrot, the CIAM was founded on some revealing anomalies and widespread contradictions. On a positive note, the Weissonhof exhibition of the previous year had just established 'Modern Architecture' as *the* style of the twenties, but negatively, Le Corbusier had just lost the League of Nations Competition because of his uncompromising modernism. Furthermore, CIAM was torn internally between the 'formalist' French architects and the 'functionalist' Germans, or to put the same opposition in the political terms which were used – bourgeois reformists and Marxist revolutionists. As a result, its foundation charter carried such political mixed salad as the following proposition:

This redistribution of the land, the indispensable preliminary basis for any town planning, must include the just division between the owners and the community of the *unearned increment* resulting from works of joint interest.[10]

Thus one would redistribute the land (revolutionist), but one would still have owners (capitalist) plus an increase in profit due to large densities (pragmatic), which would yet be divided equally (socialist). No wonder Le Corbusier and CIAM were accused of every political sin in the book. Their position nicely straddled most of the surrounding extremists (who also formed their internal ranks). Thus, to fill out the remaining points of their 1928 *Declaration*, they appealed to the interests and 'needs of the greatest number' (a clear concession to the Marxists Ernst May and Hannes Meyer who were attending the congress);

they came down unequivocally in favour of their 'professional obligations towards society' as improving 'efficiency' through 'rationalization and standardization' (to cover the interests of the manager and technocrats in their midst); like the liberals, they wished to change society through moulding 'public opinion', and like the Fascists they saw the means of control as coming from above – as the 'State'.

IV. Architecture and its relations with the State . . . If States were to adopt an attitude opposite to the present one they would bring about a veritable architectural renaissance . . .[11]

In at least one case, that of Frankfurt in Germany, it looked as if 'the State' or at least the City could indeed bring about this architectural renaissance. Ernst May was appointed City Architect in Frankfurt and during his reign, from 1925–30, 15,000 mass-produced dwelling units were built along the lines of Le Corbusier's Freehold Maisonettes – with built-in furniture and multiple services [**15**]. This vast public housing strategy established

the virtues of pre-cast slab construction (called the 'May System') along with its aesthetic the 'International Style' (as it was later named by the historians Hitchcock and Johnson in 1932). The second CIAM Congress, called by Ernst May in 1929, took place amidst this triumph of completed mass housing in Frankfurt. Its subject was the *Existenzminimum*, or the dwelling of minimal size and cost.

Before leaving this triumph of the idealist tradition, its 'Heroic Period' during the twenties, two more of the idealistic and hopeful qualities should be mentioned. On the one hand, there was the 'heroism of everyday life', the celebration of the familiar objects of daily use (*objet-types*) such as the briar pipe, wine bottle, doorknob or type-writer – which the Purist painters Ozenfant, Leger and Le Corbusier incorporated into their paintings. For the Purists, these objects had a strong, anonymous, 'heroic' quality because they had been perfected by countless years of reworking. In Paul Valéry's words – 'the best efforts of thousands of men converge towards the most economical and certain shape'. On the other hand, the 'Heroic Period' meant the herculean task of particular individuals transforming society. This sense of the word hero is much better left to later discussion of the activists, but it did also permeate the idealist tradition. For instance there is Mies van der Rohe's monument [16] to the Communist martyrs Karl Liebknecht and Rosa Luxemburg.

15 (*opposite*). **Ernst May: Bruchfeldstrasse low cost apartments, Frankfurt, 1926-8.**
The zig-zag blocks enclose a U-shaped garden court and culminate in the community centre. The 'sun, space and greenery', along with the white planes, flat roofs and ribbon windows, became conventional signs of socialist architecture and were attacked by Hitler as '*Kulturbolschewismus*'.

16. **Mies van der Rohe: Monument to Karl Liebknecht and Rosa Luxemburg, Berlin, 1926.** Hovering, purist shapes with a tacked-on conventional emblem carrying out the dual aesthetic of the Constructivists.

These two Communist leaders were shot by German officers following the Spartacist uprising in 1919. Rosa Luxemburg, in particular, illustrated the qualities of a heroine dedicated to a single idea – the transformation of society by revolution and leadership of the workers rather than some vanguard party. This commitment to the self-transformation of the masses placed her in opposition to other Communist doctrines, notably Lenin's élitist 'dictatorship of the proletariat' and the Bolshevik Party. However, for Mies van der Rohe the commission was merely pragmatic and a problem of form – an 'accident from beginning to end' as he described it.

> The [initial project by another architect] was a huge stone monument with Doric columns and medallions of Luxemburg and Liebknecht. When I saw it I started to laugh and told him it would be a fine monument for a banker . . . I told him I hadn't the slightest idea what I would do in his place, but as most of these people were shot in front of a wall, a brick wall would be what I would build as a monument.[12]

The casual, even jocular, tone of Mies towards this monument and these martyred Communists is revealing, inasmuch as it shows his uncertain grasp of who the 'heroes' of the period actually were and what they stood for. Mies, like so many other architects, was so confused about politics as to be completely apolitical, pragmatic and hence fatalistic with respect to the existing power structure. Thus he could design this Communist monument, put up a building for the editor of *The Red Flag*, and then go on to purge the Bauhaus of its Communist students in 1930 – when it was politic to do so. When the Nazis came to power he worked for them up until 1937, then left for the United States where he worked for widely different interests. When I questioned the architect Philip Johnson about this he said, 'How apolitical can you get? If the devil himself offered Mies a job he would take it.'

This politics of the apolitical is very important in considering the decline of the idealist tradition after the Heroic Period. Basically, the social Utopianism which existed in the work of Le Corbusier, Gropius and the CIAM architects became deflected just as their modern aesthetic – the International Style – triumphed around the world in the fifties. In effect, what was known popularly as 'Modern Architecture' became accepted by most national governments as well as the leading international corporations and it was, most importantly, stripped of its social idealism. As a result of this mixed success, modern architecture became identified with the bureaucracies that commissioned, inhabited and sometimes even designed it. The ambiguities that this could produce were extraordinary, since much of the International Style had previously been associated with progressive social institutions. In the fifties, this style reached a kind of penultimate development and acceptance with the final working out of the curtain wall. In essence, the curtain wall is a non-supporting skin made up from window mullions and in-fill panels which is cantilevered from a frame structure. It starts its final development with the Lever Building on Park Avenue in New York City, 1951 [**17**], and reaches two

17. Skidmore, Owings and Merrill: Lever Brothers Building, New York City, **1951/2.** A low and high slab juxtaposed to break down the mass close to the pedestrian. The windows are capped top and bottom by spandrels which reflect the mechanical services behind them.

opposite visual conclusions seven years later, across the street, with the Pepsi-Cola and the Seagram Building [53]. But two questions emerge. Is it more important that the curtain wall develops aesthetically from a light, close-mesh pattern to a heavy articulated one, or the fact that Mies van der Rohe and some of the best American architects spent their greatest energies in refining the exterior wrappings for monopolies which produced soap, whiskey and soda-pop? Secondly, is this repeated use of a curtain wall sufficient to articulate the rich and diverse content which occurs behind them?

As Park Avenue became a street lined with such anonymous expressions of Corporate America [18], the Inter-

18. View down Park Avenue, New York, 1970.

national Style became equated with the Bureaucratic School of architects that produced it [11]. This contradiction between the technical and visual excellence on the one hand, and the undeniable banality of the building task on the other, became so obvious by the early sixties that the curtain wall and its related aesthetic fell into disrepute, to be replaced by other approaches. In the idealist tradition, these were the New Brutalism, the transition from CIAM to Team Ten, and the various work of architects such as Louis Kahn, Aldo Van Eyck and James Stirling – all of which will be discussed in later chapters.

What this heterogeneous work had in common was its derivation from the principles which were laid down in the Heroic Period, without, however, any of the architects being actively engaged in social or political thinking. Rather, they shared with Le Corbusier the belief that architecture could socially transform men as well as the idea that it should reflect certain ordering principles found throughout nature. This placing of architecture on a cosmic scale was the underlying shared assumption of what could be called, for want of a better word, the Metaphysical School of architecture. Its major prophet was Louis Kahn, who spoke about the quasi-mystical spirit of 'what the building wants to be'.

> The nature of space reflects what it wants to be . . .
> In the nature of space is the spirit and the will to exist a certain way . . .
> Through the *nature* – why
> Through the *order* – what
> Through *design* – how
> A form emerges from the structural elements inherent in the form
> A dome is not conceived when questions arise how to build it
> Nervi grows an arch
> Fuller grows a dome . . .
> *Order is intangible*
> It is a level of creative consciousness forever becoming higher in level . . .[13]

This laconic manifesto called *Order Is* was written in 1960, and it reflects with fair precision a belief held by most idealist architects at this time – to wit the idea that a form can grow almost *naturally* out of primary structural elements (such as Nervi and Fuller find) and that this archetypal form provides the ordering device for a whole building.[14] The kind of architecture produced by this Metaphysical School was primitive in expression, if not fundamentalist, and unequivocally made up from ordering elements which the architect produced conceptually. Thus, like the Purists' *objet-type*, these architects tended to produce *the* dome, *the* tetrahedron, *the* arch – or the generic element which seemed to have just arrived perfected from Plato's ideal realm. For instance James Stirling's St Andrews Residence is compiled from a repetition of *the* bedroom unit and it has all the qualities of a reduction to essentials and functional expressiveness which also identifies these architects [**19**]. But what has all

19 a, b, c. James Stirling: St Andrews Residence, Scotland, 1964-9, made up from pre-cast walls organized along a circulation deck. The basic idea was derived from the Constructivists' Communal Housing projects of 1928-9 – [**45**].

this to do with politics? On the one hand, there is an attempt to influence the lives of those who use the architecture by indirect means – the ordered, disciplined forms evoking corresponding mental states in the people who use them – and, on the other hand, an attempt to construct 'contributions to a fragmentary Utopia' as the Smithsons, Guirgola and so many other idealist architects phrased it in the sixties. This might mean, as in Stirling's case, the re-use of an ordering principle which the Russian Constructivists used in their communal house schemes of the twenties or, as in the Goodmans' case, offering ideal-type alternatives from which society can choose.[15] In all these cases, the emphasis is put on the mentality and volition of the society rather than its material base.

THE SELF-CONSCIOUS TRADITION

Another coherent movement of architecture takes this idealist premise to extreme lengths, placing so much emphasis on will-power as to become hyperconscious, if not sometimes even inhibited. The self-conscious tradition of architecture often shows an attention to its own actions which is so self-reflective as to be paralysing. There are in general two directions which this has taken: the submission to past models of architecture in the belief that these contain some universal ordering principles, or the obsession with past ages and previous buildings with the idea that these may confer some kind of earthly immortality on the builders. Auguste Perret's belief in the universal properties of classical architecture with its principle of column and entablature exemplifies the former, whereas Hitler's idea of a classical, thousand-year Third Reich is typical of the latter. Both beliefs have enjoyed a wide audience in the twentieth century, reaching their heights in the thirties with the various forms of Fascism, and once again in the sixties with the triumph of the Bureaucratic School. The politics of the self-conscious tradition, as one could guess, are conservative, élitist, centralist and pragmatic with an occasional element of mystical fundamentalism thrown in to catalyse, or brutalize (as the other traditions would put it) the masses.

The arguments which Hitler put forward in *Mein Kampf* (1924) were simple in the extreme: 'degenerate art' was due to the influence of the Jews: 'the house with the flat roof is oriental – oriental is Jewish – Jewish is bolshevistic'. Therefore the Bauhaus, CIAM, Le Corbusier were Jewish, Communist conspirators. The racist interpretation of architecture was further developed in 1928 by the very influential architect Paul Schultze-Naumburg, with two basic books, *Art and Race* and *The Face of the German House*. The latter book carried forward the idea of there being a racial character of the German house different from other races ('Flat Roofs, Flat Heads' as one article put the equation), whereas the former put forward the positive characteristics of German architecture: a pitched roof, an harmonious expression, 'out of [which] there seemed to gaze the features of men upright, good and true'.[16] Beyond having this beneficent expression, the best German architecture, that of the past,

gives one the feeling that it grows out of the soil, like one of its natural products, like a tree that sinks its roots deep in the interior of the soil and forms a union with it. It is this that gives us our understanding of home, of a bond with blood and earth; for one kind of men [this is] the condition of their life and the meaning of their existence.[16]

This argument for a nationalist, organic architecture resulted in a city planning which was anti-urban and visually very similar to the curvilinear-planned garden cities of England. Opposed to the German race rooted in its past culture was placed the uprooted, materialist urbanite, and opposed to their anonymous, industrialized housing, which looked to the Nazis like sterile factories, were placed monuments to the State. Although these oppositions were directed against architects of the Heroic Period, this did not in fact stop them from compromising with the authorities for pragmatic and other reasons. Thus Mies signed a patriotic appeal put forward by Schultze-Naumburg even though the latter was so unequivocal in his position in 1932 as to give racist lectures with storm-troopers present who would 'bludgeon' dissenting artists.[17]

20. Mies van der Rohe: Reichsbank Elevation, 1933. The later associations of the curtain wall are already here.

When he [Mies] accepted in July 1933, after the coming to power of Hitler, the Commission for the Reichsbank [20] he was a traitor to all of us and a traitor to everything we had fought for. He signed at that time a patriotic appeal which Schultze-Naumburg had made as Commissar to the artists, writers, and architects of Germany to put their forces behind National Socialism. I would say that, of the leading group of the Bauhaus people, Mies was the only one who signed. And he accepted this commission. This was a terrible stab in the back for us.[18]

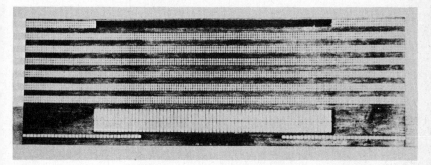

Although it appeared to such historians as Sibyl Moholy-Nagy that Mies's compromise was the exception, it was in fact more like the rule. Thus as late as June 1934 Gropius wrote letters to Goebbels defending the 'Germanness' of the new architecture and calling it a synthesis 'of the classical and Gothic traditions',[19] and he designed exhibition structures for the Nazis. Wassili Luchardt, Herbert Bayer, Hugo Häring and other uncompromising figures of the twenties took on very questionable work. Le Corbusier spent the year of 1941 in Vichy trying to persuade the puppet régime to give him work;[20] Frank Lloyd Wright happily toured Russia at a most unfortunate period in its history – during the purges; Philip Johnson, supporting one demagogic group after another, even paid a visit to Hitler in Danzig just after the latter had invaded Poland to start the Second World War.[21] I give these heterogeneous examples because the common historical opinion is that the architects of the Heroic Period were utterly opposed to Fascism; a closer look at their pragmatic statements and emphasis on 'the State' (see above, page 38) and other authoritarian means should have suggested otherwise.

The case of Italian Fascism is particularly interesting in bringing out this ambivalence.[22] For instance Le Corbusier, while fully disliking the pomp and monumentality of a centralist state (he even joined the Popular Front in 1935 to fight with the Communists against the Nazis), still admired the Fascism which 'could make the trains run on time'. The sentiments of the Italian ration-

21a. Guerrini, Lapadula and Romano: Palace of Italian Civilization, EUR, Rome, 1942. Stripped classicism with repetitive arcades again became a favourite motif twenty years later; see, for instance, illustrations 115 and 118.

21 (b). Gio Ponti: Pirelli Building, Milan, 1961, and (c). Alberto Rosselli; Lightscraper Project, 1965. Architecture as elegant and formally brilliant advertisement.

alist architects such as Pagano and Terragni were similar. They all built for Mussolini even if they had some doubts about the monumental classicism which became the signature of his régime. The greatest examples of this were the Mussolini Forum in Rome (1937) and the Universal Exposition in Rome (1942) [21a], both of which tried to make equations between the old and new architecture of Rome. As in later efforts of the self-conscious tradition, the mediating terms between these two extremes were such things as the glory of the Caesars, immortality and the universality of classicism. Because this classicism was so clear and spare, even such defenders of the International Style as Nikolaus Pevsner could ask for its future rehabilitation:

> ... Much [of the buildings] that went up ... will one day again come into their own. They all combine a convincing rectangularity with fine shows of shining marbles inside and out.[23]

The buildings of Gio Ponti fall under this description, and his explanation twenty years later about the political forces at work is as apt for his Pirelli Building [21b] as his previous work under the Fascists.

> I grant, and am pleased, that architecture (good architecture) should be a means of advertising, and I recommend it to all . . . when I happen to meet people who are ambitious to live on in History I never fail to advise them to invest in the 'Bank of Architecture' which will assure them of a 'security', which is their name, of unfailing quotation; and I quote the benefits obtained by Popes, Kings, Princes and Patricians who 'loved architecture' and whose names . . . have remained . . . in the splendour of History . . . And I quote what Mies and Skidmore, Owings and Merrill have meant for Seagram and Lever respectively.[24]

That we are dealing here with archetypes of modern thought and not a vagary of a particular culture can be shown by quoting similar passages from the major architects of the Bureaucratic School, whatever country they come from: Yamasaki (USA), Spence (England), Niemeyer (Brazil), etc. It was left to Philip Johnson, in a pronouncement typical of the Camp movement in architecture, to take this to its ultimate, droll conclusion.

> The only real urge is immortality – not sex. Plato had it right – and Freud and Horace had it wrong. What did Horace say by the way? Well it doesn't matter. Monuments last much longer than words. Civilizations are remembered by buildings. There's nothing more important than architecture.[25]

One of the ironies that has resulted from this position is that the monuments which were meant to convey their author's immortality have ended up looking alike and hence have been quickly lost to the collective memory. Thus the Palace of the Congresses constructed in Russia in 1961 [22] could be mistaken for Niemeyer's 1966 Foreign Office in Brasilia or any number of Washington bureaucracies. But what are the psychological factors which bind the self-conscious tradition together and make it continually subservient to the reigning powers? To pose the question is almost to answer it, for the factors which lead to acquiescence in any field have something to do with the related ideas of pragmatism, fatalism, a belief in the *status quo* and the *Zeitgeist*.[26] But the architect is particularly

22. Moscow, Palace of the Congresses, 1961.

prone to the influence of such factors because he has to depend more directly than any other kind of artist on social patronage and he also has to keep relatively up to date with a fast changing technology: two factors which encourage him to remain acquiescent to external forces. If Mies could say 'the individual is losing significance; his destiny is no longer what interests us' in appealing to the *Zeitgeist* of industrialization, he could then obviously find a response in Goebbels's appeal to the social *Zeitgeist*: 'It is the most essential principle of our victoriously conquering movement that the individual has been dethroned.'[27] Fatalism, whether social or technological, seems to be the bane of the self-conscious tradition.

DOLCE VITA OR THE SUPERSENSUALISTS

By the middle sixties, part of this tradition had undergone a metamorphosis which changed its character quite considerably. It merged with parts of the intuitive tradition – over their common area of fashion and formalism – to become a kind of movement that hadn't existed since the turn of the century and Art Nouveau. This movement, like its predecessor, was based on the double aspect of attacking the dull industrial environment for its monotony and, at the same time, living off the most advanced fruits of its technology. On the one hand, the Supersensualists unleashed an orgy of colour exploiting the latest processes – eye-ease green against dayglo orange, nickel-plated purple set off against frosted, polarized baby-moon-blue-glint – and on the other hand, they produced prestige commissions for the pampered sophisticates of the urban élite: night clubs, candle shops [23],

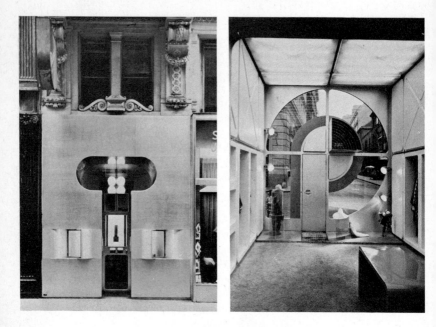

boutiques, private houses for art lovers, exhibitions such as the Biennale in Venice and the Triennale in Milan and above all consumer products varying from polychromatic furniture to 'Dream Beds' [24]. What was their major outlet? The annual *Eurodomus* show which exhibits such futuristic hybrids as M-Design, Stil Novo, O-Luce as well as the more established fashion firms such as Marie Claire and Rinascente. As one can see from this list, the Supersensualists were dependent on the kind of sophisticated outlets which supported Art Nouveau (such as Tiffany's) except that they were far greater in number and willing to pay for experiments with the latest technologies. What was the major goal of the Supersensualists? To achieve a full colour layout in one of the more fashionable 'glossies' such as *Domus*, *Vogue* or *Studio Inter-*

23a, b, c. Hans Hollein: Projects, Vienna. A candle shop, boutique and exhibition, 1965–8. The use of such technical means as polished aluminium and the treatment of industrial objects (the cantilevered air conditioner) as if they were jewels.

national. What was their unacknowledged epigram? 'It's so beautiful it's killing me', or 'It's so luscious I could eat it'.

Thus it looks at first as if the Supersensualists were a cross between British Pop and American Camp: the cool techno-sophistication of the one and the sensual, homosexual sweetness of the other. And yet this architectural and social movement is quite different from either, being really the outgrowth of the Milanese Borghese culture, the economic miracle, overripe Catholicism and the Italian love for the saccharine – the 'sweet life' – *dolce vita.* In fact probably the best portrayal of this movement comes from the movies: Pasolini's *Theorem* (Christ as the fornicator of Milanese *nouveaux riches* who nevertheless may spout Marxism) and of course Fellini's *Dolce Vita* itself (with the statue of Christ in benediction being

24. Archizoom: Dream Bed, 'Presage of Roses', Florence, 1968. An hermetically sealed environment made from rarefied images of Bob Dylan's portrait, the Art Deco of the twenties, Mies, etc. The ritualistic nature of this bed as sacrificial altar recalls the metaphysical paintings of De Chirico.

shuttled over Italian superblocks by a spluttering helicopter).

It is this image of absolute technology contrasted with cultural artefacts and traditional values which achieves such compelling force. Indeed the most convincing of the architectural Supersensualists, Hans Hollein, has made this juxtaposition the basis for his architecture [25]. In a manifesto prophetic of his work to come, Hollein summarized the intentions of the Supersensualists.

25. Hans Hollein: Aircraft Carrier in the Austrian Wheatfields, 1964.

A sensual beauty . . . architecture is without purpose. What we build will find its usefulness. Form does not follow function . . . Today for the first time in the history of mankind, at the moment when immensely developed science and perfected

54

technology offer the means, we are building what we want, making an architecture that is not determined by technique, but that uses technique – pure absolute architecture.[28]

Pure absolute architecture dependent on the patronage of psychedelic boutiques, fashion magazines and the tri-annual design exhibitions. The political assumptions of this work are evidently élitist, a point which Hollein faces unequivocally:

> Architecture is not the satisfaction of the needs of the mediocre, is not an environment for the petty happiness of the masses . . . architecture is an affair of the élite.

26. Haus Rucker Co: Pulsating Yellow Heart, Vienna, 1968. A moveable pneumatic enclosure covered with red stripes and dots that can be attached to any part of the environment to provide a change in air pressure, touch and reverberation time – a new sensual experience.

And another Viennese who has also written a manifesto on 'Absolute Architecture', Walter Pichler, takes this even further, with the machines themselves becoming the new élite.

> Architecture is an embodiment of the power and longings of a few men . . . It never serves. It crushes those who cannot bear it . . . Machines have taken possession of [architecture] and human beings are now merely tolerated in its domain.[29] [26]

It is hard with all these pronouncements to decide whether they are elaborate jokes or just too serious. This ambivalence is shared by all the Supersensualists and can be considered their peculiar virtue. Thus in Pasolini's *Theorem*, the wealthiest members of society can often be counted on to enunciate Marxist slogans as they step into their Lamborghinis and, for instance, the groups Archizoom and Superstudio consider themselves to be leftist revolutionaries while working entirely within the established framework of the consumer society (they call it 'revolution from within'). Superstudio has designed 'The Continuous Monument', which 'is a single piece of architecture to be extended over the whole world' – like a proposition in *Theorem* taking a bizarre idea to its logical conclusion [27]. In this case the idea is a mixture of

27. Superstudio: The Continuous Monument, Arizona Desert, 1969. 'We presented an architectural model for total urbanization as the logical result of an oriented story: the history of monuments which began with Stonehenge and, passing on to the Kaaba and the VAB, found its completion with the continuous monument.' One of their more modest claims.

'Fascist' 'total urbanization' (as they call it) and absolute egalitarianism. Everyone has exactly the same room, or the same white square gridiron which is used for all functions. Like Hollein's work, this monument is placed in striking contrast to nature and it is meant to convey a state of supreme calm and serenity; its 'static perfection moves the world through the love that it creates', or so the hope is. Like some tantalizing paradox, the enjoyment consists in being persuaded of something one knows to be questionable, if not entirely false:

> We are working on an architecture which we hope to render sacred and immutable, we design our architecture as a sign in the desert, architecture pitted against death, architecture as serene happiness, architecture as sweet tyranny.[30]

If one were to look for positive political implications in this movement (cutting away the 'sweet tyranny'), they could be found on probably only a semi-conscious level: an insistence on artistic autonomy approaching unlimited creative freedom and a creative play or amusement which

28. Ricardo Bofill and Partners: Xanadu, Calpe, Spain, 1967. A complex of seventeen apartments set off against an untouched landscape. Bofill, a follower of Gaudi, achieves an expressive use of structure – such as the hyperbolic roofs here.

exploits each new technique and invention for its sensuality. The nature of this sensuality can be grasped in any issue since 1965 of *Domus* – the Milanese magazine edited by Gio Ponti, which includes almost all the Supersensualists with the exception of some Spanish and Japanese architects.[31]

It is a Spanish architect, Ricardo Bofill, who has come the closest to analysing the contradictions involved in this movement, perhaps because he is so involved in the contradictions themselves – being an activist living under real Fascism who designs luxury villas when he isn't involved in agitation [28].

I consider it necessary to know this new form of pseudo-fascism, different from any other, complex and contradictory, advanced in certain fields and backward in others . . .[32]

Bofill shows that it is a mixture of the 'economic miracle', brought about by tourism and industrialization, overlaid on a conventional, covert dictatorship which has disoriented and co-opted the opposition.

We have, finally, the wildest arrivism in certain architects known for their 'classicist' convictions, who have been put to modernize their 'façades', in order to continue to maintain their eight sons. The new government ministers did not take long to understand this new situation and to become patrons . . . of the most modern architecture, converting it into the official architecture. The most recent examples are: the [Spanish entries] at the World's Fair, Brussels, 1957 and New York, 1964. Francoism now can allow itself the luxury of *avant-garde* architecture for its propaganda, even though this is not what is normally meant as fascist . . . The architects are very close to the Beaux-Arts, to *Architecture d' Aujourd' hui*, to the motive idea of Brasilia.[33]

This incisive commentary on the political compromising of the *avant-garde* obviously has its parallels in other western countries with what is termed by Herbert Marcuse as 'repressive toleration'. The potentially critical elements of society are defused by being occasionally presented through the media as an integral part of the culture, or a marginal variation from it. Few architects escape this compromising and watering down of their position. But one group, made up of expressionist architects in the intuitive tradition, has usually kept its autonomy, because most ruling élites have found its architecture too unpalatable and undignified.

Perhaps the greatest reason for the critical independence of the expressionist architects is their ideology of individual creativity which is often mixed with a form of anarchism. The Art Nouveau movement and such architects as Gaudi and Van de Velde all preached the autonomy of the artist's imagination and they combined this with a romantic socialism based on cooperation and fellowship. The medieval guild system was a model for the socialism of William Morris; the anarchist writings of Kropotkin, Stirner and even Tolstoy were much admired and propagated by the designer Van de Velde; the Bauhaus in its expressionist phase, from 1919 to 1923, was loosely based on the Mutual Aid ideas which go back to the Anarcho-Syndicalism of Proudhon. In fact Gropius's foundation manifesto of 1919 reads like a cross between Guild Socialism, the Arts and Crafts Movement in England, and Mutualism:

> Let us then create a new guild of craftsmen without the class distinctions . . . a working community . . . [based on the] collaboration by the students in the work of the masters . . . mutual planning of extensive, Utopian structural design . . . aimed at the future . . . [in] contact with public life, with the people, through exhibitions and other activities.[34]

The Bauhaus was even run by a *Council* of Masters (with student participation) and 'friendly relations between masters and students' would be 'encouraged by plays, lectures, poetry, music, fancy-dress parties'. Gropius said in another proclamation at the same time:

> Our time will throw aside respect for the dead mask of organization which blinds us and leads us into error. The relationship of man to man, the spirit of small communities must conquer again. Small fruitful communities, secret societies, brotherhoods . . . building guilds as in the golden age of cathedrals.[35]

Actually, many of these ideas were orthodox in Germany right after the republican revolution of November 1918 when the Kaiser had fled and the social democrats had formed the Workers' and Soldiers' Councils which brought about the general strike. The *Novembergruppe*, to which Gropius, Mies, Bruno Taut and other *avant-garde* architects belonged, formed a Workers' Council for Art which proclaimed the creation of collective art works, mass housing and the 'destruction of artistically valueless monuments' (a parting shot at the élitist militarism which, to all the German *avant-garde*, was responsible for the First World War). Workers' Councils for Art formed in nearly every German city, quite consciously modelling themselves on the Soviets (a form of organization which seems to spring spontaneously into existence with every popular revolution). They demanded a 'spiritual revolution' which would accompany the political one and hence they tended to attach what was known as Utopianism or Expressionism to a leftist programme.

Perhaps the greatest exponent of this double revolution was Bruno Taut who allied the 'new crystal architecture'

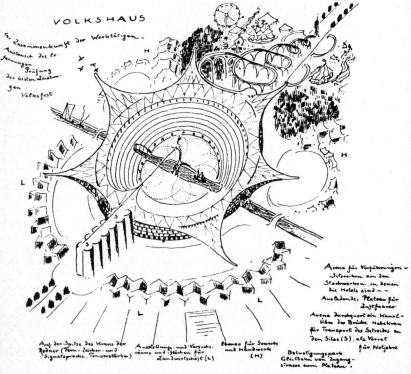

with the new community spirit. In fact often in his Utopian sketches, the central community building would be a 'house of crystal' or at least an expressive application of the latest technologies [29]. Taut, in his manifestoes, demanded 'no distinction between public and private buildings . . . [they] may be built by anyone' – thus anticipating later polemicists of the self-build environment. Architects were to form into 'corporations' where 'Mutual Aid' was to be the binding power.

These corporations are to exercise to the limit the principle of *mutual aid* . . . Mutual aid alone makes an association fruitful and active. It is more important than the number of votes, which means nothing without social concord.

Taut then ends this little panegyric on the virtues of brotherhood and mutual aid with a complete non-sequitur and improbable answer to Marxism.

[Mutual aid] excludes inartistic and hence unfair competition.[36]

29. Bruno Taut: Design for a Community Centre, 1918. The expressionist glass architecture tied to mutualist ideas. 'Public address equipment at the top of the crane . . . Exposition and experimentation areas for agriculture (L). Same for the trades and crafts (H). Arena for performances – rows of seats in front of the floors in which the hotels are located [sic] – projecting plateau for pleasure drives. The arena is crossed by a canal. Above its bridge a loading crane for transporting grain to the silos (S) as a reserve for years of scarcity. Amusement park, chute from the access road on to the plateau. Arrival by water, land, air.' (Quoted from *The Dissolution of Cities*, 1920)

It wasn't just the Bauhaus which was organized and run along the lines of social concord and mutual aid, but also Frank Lloyd Wright's community workshop called 'Taliesin', and the ateliers of Le Corbusier and Alvar Aalto. All these architects ran their offices with a strong central control, but this was matched by a self-organizing teamwork which was fairly autonomous. Indeed, Le Corbusier projected anarchist forms of organization based on the federation of workers' syndicates where control was to be exercised from the bottom up,[37] while Aalto claimed to have organized his own firms along Kropotkin's mutualist lines. Of course the political theory and practice of these architects was by no means entirely anarchist. Thus Frank Lloyd Wright in his Utopian designs for *Broadacres* projected a system which was individualist and based on self-help, home economies, social credit and communal control of big machinery – e.g., transportation and power – but all this was also mixed with corporate capitalism and a built-in class distinction.

In any case, the Utopian movement of the early twenties definitely had anarchist ideals to which the major Expressionist architects subscribed. These ideas were, unfortunately, never carried very far in practice, just as very few Expressionist buildings were actually constructed

61

(except those of Taut, Mendelsohn, Poelzig and Häring). As a result, when Expressionism was reborn as 'Fantastic Architecture' in the sixties the political and ideological roots had eroded, and it had become merely a rather significant movement in architectural history.

This movement was started by exhibitions and books: Conrads and Sperlich's *Fantastic Architecture* (in German 1960, English 1963), an issue of *L' Architecture d' Aujourd'hui* also called *Fantastic Architecture* (1962), and an exhibition at the Museum of Modern Art in New York on 'Visionary Architecture' (1960). If there was any ideological justification, it concerned the freedom of the architect's imagination as against the conventional building of society and a sterile rationalism in architecture.

The Viennese painter Hundertwasser put forward two basic themes in his 1958 *Mould Manifesto Against Rationalism in Architecture*. The first one recalled the extreme pronouncements on individual freedom of the anarchist Max Stirner:

> Everyone should be able to build, and so long as this freedom to build does not exist, the planned architecture of today cannot be considered an art at all. Architecture with us is subject to the same censorship as painting in the Soviet Union.[38]

The second thesis, with sustained polemical wit, attacked the rationalist convention of the straight line as the symbol of efficiency and rectitude:

> Merely to carry a straight line about with one ought to be, at least morally, forbidden. The ruler is the symbol of the new illiteracy. The ruler is the symptom of the new sickness of decadence.
>
> We live in a chaos of straight lines . . . Anybody who doesn't believe this should take the trouble to count the straight lines all around him and he will understand; for he will never stop counting . . .[39]

After counting 3,000 straight lines on his razor blade, Hundertwasser goes on to propose a universal antidote – 'mould', 'microbes and fungi', and various 'disintegrating agents' which can reduce all the straight architecture to flowing, free-form curves. The kind of building that was actually being produced which could fit this description was that 'Fantastic Architecture' of Bruce Goff [119], Juan O'Gorman, Simone Rodilla and Amancio Guedes.

They would collect every kind of buildable material from bottle caps and broken glass to chicken wire and shingle and use them as an abstract painter uses paint: as an open means of expression which has its own natural strengths and rules.

Another naturalist approach termed 'fantastic' was that of the structural engineers such as Morandi, Nervi and Castiglioni. They pushed structure to its expressive limits. For instance, Frei Otto designed tension cables which could span from one mountain to another across twenty-five mile valleys, holding up tent-like cities below them [30]. Felix Candela pushed the hyperbolic paraboloid to its constructional capacity in achieving large vaults, only

30. Frei Otto: German Pavilion, Expo 67, Montreal. The tent-like forms of these tension nets were in fact a most efficient distribution of structural forces.

31. Felix Candela: Church of the Miraculous Virgin, Mexico City, 1954. The expression of forces in opposition actually makes structural sense in a shell.

five-eighths of an inch thick, spanning thirty-three feet. But neither Candela's work [31] nor Otto's hanging cities contradicted basic laws of statics. In fact, like the architecture of Gaudi before them, they made a positive expressive virtue of the inherent logic of structure.

Taking this structural logic as his departure point, the German architect Hans Scharoun showed just how expressively appropriate this fantastic architecture could be on a metaphorical level. For instance his Berlin Philharmonic

Hall catches the frenetic mood of the pre-concert crush in the circulation space [32]. And on the inside of the auditorium the cascading forms (what Scharoun called the 'vineyards of people') are also appropriate to the spirit of musical performance. In fact, music is the generator of form even on a literal level as the convex and broken interior shapes diffuse the sounds around to the surrounding seats. In the twenties, Scharoun was a member of the Utopian group of architects and, like them, a strong exponent of individual creativity as the sole measure of quality and judgement:

Our work is the ecstatic dream of our hot blood, multiplied by the blood pressure in the millions of our fellow human beings.

**32a, b, c. Hans Scharoun:
Philharmonic Hall,
Berlin, 1956–63,** exterior,
interior gangways and
auditorium.

Our blood is the blood of *our* time, of the possibilities of expression in our time.

We create, we must create just as the blood of our ancestors brought on waves of creativity . . .[40]

The point at which this insistence on individual creativity became politically and functionally 'fantastic' was reached by Jorn Utzon in his Sydney Opera House

[33]. This extravagant building led to a parliamentary debate in Australia, several large lotteries, and finally the resignation of the architect because various economies and changes in the programme were introduced. On an architectural level, the appropriateness of the shell vaults could be questioned for not relating either to the acoustic ceilings underneath, or to the function of opera. In fact they were conceived by analogy with the surrounding sailboats and by geometry from the surface of a sphere – neither origin having anything specific to do with an opera house, or with music as in the case of Scharoun. On a

political and social level the project was equally questionable, as it elevated opera to a position of priority within
the spectrum of civic activities – a place usually reserved
for religious buildings or some kind of community centre.

It is at such a point as this that abstract formalism – the
specialty of the intuitive tradition – merges with the preoccupations of the consumer society to bring about the
co-option or domestication of the *avant-garde*. Some
architects in the intuitive tradition such as the Situationists, or extreme individualists like Bruce Goff, managed to keep their ideology of creativity from being
compromised by society. The Situationists demanded a
'collective creation', a 'total participation', 'an art of
dialogue' which kept their defence of the individual
imagination relevant for the rest of society.

The exercise of this playful creativity is the guarantee of the
freedom of each and all, within the framework of that equality
which is guaranteed by the absence of exploitation of one man by
another. The freedom to play means man's creative autonomy,
*which goes beyond the old division between imposed work and passive
leisure* . . . As opposed to spectacle, Situationist culture, when put
into practice, will introduce total participation.

As opposed to the preservation of art, it will involve direct
organization of the lived moment . . . collective . . . an art of
dialogue . . . everyone will become an artist . . . everyone will
construct his own life.[41]

It is also interesting that this plea of the Situationists in
1960 for populist, spontaneous creation harkens back to
the anarchist manifestoes of the twenties, asking, like
them, for the reorganization of 'production on the foundation of a free and equal association of producers'. These
political ideas bring us close to the more revolutionary
concepts of the activist tradition which will be discussed
later, just as the ideas on expressive creativity carry us in
another direction to a half-way house between the self-
conscious and logical traditions.

THE LOGICAL TRADITION

The recent architectural movement in Japan led by Kenzo
Tange fits between many of the traditions and categories
adopted here. In one sense it is an outgrowth of the Heroic

33. Jorn Utzon: Sydney
Opera House, Australia,
1957. The shell vaults,
inefficient as structure, were
to hold acoustic ceilings
some distance below and
were meant to recall the
billowing sail boats and
waves of the harbour – a
quite fantastic association
both in terms of cost and
appropriateness. The cost
grew from an underestimated
$7 million in 1960 to over
70 million

67

Period and Le Corbusier's later work, while it is also very similar to the Supersensualists and, what it is now classified as, part of the logical tradition. The reason for placing the Japanese 'Metabolists' here is that they take many of the ideas and images from other sources and *systematically perfect* them so that they are often superior to their origins. A case in point is Kenzo Tange's Theme Pavilion at Expo 70 [34] which is a realization of the English group – Archigram's – Plug-In-City, 1964, and Yona Friedman's Spatial City, 1961 [208]. What started off as extravagant Utopian visions of the early sixties has ended up as a rationalized discipline by the seventies. The robots are still present and the mechanical equipment is still celebrated in visual terms as a military arsenal of considerable explosive power, and yet this gigantic pavilion was actually the result of a systematic design process (a team under Tange) which bears comparison with that of the US space programme. That this is not an unusual example can be

34. Kenzo Tange: Theme Pavilion, Expo 70, Osaka. Above: a giant megastructure with plug-in capsules, moving lighting booms and stage setting robots on telescoping arms. Below: a performance robot carries people and partially movable seating. Many of the ideas which Archigram projected six years previously have been rationalized by the systematic design process.

35a. **Kiyonari Kikutake:**
Landmark Tower, Expo
70, Osaka, on a triangular
base, consists of three silver
pipe ladders supporting
polyhedral viewing galleries.

35b. **Peter Cook: Montreal**
Tower Project, 1964. The
geodesic net encloses
entertainment areas, the
domes enclose auditoria and
restaurants, while the pods
indicate hotel rooms.

seen in Kiyonari Kikutake's Landmark Tower [35a] which
is also a logical working out of previous projects: the
geodesic experiments of Buckminster Fuller and Archigram's Montreal Tower Project of 1964 [35b]. Again, as
with Tange's structure, we have a lattice grid made up
from ball joints and steel tubes all prefabricated at a factory and quickly bolted together on site. Although some
expressive strength of Archigram remains – the polyhedra
offset by the vertical ladders – the building is still an essay
in rationalized design and efficient logistics (moving the
parts to the site for construction and away, after Expo,
for destruction). This emphasis on the cycles of growth,
change and decay is the basic idea of the Japanese Metabolists and finally, with Kisho Kurokawa's Takara
Beautilion [36], the philosophy can be said to have reached
a level of lyrical expression. Basically, Kurokawa's structure consists of a single unit, repeated 200 times, which is
made up of twelve steel tubes bent to a common radius.

These have end joints which can accept new units in any direction of desired growth. Into the unit structure are slung various capsules, mechanical equipment and circulation systems. The whole metabolic building was assembled in a week – presumably also the time of disassembly.

Although Kurokawa has been unusually successful as an architect, his situation in a way typifies the Japanese 'economic miracle'. By 1971, at thirty-six years old, he had designed numerous buildings, had three pavilions at Expo 70 and two new towns under construction. Like the other Metabolists and unlike the European *avant-garde* of the twenties, his architecture has been accepted by society and actually built. This success, combined with

36a, b. Kisho Kurokawa: Takara Beautilion, Expo 70, Osaka. A grid of bent steel tubes which have flange ends so that new units can be added or subtracted with a change in function. Capsules, stairways, etc. are suspended within the three-dimensional grid.

the fast technological innovation in Japan, has quite naturally generated a political philosophy of meritocracy, managerialism and technocracy. Kenzo Tange has become the major spokesman, both in his work (for instance the City for Ten Million based on a tertiary economy [200]) and in his pronouncements:

In challenging reality, we must prepare and strive for a coming era which must be characterized by a new type of technological revolution . . . the control and planning of the production and distribution of energy while creating productivity far surpassing that of the present . . . In the not too distant future the impact of a second technological revolution will change the basic nature of overall society . . .[42]

This emphasis on systematic planning, continuous growth and the impact of the cybernetic revolution was so characteristic of the logical tradition as almost to constitute its ideological trademark. Buckminster Fuller, the inventor-architect, took the position to its furthest ex-

treme designing geodesic structures [37] and proclaiming the final triumph of technocracy (or administration) over politics:

> It seems perfectly clear that when there is enough to go around man will not fight any more than he now fights for air. When man is successful in doing so much more with so much less that he can take care of everybody at a higher standard, then there will be no fundamental cause for war . . . Within ten years it will be normal for man to be successful . . . Politics will become obsolete.[43]

The next argument of Fuller parallels almost verbatim *Saint-Simon's Parable* of 1832 where the disastrous effect of taking away industry and its experts is contrasted with that of getting rid of the politicians.

37. **Buckminster Fuller:** **Union Tank Car** **Company, Louisiana,** **1958.** Diameter 384 feet, height 116 feet, this was when built 'the largest clear-span enclosure ever built anywhere'. Fuller's principle of maximum efficiency per pound often produces, as a by-product, a visually homogeneous and striking image.

On the other hand, supposing that we take away instead every politician, all the ideologies, all the books on politics – and send them into orbit around the sun. Everybody would keep on eating as before, down will go all the political barriers and we could begin to find ways in which we could send the goods that were in great surplus in one place to another.[44]

As always in the logical tradition, the self-effacing virtues of the engineer, his service-orientation and efficiency are contrasted with the closed-mindedness of the bully politicians. Fuller proposes a system of world organization where his noble savage engineers, 'The Universal Architects', replace the government of men with the administration of efficiency. This ideology of 'the Post-Industrial Society' or even 'the end of ideology' became paramount in the early sixties and, oddly enough, very popular among architectural students in the late sixties in spite of the fact that its drawbacks had become obvious and criticized in such devastating works as Noam Chomsky's *American Power and the New Mandarins* (1969). Where there was no ideological restraint, the self-effacing technicians were just as likely to work for destructive as constructive ends.

Another set of justifications coming forth from the logical tradition concerned the nature of universal truths and the doctrine of Functionalism (roughly that form should follow it without deviation). Pier Luigi Nervi brought out the Platonic assumptions of this approach in an article entitled 'Is Architecture Moving Towards Unchanging Forms?' (the answer was, basically, 'yes') which had the following injunction:

To approach the mysterious laws of nature with modest aspirations and try to interpret and command them by obeying them, is the only method to bring their majestic eternity to the service of our limited and contingent goals.[45]

His architecture was visually convincing enough to persuade many that a modest and inquiring approach towards function and 'the laws of nature' (in his case structure and logistics) would result inevitably in 'majestic eternity' or at least beauty [38]. Yet there were a few examples where the reverse was also true, where his straightforward commitment to the programme of the building led to a pompous monotony not unlike that of the selfconscious

73

tradition. Indeed one should point out that there seems to be a definite correlation between this latter tradition and the logical. When there are strong central governments, then large mega-structures, stadia and autobahns tend to get built, as in the thirties and sixties. In fact, Nervi built some of his most beautiful structures, such as his airplane hangars and stadia, under the Fascists in the late thirties.

A last set of attitudes and values in the logical tradition concerns the question of solving complex problems with systematic design methods and the writing of 'performance requirements' as opposed to concentrating on the finished object. The Parametric School of design, which grew up in the middle sixties to become a major movement around the world, will be discussed in Chapter 8. This school placed primary emphasis on the analysis, measurement and reconciliation of all the elements which could be called parameters in a building. That is to say, in the most sophisticated models of Christopher Alexander, anything that could be thought about or perceived – even such things as marital relations and kinship systems.

38. Pier Luigi Nervi: Palazetto dello Sport, Rome, 1958-9. Pylons which support the central ceiling and seating are tapered in three dimensions following the complex structural forces. Compare with [31].

One school to have a strong basis in systematic design was the 'New Bauhaus', the *Hochschule für Gestaltung*, which opened in Ulm, Germany, in 1955 and ran until its governmental funds were cut off in 1968. Led by such designers as Max Bill and Thomás Maldonado, this school produced a very distinctive *style* of parametric design: the results were always recognizably smooth, understated to the point of reticence, crisply detailed and coolly antiseptic. When parametric design took on particular visual metaphors they were those of the computer and hospital with their overtones of precision and neutrality. Ulm's emphasis on a rigorous approach to science and technology combined with New Left politics led to its being suppressed by the conservative and provincial government of Baden-Württemberg. The radical design theory which was being evolved at this time, based on computer analysis and semiology (the theory of signs), was unfortunately fragmented as the teachers left.

Another approach of the Parametric School, led by the systems designer Ezra Ehrenkrantz, concentrated on

39. Ezra Ehrenkrantz: S.C.S.D., 1964. A system of four elements: structural roofdeck, air conditioning, lighting and partitions. These four systems account for about half of the total cost of a school.

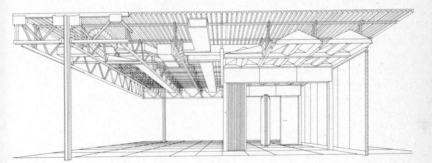

more prosaic requirements, such as designing four major components for a school building system [**39**]. Basically, these components concerned only the environmental servicing and left the architect or builder free to finish off the appearance of the building in any way he pleased. Called by the acronym SCSD (Schools Construction System Development), this system became both successful in California and influential throughout the world. In California at least thirteen schools had been built with it by 1966, at substantial savings, and thousands of entrepreneurs had appropriated the sub-systems for their own particular requirements. In this sense, one of the political ideals of the logical tradition came true: the technical services offered by a team of engineers resulted in a product that increased efficiency and was socially productive. Not surprisingly, Ezra Ehrenkrantz had previously studied the Hertfordshire Schools in England, where a supporting idea had become a major orthodoxy: the unselfconscious and restrained approach to design.

THE UNSELFCONSCIOUS TRADITION

In 1946, Stirrat Johnson-Marshall and his design team produced the prototype for the mass-produced system of Hertfordshire Schools. Two years and twenty-nine schools later, Johnson-Marshall and his team were appointed by the Ministry of Education to centralize research and formulate official policy.

> What is needed [they stated] is a *team* of experts, with the architect responsible for maintaining a balance between all aspects, ensuring that the contribution of each specialist is properly related to the whole . . . This approach and building will lead us to . . . new architecture which is a simple and unselfconscious expression of present-day requirements.[46]

This emphasis on a 'simple and unselfconscious expression' which would naturally grow out of group design was a selfconscious attempt to invent a new vernacular which would be as restrained, anonymous and dignified as Georgian architecture. The other model was the common vernacular of nineteenth-century industrial buildings – the 'functional tradition', as J. M. Richards termed it. Both historical styles were exemplified for their relevance to large building programmes and mass housing, to which the English Welfare State was initially committed in 1946. The situation was similar in other countries. In Sweden, New Towns such as Vallingby were constructed in a modern vernacular suitable to background building. The Russians undertook a programme of mass-producing large-scale housing units that could be factory-assembled, driven to the site, and put in place by a travelling crane [40]. They also applied aviation technology to the housing

40. Russian prefabricated dwellings, 1965. Heavy, inflexible units are self-supporting and can be stacked like bricks by a travelling crane.

problem, coming up with units that had great strength and size but, unfortunately, little opportunity to alter with the change in family life and technology. Nevertheless, as one architect put the advantages:

It will take Moscow builders about fifteen years of vigorous effort to put an end once and for all to the housing problem . . . another two million flats by 1980. All Moscow families will then have a room for each member of the family plus one common room . . . There will be on an average about twenty square metres of useful area per each inhabitant in a flat.[47]

This ratio, as against six square metres per inhabitant in the twenties, gives one a crude idea of the progress made. And yet, taken as a whole, these developments of the unselfconscious tradition had two great faults: the actual welfare programmes were always inadequate in size and inflexible, not to say inhumane, in practice. At best they could produce New Towns such as Cumbernauld [211]

and the CLASP system of school building [41], while at worst they were monotonous, paternalistic and 'closed'.

Opposed to these attitudes and methods of welfare were two others in the unselfconscious tradition. One, which could be called libertarian anarchism, has already been briefly mentioned in the pronouncements of the Situationists and Hundertwasser:

> Only when architect, bricklayer and occupant are a unity, i.e. one and the same person, can one speak of architecture. Everything else is not architecture, but the physical incarnation of a criminal act.[48]

The other is consumer power where the design initiative is decentralized and everyone is (theoretically) given the opportunity to buy what sub-systems he can find on the open market. An example of this is the Do-It-Yourself industry which has grown since 1950 to a point where more than 20,000 shops exist in Britain, and in the United States it is a multi-billion dollar business. In the beginning it started off catering to relatively unskilled labour in the house – such as painting, decorating, wiring – after

41. Matthew, Johnson-Marshall: University of York, 1965. The CLASP system, was adopted for quick and cheap erection. The result has Georgian-like qualities as demanded in 1946.

which it moved into all constructional areas including the most complicated ones. By 1970 it accounted for most of the internal work in the house and was serviced by 'How to-do-it' magazines, annual exhibitions, drive-in department stores, cataloguing and information centres, and a gigantic mail order business.

The relevance of such things as the Do-It-Yourself industry for the question of mass housing and welfare was that they showed a possible alternative to the inflexible paternalism of centralized systems. Instead of a monotonous repetitive grid of mass housing, one might have the more significantly expressive hodge-podge of Las Vegas, Route One or Main Street. Instead of the personalized elements being supplied from above, the individual, who is the only one capable of making local design decisions, could make the choice from below. At least this was the major idea of Nikolaas Habraken, the Dutch architect who developed a very influential theory of housing in the early sixties. Habraken's main contribution was very simple and quite obvious, but nevertheless impressive for its relevance. He continuously insisted on the major distinction between what he called 'structural supports and detachable units' or those things which are public, relatively inflexible, long term and those which are private, responsive and short term. Since most high-rise housing glosses over this distinction, there is a natural antagonism between the two sectors within it. Supports are not built and private space cannot be changed or moulded by the individual. By placing responsibility for the supports in municipal and architects' hands and leaving detachable units to the individual in the consumer situation, Habraken proposed at least one way out of the housing impasse.

Another related way was proposed by Ezra Ehrenkrantz and his various design teams. Significantly enough, Ehrenkrantz moved, after his initial success with SCSD, from designing components to merely specifying which existing systems were *compatible*. This evolution was a natural result of the consumer society: the movement from a designer to a 'coordinating cataloguer'. Ehrenkrantz's two design teams in Britain and the US would merely show in a cross-referenced table which lighting systems were compatible with which structures and so on.

From this one would have an 'open' rather than 'closed' system, or in another key-word of the late sixties, a 'kit-of-parts' which could generate a near infinite amount of unique buildings. Also, Ehrenkrantz and his team developed for the US Government's 'Operation Breakthrough' a fibershell system based on new plastic technologies which was itself a 'kit-of-parts plus rules and a process by which the parts can be joined' [42]. It is not far from this, conceptually at least, to see the point reached where everyone could design his own unique shelter or detachable unit within some larger support structure.

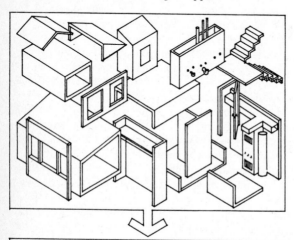

42. Ezra Ehrenkrantz and BSD: Fibershell Kit-of-Parts, 1970, generates different house types. Because all the elements are wrapped as a single shell on the site there are no joints within the parts.

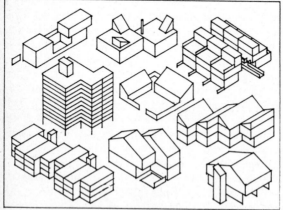

Although certain of the other traditions – the intuitive and idealist – recognize that a large part of the environmental problem comes from the nature of society, and seek to transform that society, it is only the activists who concentrate on the social means and agencies of change. The housing problem? As Engels put it unequivocally in the nineteenth century, there is no problem if one divides the existing amount of shelter by the number of people. Of course this necessitates, in practice, a social revolution and an expropriation of the present owners and the occupation of their houses by homeless workers or people living under excessively crowded conditions. But:

> There is only one means of ending this housing crisis: that is simply to abolish the exploitation and oppression of the workers by the ruling class . . . Solving the housing question will not simultaneously solve the social question, but solving the social question, that is, abolishing the capitalist mode of production, will make it possible to solve the housing question.[49]

Such measures of expropriation and redistribution were carried through by the Bolsheviks after the October revolution of 1917, but in the rest of the world where revolutions did not occur, Engels's straightforward logic turned out to be actually brutal: because what he proposed in *The Housing Question* (1872) was that new housing for the proletariat should be rejected, since this would ameliorate the conditions of the poor and thereby break their revolutionary spirit. Such all-or-nothing logic which regards reformism as counter-revolutionary tends to be a prevalent attitude of the activist tradition, both its moral strength and pragmatic weakness.

In terms of its own fortunes, the tradition underwent its great period during the early twenties with Communist-Constructivism, before this was killed by the Stalinist reaction from within and by conservative and liberal reformism from without. The activist tradition only came to life again thirty years later with the rebirth of the New Left, the student activists, drop-out communities and other fragmented, revolutionary groups.

Soon after the Russian Revolution of 1917, the live art and architectural movements which existed, such as Cubo-Futurism, made their alliance with the social movement in a single, if unstable, *avant-garde*. The Futurist-Constructivist poet Vladimir Mayakovsky demanded a socially active street art:

> We do not need a dead mausoleum of art where dead works are worshipped, but a living factory of the human spirit – in the streets, in the tramways, in the factories, workshops and workers' homes.[50]

Out of the museum, into the streets and factories, was also the demand of the new broadsheet *Art of the Commune* in 1918:

> The proletariat will create new houses, new streets, new objects of everyday life ... Art of the proletariat is not a holy shrine where things are lazily regarded, but work, a factory which produces new artistic things.[51]

43. Vladimir Tatlin: Monument to the Third International, 1919-20. A 'construction' or putting together of various sub-systems: two interlocking helices, and four Platonic solids which hold assemblies, executive and agit-prop centres. The helices on the diagonal symbolized the Marxist dialectic which develops 'in spirals ... in leaps and bounds, catastrophes, revolutions'.

In fact much of the available surface on the streets and articles of everyday use such as trains and boats were covered with a mixture of Cubo-Futurist art and written slogans. This combination produced Constructivism and its first 'monument' in the winter of 1919, Vladimir Tatlin's Monument to the Third International [43]. Made up from a lattice structure reminiscent of the Eiffel Tower and four gigantic primary forms which were meant to revolve on their axes, this tower became the symbol of Constructivism for both its adherents and detractors. Among the latter were Lenin and Trotsky. Trotsky attacked the monument for its functional in-adequacies – 'we would answer that meetings surely need not take place in a cylinder, and that the cylinder surely need not rotate'.[52] Lenin, although not specifically attacking Tatlin, denounced all the *avant-garde* movements, having Constructivism in mind as well.

> I cannot value the works of expressionism, futurism, cubism, and other isms as the highest expressions of artistic genius. I don't understand them. They give me no pleasure.[53]

What gave Lenin pleasure, like Marx and later the Stalinists, was the social realism of Courbet in painting, Balzac in literature and the classicism of the Greeks in architecture. Perhaps another reason for Lenin's distaste for all the 'isms' was that when he was in Zurich planning the Russian Revolution in 1915, right down the street, at the Café Voltaire, were the Dadaists planning the artistic revolution that would leave art dead. When the news of Tatlin's monument reached Germany, the Dadaists made him the centrepiece of their exhibition, in June 1920: 'Art is Dead, Long Live the New Machine Art of the Tatlins'. Lenin was not amused either by the antics of the Dadaists or the anti-art position (really just anti-*bourgeois* art) of the Constructivists. The architect, polemicist Alexei Gan, a major exponent of this view, called for an end to salon art.

> The social-political set-up dictated by the new economic structure brings to life new forms and means of expression. Intellectual-material production will be expressed in the rising-up of a culture of work and the intellect. The first slogan of Constructivism is 'Down with speculative activity in artistic work! We declare unconditional war on art.'[54]

Work, construction and propaganda versus bourgeois, speculative art privately owned and viewed in dead museums – such were the antitheses. Several of the Constructivists, such as Gabo, Pevsner and Lissitsky, were caught in the middle of these antitheses, so they left Russia in 1921 for the West.

The next major steps in the Constructivists' evolution were two architectural projects of the brothers Vesnin – the Pravda Building, 1924, and the Palace of Labour, 1923 [44]. The Palace of Labour project really marked the consolidation of the Constructivists' style. Here were all the striking contrasts which had typified their previous work: the street slogans, the large-scale graphics advertising a meeting for 9.30 in the hall for 8,000 spectators, the incredible use of tension cables and radio antennae as if they were spun-steel spider webs and liquid propulsion rockets – all this set off against a strongly disciplined concrete frame and steel girders. The programme imagined for this Palace celebrating work was equally fantastic: two auditoria which could be combined into one for 10,500 spectators; administration offices, the agit-prop radio station, a restaurant for 6,000 diners to eat at once [sic], a social science museum, a museum of labour, a library, a meteorological observatory and, even, an astrophysical laboratory – presumably for the Communist astronomers to see that the earthly dialectic was keeping time with the cosmic revolutions. It was this great social imagination which typified the best work of the Constructivists. They took every opportunity to create new forms of social experience which would actively transform life. Prime among these were the new film and theatrical experiments, the communal housing, the disurbanized city and the workers' club. Indeed the workers' club, which grew out of the Palace of Labour, was looked upon as the successor to the Renaissance palace and the bourgeois church – a 'social power plant' into which the major activities were drawn in order to create the multifaceted and fully developed man of Communist life.

Another new form of life created was the communal house which also contained a spectrum of different functions. The Constructivist group, termed OSA, described in their 1928 manifesto the intentions of social transformation behind this type of housing:

44. Alexander, Leonid and Victor Vesnin: Palace of Labour, 1923. A reinforced concrete frame, reminiscent of Perret's work in France and a Gropius project, shows the international awareness of the Constructivists at this time. The use of advertisement, super-radio technology, and lattice columns in dynamic confrontation, is unique to them.

We are opposed to such prerevolutionary building types as the speculative apartment house, the private residence, the 'nobleman's club', etc., all products of prerevolutionary social, technical and economic circumstances, but still serving as a model for buildings now being erected in the U.S.S.R.: [instead we propose] new types of communal housing, new types of clubs, palaces of labour, new factories, etc. which in fact should be the conductors and condensers of socialist culture.[55]

'Conductors and condensers of socialist culture', 'a social power plant' – the metaphor of the electrical condenser was seriously used to suggest that such new forms would transform the old self-centred individual of bourgeois culture into a responsible, altruistic citizen. The woman would be liberated as well, finding the daily round of

45a, b. Moses Ginzburg and I. Milinis: Narkomfim Communal House, Moscow, 1928-9. Like Le Corbusier, with whom he was corresponding, Ginzberg designed a unity which included collective facilities such as a kitchen, gymnasium, library, nursery, roof garden, canteen and heating services. The standard unit includes a double-height living-room, as in Le Corbusier's Unité [3].

chores which kept her enslaved – cleaning, cooking, washing, nursing – taken over in part by the collective facilities [45]. Unfortunately, not enough of these communal houses were built and the few that were put up created a disastrous reaction. Whereas an extended family could move into an expropriated bourgeois apartment and not be too overcrowded, when they inhabited the closely-packaged spaces of the communal house, it became a 'behavioural sink' – to use the bourgeois metaphor of condemnation.

In fact there was a curious parallel at this time in the Russian and Western reactions to the new architecture and its social Utopianism: they both started rejecting functionalism and communal living for being inhumane

and too materialistic. In part this reaction was brought on by the unequivocal materialism of Marxist architects, such as Hannes Meyer, who was forever denouncing all types of sensuality as a formalism unsuited to scientific socialism. Hannes Meyer had taken over the Bauhaus for two years, from 1928 to 1930, and triumphed on such trenchantly tough-minded slogans as –

All things in this world are a product of the formula: function times economics.

So none of these things are works of art.

All art is composition and hence unsuited to a particular end.

All life is function and therefore not artistic.

The idea of the 'composition of a dock' is enough to make a cat laugh.[56]

These materialistic epithets didn't make the conservatives of Dessau laugh (they threw Meyer out) and they even brought on a rare ironic invective of the liberals. Gropius said later:

[Hannes Meyer] was a radical petit bourgeois. His philosophy culminates in the assertion that 'life is oxygen plus sugar plus starch plus protein', to which Mies retorted: 'Try stirring all that together, it stinks'.[57]

What stank, in particular, were the polemics of Meyer (and the Swiss magazine of architecture, *ABC*), which proposed a mechanistic determinism devoid of ideological and spiritual influence. One witty and peevish manifesto of 1928 was called *ABC Demands the Dictatorship of the Machine*. Nevertheless where almost everyone else was polite and evasive about certain aspects of contemporary architecture, Meyer tried to be realistic (even if sectarian):

The Leninist architect is not an aesthetic lackey and, unlike his colleague in the West, not a lawyer and custodian of the interests of the Capitalist ruling class there . . . For him architecture is not an aesthetic stimulus but a keen edged weapon in the class struggle.

Or later, to Mexican students in 1938:

Remember: architecture is a weapon which at all times has been wielded by the ruling class of human society.[58]

Even if there were a false antithesis between aesthetics and social commitment, Meyer was still pointing here to an unpopular truth about who actually controls architecture. Indeed this truth was brought home particularly in Russia where the ruling class of State Capitalists crushed Constructivism in 1932 in favour of Socialist Realism. (They also made it necessary for Meyer himself to leave once again, this time for the West.) The actual theoretical

arguments that the Stalinists used to eliminate Constructivism paralleled in essence their political purges. Instead
of Bukharin's 'right-wing deviationism', the sin was the
formalism of those such as Tatlin; instead of the 'left-
wing deviationism' of Trotsky, the sin was the functionalism and mechanism of those such as Ginzburg.
Naturally Stalinism occupied the only true, balanced
centre without deviationism, although in fact it used all
its epithets of abuse interchangeably when it was convenient to do so. Stalin: 'We have always said that the
"Lefts" are also "Rights", only they mask their Right-
ness behind Left phrases.' In other words, 'heads I win,
tails you lose'. The final victory for Socialist Realism was
achieved in the Palace of the Soviets Competition of
1932 when the Constructivist entries, along with Le
Corbusier's, etc., were thrown out for a 'classical' solution
and branded as part of the international bourgeois conspiracy of formalism, functionalism, individualism, col-
lectivism, all the opposing deviations which the Stalinists
used interchangeably.

Thirty years later, the activist tradition began to
recover somewhat. On a political level, there were the
various fragmented groups I have already mentioned,
which managed to accomplish slight changes. For instance, the student uprisings in France in May 1968
brought about minimal reforms in architectural education, such as the decentralization of the *Ecole des Beaux
Arts* and, in England, there were hints of a greater student
participation and self-government after the sit-ins at the
Hornsey and Guildford Colleges of Art in 1968. Yet
besides some new ideas in planning, which will be discussed in Chapter 8, the only unique and successful
creations of the activist tradition concerned the squatter
housing and drop-out communities.

The squatting movement started right after the Second
World War in a large way in almost every industrialized
country. It wasn't simply the influx of returning soldiers
which caused it, but more, the rapid urbanization that
attracted many people in from the country. Around all
the major cities in South America, including Brasilia,
these squatters set up their *ad hoc* arrangements. In
France, *bidonvilles* were formed (the name came from
bidons – petrol cans – hammered flat to provide building

material). And like their counterparts in South America, they were often formed right next to new housing, ironically, inasmuch as their major inhabitants were the underpaid building workers.

The actual squatter housing varies from country to country since it all depends on finding a quirk in the law, a strange custom or a particular cultural attitude. In Greece squatters settle quickly outside Athens on property which is divided up by speculators either at night or on a religious holiday. In the United States, where the police force is much stronger and more efficient, there is no illegal squatting. One of the infrequent examples which did occur was Tent City in Boston, which lasted for only four days and was located on a parking lot. The more usual American example was either the movable commune such as Hog Farm, which lived off light and sound shows performed for various tolerant communities, or the legal drop-out communities which paid for the land and discarded junk [46]. In Britain,

46. Drop City, Arizona, 1966. Geodesic domes made from used car bodies and other consumer durables. The semi-agrarian commune became for many young either a weekend trip or a somewhat more permanent experience.

squatting developed later, in 1969, in its own peculiar way. The particular gimmicks involved here were a medieval law going back to the Crusades, newspaper reporters looking for a good story, and a relatively kind-hearted Ministry of Housing which disliked nothing so much as a scandal. Basically, the squatters would move into unoccupied houses due to be pulled down. Then when the police came to evict them, the squatters would point to the crusaders' law denying forcible entry . . . and use it against the police! Naturally, the courts were not completely convinced by this *ad hoc* extension of a statute, but the newspapers were and so for a moment was the Ministry, which put pressure on the local councils to allow the squatters to remain. By 1970 over a hundred families were housed in temporary accommodation and the squatting movement was determined to become legal and massive.

However, it was the situation in Peru that was the most successful and bizarre. About one-fifteenth of the population, or 700,000, live in squatter settlements, or *barriadas*, as they are called. The way a *barriada* comes into being is instructive.[59] During the night an advance guard made up of lay-out men draws the boundaries for streets and lots.

47. Barriada, outside Lima, Peru, in its first stage made from mat sheds. The two later stages of development resulted in more permanent masonry structures and a minimal infrastructure of services.

In the early morning, up to a thousand squatters arrive by truck, bus and taxi, accompanied by lawyers who have chosen suitable sites, and a woman, known as 'the Secretary of Defence' who is a good typist and a buffer to the counter-attacking police (who in turn arrive on the scene at about 10 o'clock). By lunch time, when the police have managed to lose their struggle, a small town of mat sheds is laid out with future provisions for growth and zones for churches, clinics and other facilities [47]. Thereafter starts a two-stage process where more permanent abodes are built and a democratic form of government is introduced – in a country where local democracy had disappeared sixty years before. Beyond this political advantage, the *barriada* also introduces a very strong community spirit based on self-help and popular initiative. Where everyone constructs and destroys his own house according to need and desire and where communal services have to be created by popular initiative, there grows a kind of fraternal feeling which was predicted by Mutualist doctrine. Indeed the *barriadas* became so successful that they were featured in the architectural magazines, major European architects, such as Aldo van Eyck and James Stirling, were asked to design them and the Peruvian government gave up repressing them and actually re-christened them 'Young Towns'.

Other events in the activist tradition bore out the advantages of direct, spontaneous action as a catalyst for participation. Such things as the 'instant city', produced by rock festivals, showed what potential existed within society for self-organization – at least for a long weekend, as at the Woodstock festival where half a million lived for four days. An instance of such a festival merging with a public, political realm was the May Events in France. The emphasis was again on *ad hoc* self-organization for specific goals, such as feeding the Parisian population when supplies had run short. Paris was divided up into 460 Action Committees which were coordinated as a federal body, but the revolutionists, such as Daniel Cohn-Bendit, refused to allow this coordination to degenerate into political control from above and they refused to be swayed by previous revolutionary theory – above all the Marxist–Leninist emphasis on the vanguard, élite party. The emphasis was on spontaneous organization.

The organization of the local Action Committees did not precede the events but followed them step by step. New forms were evolved as we went along and as we found the old forms inadequate and paralysing . . . [The Action Committees] were born for the purpose of solving concrete common problems and sharing life in battle, rendering aid to the strikers, and helping wherever help was most needed.[60]

In terms of architectural and environmental expression, the May Events produced the kind of street art and wall slogans which were seen in 1917, except that they were less idealistic and more humorous: 'It is forbidden to forbid; TOUT EST POSSIBLE: The Reign of Imagination; The more I make the Revolution, the more I want to make love, the more I make love, the more I want to make the revolution', etc. The hardware architecture was made up of paving stones, street signs, garbage cans and automobiles which were instantly 'liberated' of their first-hand status and turned into 'used cars'. The relation of these *ad hoc* barricades to the usual scrap heaps of consumer society was not without its ironic side.

On a more conventional architectural level, and well within the political doctrines of Marxism, the French *Utopie Group* produced a series of satirical collages which attacked the reigning architectural ideologies of liberalism and futurism and offered a transient, mobile architecture totally made from pneumatic, inflatable products – walls, floors, partitions, furniture, even the mechanical equipment was inflatable [48]. Because of its cost, responsive-

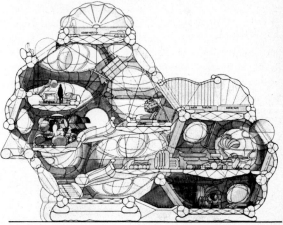

48. J. P. Jungman: Dyoden, 1968. Totally inflatable architecture resembles in its bulbous, rubber rings the shapes of the Michelin man. A similar-looking structure was erected by the Japanese at Expo 70.

ness and quickness, this pneumatic architecture naturally connected up with *Utopie*'s leftist politics. Like clothing, pneumatic architecture could be put on and off in a short time. Like the human body, it was responsive, warm, squashy and pleasant to touch. Like dirt, it was cheap. These values reflected, in a symbolic sense, the new ideology of the activist tradition in its departure from nineteenth-century theories of revolution, just as did Woodstock and the May Events.

It would be oversimplifying matters to reduce the politics of these six traditions to certain common denominators: anarchism does not reduce to Fascism, in spite of the fact that Mussolini and Marinetti went from one to the other. Nevertheless there are some shared assumptions which cut across the traditions and have positive implications. For instance, the idea of artistic freedom and autonomy is shared by the selfconscious, idealist and intuitive traditions, while the idea of social equality is common to the activist, unselfconscious, logical and idealist traditions. Freedom and equality – a dualism which tends to be ideologically unstable and difficult to attain in practice, but which, once reached, is self-reinforcing, since the political freedom protects the socialism and the equality allows a full democracy to emerge. In addition, these complementary qualities are in a sense ultimate, inasmuch as it is hard to conceive of a greater justice than equal social opportunity combined with political freedom. Most of the modern movements in architecture are concerned with these two interrelated ideologies and define their positions with respect to them. Yet the major protagonists – Mies, Gropius, Wright, Le Corbusier and Aalto – often had a tenuous grasp of these ideologies, especially towards the end of their careers, and we will now consider the effect of this slackening, where it did occur.

2. THE PROBLEM OF MIES

Less is more. (MIES)
Less is a bore. (ROBERT VENTURI)

The problem of Mies van der Rohe for critics and inhabitants of his architecture alike is that he demands an absolute commitment to the Platonic world-view in order to appreciate his buildings. Without this commitment, the technical and functional mistakes which he creates are so damaging that one can no longer accept the Platonic form as being 'perfect' or 'ideal' or even 'plausible'. Rather it becomes merely beautiful and sometimes even just trite. There are a few cases – the Barcelona Pavilion and the Farnsworth House – where this is not true, where his Platonic statements of pure form and transcendental technology are plausible and even appropriate, because the purpose and surrounding landscape provide the context for an 'ideal' solution. But in other cases – the Chapel at Illinois Institute of Technology or the town houses at Lafayette Park – the purity of form leads to an inarticulate architecture, or one extraneous element, a bathroom vent, leads to monumental bathos [49]. There

49. **Mies van der Rohe:**
Lafayette Park, Detroit,
1955-63. Bathroom vents,
television aerials, etc.
shatter the pretensions of a
'perfect form'.

is no place for a mistake in his absolute universe, because extreme simplicity makes one hypersensitive to each inch of a structure and the Platonic form, with its transcendental pretension, demands utter perfection.

THE CRITICS' VIEWS

Lewis Mumford speaks for many critics of these sublime failures when he says in 'The Case against "Modern Architecture"' that:

> Mies van der Rohe used the facilities offered by steel and glass to create elegant monuments of nothingness. They had the dry style of machine forms without the contents. His own chaste taste gave these hollow glass shells a crystalline purity of form; but they existed alone in the Platonic world of his imagination and had no relation to site, climate, insulation, function, or internal activity; indeed, they completely turned their backs upon these realities just as the rigidly arranged chairs of his living rooms openly disregarded the necessary intimacies and informalities of conversation. This was the apotheosis of the compulsive, bureaucratic spirit. Its emptiness and hollowness were more expressive than van der Rohe's admirers realized.[1]

This seems to be a damaging indictment since most of the accusations are true on a *literal* level: his architecture only relates imperfectly to site, climate, place, etc. But the defence of Mies admirers is that his architecture, like poetry, is not to be understood on the literal level. To do so would be like reading *Hamlet* for its literal statements about 'life' or 'women'.

The problem that Mies raises in an acute form is 'How much importance should one give to literal meanings in an architecture of analogy where pure form stands for other values?' The answer of most critics would appear to be 'none at all'. Thus Mies has been accepted as 'one of the three greatest architects of the twentieth century whose architecture expressed the spirit of the century' (as the American newspaper obituaries put it), because his great 'integrity of form' (as Giedion put it) exploited the 'essence of modern technology' (as nearly everyone puts it). But again these statements have to be understood on the level of analogy, because they are literally false: i.e. the essence of modern technology has moved much beyond the inefficient principle of post and lintel construction which Mies often used; form simply cannot have integrity if it doesn't relate to function or technique; and the spirit of the century is as much motivated by democratic idealism as it is by Platonic élitism. But such objections are glossed over by most of the critics and Mies admirers.

Thus Sigfried Giedion compares the spirit of Mies's architecture to the calm, crystalline interiors of de Hooch, a seventeenth-century Dutch painter, who achieved the same clear quality of light and sharp outline; the same presentation of abstract form and calm order verging on quietism. The reason why Giedion finds an 'integrity of form' here is that Mies 'has subdued all forms to the utmost purity' by bringing out the essential qualities of each material and building full-scale models of construction details until all the extraneous, visual elements have been removed.[2] In fact other critics such as William Jordy are also convinced by Mies's visual perfectionism and speak about the brilliance of solving the corner junction [50] or the refinement of the curtain wall from one project

50. Mies van der Rohe: Seagram Building, New York, 1958, external corner. The curtain wall of regularly spaced I-beams is extended out a few inches from the column lines so that there is a rich articulation of angles at the corner.

to another.[3] There is a whole world of analogous meaning
to be found in a Miesian detail, and critics and architects
are prepared to inhabit this world as if it were complete:
none more so than Peter and Alison Smithson. They speak
about 'Mies's immortality' coming from the 'neutralizing
skin and the open space structure' of the urban layout.[4]
They eulogize his essentialist use of materials, the 'thing-
ness of brick' and even go so far as saying that Lafayette
Park is 'certainly the most civilized dwelling-quarter of

51. Mies van der Rohe:
Lafayette Towers and
Court Houses, Detroit,
1955–63. The curtain wall is
applied indiscriminately to
dwellings, offices and
institutional buildings,
thereby trivializing the
functions.

this century' [51]. The problem with this kind of assertion is that it fails to note that as a civilization becomes more open, it makes more semantic discriminations between building types, a discrimination which Mies's 'neutralizing skin' does everything to obscure. Not even the connoisseur acquainted with the Miesian idiom can identify the religious building at IIT, so the lettering 'Chapel' had to be added on by way of signification; or the same 'perfect' form of a two-way horizontal grid was used indiscriminately for an office project in Cuba and then later on two different museums [52]. The justification for this repetition was that 'you can do anything you wish in this building' because the form and space were 'universal'. But again the statements of intent amounted to literal falsehoods

52. Mies van der Rohe: Gallery of the Twentieth Century, Berlin, 1962–8. The absolute form of a two-way grid supported on exterior columns was used across many different projects, and in each case the most important functions, here the permanent art collection, were suppressed in the basement.

because in fact the space was anything but universal and, as in the Crown Hall at IIT, important functions were suppressed and constricted into the basement. As to the question of semantic discrimination, the Smithsons assert that it is both acknowledged and solved in the buildings:

> By anyone truly bedded in our culture, a building by Mies can be placed with ease, certainly dated within three years by dozens of signs to do with changing building techniques and the refinement of the formal idea.[5]

However, if we examine the development of his use of the curtain wall since 1951 this assertion seems to be once again literally false, as Mies's buildings do not change purposefully with a change in technology. Furthermore, in so far as the assertion is true, it is damaging from the semantic point of view because the refinements are only discernible to an art historian or architect *already well acquainted* with all of Mies's buildings. That is, 'anyone truly bedded in our culture' could not date these buildings; only a connoisseur could.

That architectural historians continue to find the esoteric refinements of primary interest and a substitute for social and semantic problems is clear from a critique of the Seagram Building by William Jordy:

> With all odds favouring a weightless result when Mies employed the curtain wall for the Seagram, he refuted reasonable expectations. In this refutation, with what is visually, all things considered, the first weighty skyscraper to be completely enveloped in its glass window wall, lies the meaning of the Seagram [53].[6]

The reduction of 'meaning' to such formal concerns as the 'weighty' tradition of skyscrapers is not an atypical move of critics who favour and admire Mies. However, in this case the reduction obscures other concerns, such as the fact that a large amount of social content has remained unacknowledged either in expression or flexibility. The users of this building, as many as in a large town, cannot change the internal space because of its exacting precision, except at great cost.[7] However, high cost is just one of the many 'problems' created when Mies reduces 'more' to 'less' in order to achieve his Platonic essentialism.

Consider, even in Mies's own terms of visual refinement, how far he has failed to reach a 'perfect' visual solution to

53a, b. Mies van der Rohe: Seagram Building, New York, 1958. Façade of bronze sections with tinted glass to match creates a 'weighty' solution to the glass skyscraper. The lighting and window blinds are automatically controlled to provide a uniform visual effect regardless of the users' needs.

54. Mies van der Rohe: Seagram Building, internal corner. One interesting aspect resulting from the commitment to 'Platonic form' is the conflict between two absolute systems. If the structural system is perfectly regular on the inside, then the mullion system has to break its rhythm on the outside if an internal corner is turned, as here. While this may seem to be a trivial inconsistency, it points to the contradiction facing those who claim to have discovered an order in the universe.

resolving the geometries on the internal corner of the Seagram Building [54]. If in formal terms the exterior corners of the building are masterful and convincing, the internal ones are indecisive and botched: they look as if a meat cleaver has sliced the two regular curtain walls off at mid-point and just joined what is left over. It appears that Mies is trying to get away with a fudge on just the very problem which would have exercised the greatest skill and passion of past, classical architects. The architects of the Parthenon and the Italian Palazzi of the Renaissance were obsessed by the 'problem of the corner' and devised many visual refinements to deal with it, there simply being no 'perfect' solution possible in the nature of the case. In the Seagram's corner the 'problem' is that if the interior columns and exterior mullions are regularly spaced, then there is no way to turn an internal corner without breaking one of the two regularities. In this case, the even rhythm of the window bay is broken by the remaining half-bay, a result which would not matter in a richer architecture or one based on a botched aesthetic, but which is a near disaster in an architecture claiming consideration in the classical tradition of perfection. If one didn't know from other works how strongly Mies believes in the Platonic universe, the laxity might cast doubt on the seriousness of that belief. However, there are too many examples where he has explored his formal propositions with utter conviction for us to take this as anything more than a momentary lapse, and there is at least one case, the Farnsworth House, where this conviction has resulted in a work which will stand up to technical and functional analysis as well.

THE FARNSWORTH HOUSE

The Farnsworth House, like so much of Mies's late work, is simply made up of two horizontal planes suspended above a natural ground level. However, unlike his other late work, there is no gross functional distortion caused by the *a priori* decision to create two absolute planes of reference with an 'universal' open space between. The reason is that the Farnsworth House is a weekend retreat

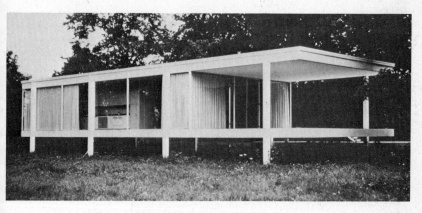

55. Mies van der Rohe: Farnsworth House, Fox River, Illinois, 1945-50. Two white, horizontal slabs suspended in nature by welded I-beams. The glass areas change in colour with the seasonal foliage, a reciprocal acknowledgement of nature and culture.

for a single person located in the woods and isolated from a disturbing environment [55]. Thus the large, open glass areas are possible and the 'ideal' solution of a refined symbol of technology is plausible because of the contrast with a natural richness. The two pure white planes of painted steel contrast with the green, red or brown background depending on the season; this theme is then reinforced by further white planes of different dimension –

the platform and steps [56]. In fact these planes are actually held in space by what *appears* to hold them in place: in most Mies architecture the I-beams are 'symbols' for structure or 'make visible' the structure rather than being actually the thing itself. In effect the I-beams are both structural supports and visual dividers at the same time, just as the glass area is at once window, wall and reflective plane. Hence the delight in finding an ambiguity or multivalence of determining meanings; we can intuit this complexity of factors rather than explain it away with a single answer. Perhaps the mystery that is often felt to lie behind a Miesian work is here at least caused by the fact that no sequential listing of determining factors will be adequate to the multilevelled experience because they are all experienced at once as a compact whole. In any case, in spite of the fact that Dr Farnsworth found this house too expensive to live in and actually sued Mies (but lost the case), it remains a coherent statement of transcendental technology which is not immediately destroyed by tech-

56. Mies van der Rohe: Farnsworth House, entrance. The classical motifs of the podium and transitional platform avoid pomposity because of their domestic scale and simplicity.

nical and functional faults. The allusions which it makes to the Platonic world of eternal values are not quickly ridiculed by obvious shortcomings.

FARCE AND THE BELIEF IN ESSENCE

Hence in the best of Mies's work we are brought up to the question of belief, because, depending on our own beliefs in the existence of a transcendental world, we will experience this work as an adequate symbol of that world or, alternatively, as just a very exquisite farce. For instance, nominalist philosophers and pragmatists, who believe that universals do not in fact exist, would find the Platonic statements of Mies mostly just humorous, because they go to such terrific pains to project a non-existent reality.

To clarify the beliefs on which Mies's architecture is based, his background and some of his more revealing pronouncements are relevant. First, he was born in Aachen, Germany, the centre of the Holy Roman Empire under Charlemagne and hence the place where the temporal and eternal order, the 'Imperium' and 'Sacerdotum', were unified. In accord with this unification (even if it were a thousand years old) was his neo-Thomist education at the Cathedral School of Aachen, for it is likely that here he received the idea of intellectual clarity and the equation of beauty with truth. Beauty reveals truth or makes truth 'manifest'. Not only does Mies refer to Aquinas' formulation explicitly, but he also seems to uphold the further scholastic doctrine that all the apparent phenomena of this world are actually mere symbols for a greater reality lying behind them. To see the striking relevance of this Platonic belief in universals for Mies's work, one should remember that Plato put above the entrance to his Academy a sign that Mies might have placed above all his entrances: 'Nobody Untrained in Geometry May Enter My House' – because, it is implied, only geometry refers to the essential universals which lie behind the transient and multiform appearances.

Secondly, for Mies, as for Hegel, these ultimate universals unfolded in time according to 'the spirit of the age', and for Mies this spirit meant: 'the economic order in which we live, the discoveries of science and technology, the fact of mass society . . . and construction'.[8] Lastly, it was the role of the architect, just as it was that of the scientist and theologian, to simplify, make clear and order these universals for all time: 'We desire an order which gives everything its rightful place and we desire everything to have what is right for it according to its own nature.'[9]

Now these last two quotes taken together show with what ease Mies can slip from a belief in the *Zeitgeist* to the conservative arguments for a Closed Society – or a society where everything has its 'rightful place' according 'to its nature'. We have already mentioned how his apoliticism, verging on fatalism, led Mies to accepting Nazism. As Karl Popper has argued, a belief in essences is one of the prime convictions of those who support a Closed Society.[10] But still these points are at best inconclusive because, for instance, Karl Popper himself believes that absolute truths lie behind appearances and, furthermore, that any view of human knowledge which does not also assume this is doomed to a certain failure. Accepting Popper's arguments, we are led to a modification, not a complete rejection, of Mies's architecture and the position which it entails. First of all, contrary to Mies, one would have to

57. Mies van der Rohe: Crown Hall, IIT, Chicago, 1962. Beautifully floating stairs and terraces rise to a 'universal' open space sandwiched between two slabs. However the space is too noisy and public for the architectural students to work in; the designers are cramped into the basement and the slabs are supported by conventional piers, not just hung as it appears. When form as beautiful as this turns out to be univalent and not functional, one can only enjoy it as farce – a beautiful fairyland. The exploitation of this insight leads to the Camp Movement in Architecture. See below, pp. 185–212.

point out the fact that the universals are never known with certainty and that, secondly, they are only approached through constant and unremitting criticism as opposed to being revealed by the dialectic of the *Zeitgeist*. Hence the continual claims by Mies to have discovered these truths or to have fixed their 'rightful place' for all time would be dismissed as ridiculous and highly dangerous. Lastly, the idea that these truths happen in fact to be empty, parallelepipeds of post and lintel construction which enclose a 'universal' blank space is so obviously reductive as to be laughable [57]. Universal essences may indeed underlie all appearances, contrary to what the nominalist believes, but the idea that they are all geometrical rectangles or even geometric is farcical. In fact when we test the architecture of Mies against more developed beliefs, we find that his world, like that of farce, is based on the radical reduction of things to a few simple formulae and rigid laws which are made to stand for a richer reality. We can inhabit this truncated world where 'less' stands for 'more' and a perfected cruciform column stands for beauty, truth, God and the brotherhood of man [58], just as we can laugh when a ballet dancer slips on a banana peel. That is to say, we can enjoy both

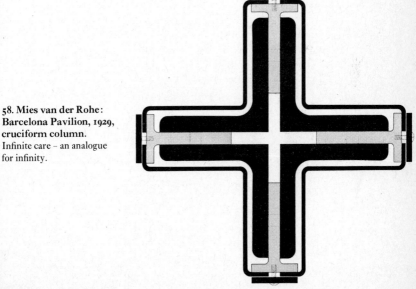

**58. Mies van der Rohe:
Barcelona Pavilion, 1929,
cruciform column.**
Infinite care – an analogue
for infinity.

these forms of farce if, and only if, we know and supply the missing area of value to which it refers: i.e. the ultimate world in the case of Mies and the organically controlled world in the case of the ballet dancer. If, however, we confuse the restricted area of farce with the real world, as critics and architects have done, we are then led back to the Closed Society and the kind of formalism evident in American Camp architecture. Paul Rudolph's statement summarizes the direct consequences of taking Mies seriously on his own terms:

> Mies, for instance, makes wonderful buildings only because he ignores many aspects of a building. If he solved more problems his buildings would be far less potent. This paradox is heightened by the various commitments to functionalism.[11]

In other words, if one does take Mies too seriously, one starts really to believe that farce is more important and nourishing than tragedy or that a half-baked, univalent architecture is better than an inclusive one.

3. GROPIUS, WRIGHT AND THE COLLAPSE INTO FORMALISM

SWARTS: These fellows always get pinched in the end.
SNOW: Excuse me, they don't all get pinched in the end.
What about them bones on Epsom Heath?
(T. S. ELIOT, *Sweeney Agonistes*)

If the later work of Mies contributed to what was called in the fifties 'the crisis of modern architecture' – the various turns of the idealist tradition towards formalism – then the work of Walter Gropius and Frank Lloyd Wright was a major cause of this event. The formalism of these two architects was more influential and disturbing than that of Mies, inasmuch as their early buildings and statements were directed against style as an end in itself and the divorce between function and form. For instance, in any number of statements Wright had put forward an 'organic architecture' in contradistinction to the prevailing Beaux-Arts method of design:

Furthermore [organic architecture] is an art of building where aesthetic and construction not only approve but prove each other. [1910]

And Gropius, reviving both futurist and functionalist ideas, had also put forward the idea of an organic architecture as an integrated approach opposed to that of the academies:

We want a clear, organic architecture, whose inner logic will be radiant and naked, unencumbered by lying façades and trickeries; we want an architecture adapted to our world of machines, radios and fast motor cars, an architecture whose function is clearly recognizable in the relation to its form. [1923]

Yet in spite of these early, unequivocal statements of intent, by the fifties both Wright and Gropius were designing non-organic images where 'aesthetic and construction' disproved 'each other' and the 'function' was clearly un-'recognizable'. It is one of the strange ironies of history that both of these pioneers should achieve their most unorganic projects for Baghdad, Iraq [**59, 60**]. But it is

perhaps understandable that this 'land of the Arabian Nights and cradle of civilization' should bring out their most extreme formalism, since the situation obviously demanded some form of historical acknowledgement. Yet these two desultory projects were not just momentary lapses; they typified much of their later work. While this retreat from their early intentions has been noticed and even applauded in some circles, it has not led to a general revaluation of their place in the modern movements. Rather the critics have been silent and kept to the standard interpretation of Gropius as the paragon of integrity and Wright as the epitome of creative genius. To some extent this silence must be attributed to the mixed quality of their late work and, in the case of Gropius at least, the inaccessibility of historical data. For it now appears, from sources which have recently come to light, that Gropius's 1923 synthesis of 'Art and Technology: a New Unity' and

59. **Walter Gropius with TAC: Baghdad University,** central area and auditorium, 1958. The image is pseudo-Arabic and the planning is haphazard sprawl. Muslim arches support nothing and shield a blank wall. The minaret is a clumsy pastiche of the traditional form.

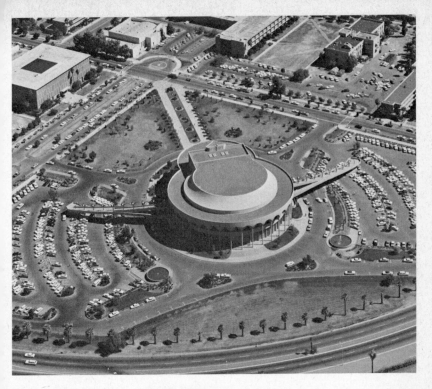

60. Frank Lloyd Wright: Grady Gammage Memorial Auditorium, Tempe, Arizona, 1959–66. Very similar to Wright's design for a Baghdad Opera House, which was to have legends from the Arabian Nights between the 'lattice crescents'. Although these crescents were kept, the building was actually surrounded by cars, not the projected 'fruit trees'. See also [68].

the whole Bauhaus method of design owes a good deal more to Theo Van Doesburg, El Lissitsky and Le Corbusier than had previously been thought. Indeed, from the revaluation that follows, it appears that much of Gropius's contribution to architecture was more the result of external pressure than internal willpower.

THE MIXED INTENTIONS OF GROPIUS

It is commonly held by most people that Gropius was a functionalist, if not *the* major exponent of functionalism in the twenties. Yet Gropius continuously denied this characterization of his work after 1930 and before the 1923 synthesis. In fact in a little-known contribution to an Expressionist manifesto in 1919 he attacked functionalism as the curse, not the spirit, of the age:

But who of those living at this time, cursed as it is with functionalism, does still understand the all embracing and cheering
character of architecture ... The grey, empty, obtuse stupidities
in which we live and work will bear humiliating evidence to
posterity of the spiritual abyss into which our generation has
slid ... Ideas perish as soon as they are compromised ... return
to the crafts ... build in fantasy without regard for technical
difficulties. To have the gift of imagination is more important
than all technology, which always adapts itself to man's creative
will.[1]

At this time and for the next four years Gropius was a
member of that group of Expressionist architects who
were sending each other letters – 'the Utopian Cor-
respondences' – that demanded a return to the medieval
integration of the building team and which proffered
highly irregular, faceted, glass monuments radiant with
light, or 'cathedrals of the future'. Gropius himself was
known in this group as 'Mass' or 'Measure' which was a
portentous pseudonym for him inasmuch as four years
later he had shifted field completely, demanded a 'functional architecture' and proclaimed in a lecture 'Art and
Technology: a New Unity'. How could a man who had
previously cursed functionalism and said 'build in fantasy without regard for technical difficulties' [61] later

61. Walter Gropius:
Monument to the March
Dead, Weimar, Germany,
1921-2. Like the
Sommerfeld house of 1921,
this was one of the few
Expressionist works Gropius
managed to get built.

bring in function and technology as prime determinants? In fact how could all the Expressionist architects, the architects who were simply known as *the* modern architects,[2] compromise their ideas in four years (and hence according to Gropius have them 'perish')? The explanations often given that Expressionism was difficult to build or that inflation changed the climate of opinion to a more sobering one do not seem altogether viable. A more convincing explanation, because it is on the level where these architects were committed, is that Expressionism had become associated with extreme Utopianism which in turn had been discredited by violence and bloodshed. Or perhaps this radical shift was made because architects were convinced that the new style, or New Unity, was equally expressive and that no compromise was involved.[3]

In any case, it appears that the reversal was made without either aggravated struggle or explicit acknowledgement. The only ostensible sign that a crisis had occurred was that the mystic, Expressionist painter Itten was forced to resign as head of the basic course at the Bauhaus in 1923, to be replaced by the Constructivist Moholy-Nagy. About forty years later, when Gropius was asked about his Utopian-Expressionist period, he gave an answer which was in fact more illuminating of his continuous intentions than he might have wished, for it underlined his basic pragmatism and willingness to compromise with the prevailing opinion or *Zeitgeist*:

A realistic call to realistic work would in those times [1918–21] have missed its aim – to offer young people, pregnant with new ideas, a broad basis for the clarification and testing of these ideas. The success of the manifesto [Bauhaus Manifesto, 1919] speaks for itself . . .[4]

If success can justify an assumed position in 1919, then what about Gropius's lack of success in trying to justify modern architecture to the Nazis in 1934 as 'Germanic'? It appears that, whenever Gropius was confronted with a choice between abstract principles and pragmatism, he invariably took the second of the two alternatives: in 1923 with his 'New Unity', in 1934 with his appeal to Goebbels and later in the sixties with his Pan Am Building, Baghdad University and Temple of Ohab Shalom. The reason why he could accept these compromises was that he believed above all in teamwork, collaboration and the *relativity* of truth:

> Science has discovered the relativity of all human values and that they are in constant flux. There is no such thing as finality or eternal truth according to science. Transformation is the essence of life.[5]

Elsewhere,[6] Gropius reiterated that he placed higher value on 'the whole social structure' than 'abstract principles of right and wrong' – again the definition of truth in pragmatic terms relative to social success. Hence, at least for Gropius, we see one of the reasons for the sudden change toward rationalism that occurred between 1922 and 1923: it was made because the *Zeitgeist* was headed in this direction and it was convenient for Gropius to follow it.

What actually occurred at the Bauhaus in the crucial months between January and June 1922 when the shift happened is still obscure because of the lack of documentation and the haziness of dated buildings. For instance, Gropius's key project for mass-production dwellings [62]

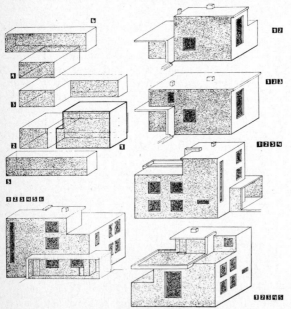

62. Walter Gropius with Adolf Meyer, 1922–3?: Mass-production housing made up of 'large-scale building bricks', along with the Chicago Tribune Competition, Fall 1922, signals the acceptance of the shift to functionalism and *De Stijl*.

is dated, by historians, from anywhere between 1921 and 1924, thus obscuring the question of influence. A further difficulty is caused by the fact that so many different movements claim primary place that it is almost impossible to achieve a balanced view of what was happening and who caused it. On the very large scale of influences, one might mention the Dadaist-Anarchist statement of Lenin on what was the essence of the Russian Revolution: 'Electrification plus the Soviets' (1917), and the parallel of this statement in Constructivism by Lissitzky, Tatlin and Gabo. Indeed Lissitzky's Lenin Tribune of 1920 [63] has all the elements of the later Bauhaus synthesis,

63. El Lissitzky: Lenin Tribune, 1920. Along with the Suprematism of Malevich, the Realism of Gabo and Tatlin's *Monument to the Third International*, 1920, the influence of this work on modern architecture has been vastly underrated by historians.

including the Suprematist shapes, the new typography, the engineering 'objectivity' and the photomontage of the revolutionist himself. No doubt the Russian Constructivists had a great influence by 1922, inasmuch as nearly all the Bauhaus students went to their Berlin exhibition of that year, but it seems that the magazines *De Stijl* and *Esprit Nouveau* had an even greater impact at an earlier date. Also an undeniably great influence (but one which has yet to be explored[7]) was that of the Berlin Dadaists with their continual Anti-Art exhibits and pronouncements on the new machine art: 'Art is dead, long live the new machine art of the Tatlins'. Not only is this direct self-contradiction of relevance to the 1923 synthesis of Gropius but it also leads to the anti-art positions of Van Doesburg and Hannes Meyer in 1926. In any case, the more direct causes for the shift are due to the polemicizing of Van Doesburg at the Bauhaus itself. He writes in a letter dated 7 January 1921:

At Weimar I have radically overturned everything. This is the famous academy which now has the most modern teachers! I have talked to the pupils every evening and I have infused the poison of the new spirit everywhere. *De Stijl* will soon be published again and more radically. I have mountains of strength and I know that our notions will be victorious over everyone and everything.[8]

Van Doesburg attacked viciously all the examples of 'morbid expressionism' which he found everywhere at the Bauhaus and then launched into a personal attack on Gropius for syncretic idealism – the attempt to compromise all values away in a premature synthesis:

One of those who goes eagerly to the attack is Van Doesburg ... he rejects handwork [the focal point of the Bauhaus] in favour of the modern means, the machine. [Letter of Oskar Schlemmer, March 1922][9]

According to Bruno Zevi, whose source was the polemically involved Madame Van Doesburg, Gropius then had a sign put up at the Bauhaus entrance threatening any student who attended Theo Van Doesburg's lectures with expulsion.[10] According to her the issues were so extreme that several Gropius supporters threw rocks at their studio window and some 'thugs' threatened them with assassination - they left Weimar and moved to Paris. Thus, even accounting for the highly-coloured nature of these documents, they still seem to point toward Van Doesburg as the major cause of the Bauhaus switch away from Expressionism, handicrafts and mysticism. Other factors, besides those already mentioned, were the Dusseldorf Congress of Progressive Artists in May 1922, a meeting of the G-group and the Constructivist-Dadaist International which met in Weimar in September 1922 and was led by Van Doesburg and Lisstzky. Finally, as great an influence as all this put together[11] appears to have been the writings of Le Corbusier-Saugnier. Another letter of Oskar Schlemmer, dated June 1922, bears this out:

> We can and must strive only for the most real, for the realization of ideas. We need 'machines for living in' instead of cathedrals - let us turn away, therefore, from the middle ages and from the concept of craftsmanship itself which during the middle ages served merely as training and a means to the completion of a construction. Instead of ornamentation which necessarily gets lost in a non-objective or aesthetic handicraft guided by concepts of the middle ages - objective objects which serve specific purposes.[12]

Nowhere is there a more flat rebuttal of Gropius's previous Bauhaus and Expressionist manifestoes, and Schlemmer's opposition between Le Corbusier's 'machines for living in' and Gropius's 'cathedrals of the future' points to a possible explanation of the Expressionists' reversal. It may well have appeared that the New Style was both more expressive and more related to machine production than Expressionism so that the shift could be made without either loss of faith or compromise. It simply looked as if Le Corbusier's equation of the Parthenon with the automobile was as feasible as *De Stijl*'s equation of straight lines and abstraction with machine production, so that 'the new synthesis of art and technology' was both rational and formally exciting. Yet almost immediately there were objections to this 'new unity' as a false compromise. Itten and Feininger subscribed to the statement of the painter Muche from the artists' side:

> Art and technology are not a new unity, they remain essentially different in their creative value.[13]

And Buckminster Fuller and Hannes Meyer said much the same thing from the viewpoint of technology. In fact it also appears (although Gropius gives other reasons[14]) that the Bauhaus students rejected this 'new unity' by 1928 and that Gropius, Moholy-Nagy, Bayer, Breuer, Schawinsky (and later Schlemmer and Klee) were forced to leave because the students wanted more 'pedagogic orientation' (in this case the scientific rationalism of Meyer) instead of 'formalism' (or the syncretism of those who left).

Whether or not the synthesis of art and technology was possible and justified for Gropius depended very much on the individual case; in some examples, such as the Dessau Bauhaus or the Chamberlain house of 1939 [64], there was a very potent and multivalent fusion, whereas

in other examples such as the Baghdad University Auditorium [59], the marriage ended in mutual compromise, being both unconvincing 'art' and mediocre 'technology'. Perhaps the most extreme compromise that Gropius attempted in his continually pragmatic efforts to smooth over differences and synthesize opposing trends was his appeal to the Nazis, to Goebbels, in June 1934, to accept modern architecture because it was above all 'Germanic' and pragmatic for the Nazis to do so:

> Can Germany *afford* to throw overboard the new architecture and its spiritual leaders, when there is nothing to replace them . . .? But above all I myself see this *new style* as the way in which we in our country can finally achieve a *valid union* of the two great spiritual heritages of the *classical* and the *Gothic* traditions. Schinkel sought this union, but in vain. Shall *Germany* deny itself this great *opportunity*.[15] [italics added]

'New style-classical-Gothic-Schinkel-valid union-opportunity'? Just as it was expedient to 'offer young people' an Expressionist manifesto in 1919 or a 'new unity' in 1923, it was now pragmatic to claim that 'the new style'

expressed 'Germanness'. Later, when Gropius was in America, he continuously denied that there was any such thing as a 'new style':

> A 'Bauhaus Style' would have been a confession of failure and a return to that devitalizing inertia, that stagnating academism which I had called it into being to combat.[16]

Clearly with such an opportunistic approach, that contradicts its intentions to suit the *Zeitgeist*, the outcome in terms of building will tend to be compromised architecture and it only remains to show that this was in fact the result. There are many projects of this nature, varying from the large-scale Rudow–Buckow Housing to the small-scale Playboy Club, but I will mention only three which are representative.

First, the Pan Am Building [**65**], which was a large volume broken up into an octagonal shape to decrease the apparent size, was like Le Corbusier's Algiers Scheme of 1938 except that it lacked the all important articulation of social content within. Gropius justified this inarticulate mass by appealing to the social pressures on New York building which, he said, it was impossible to avoid without

65. Walter Gropius with TAC: Pan Am Building, New York, 1958. Fifty-nine storey tower with precast mullions, false columns and flattened octagonal shape.

66 (*opposite*). **Walter Gropius with TAC: Temple Oheb Shalom, Baltimore, Maryland, 1957.** While somewhat restrained, the architecture is not dissimilar to that of the *prima donna* architects whom Gropius attacked in his later years.

retreating into an ivory tower escapism. In short, his defence against the various criticisms[17] consisted in the old argument that it is more honest and difficult to compromise with the real, tough world than to opt out as an armchair critic and safely chide others for failure – a tacit acknowledgement that he had in fact both compromised and failed.

The second building, which was again coupled with an inadvertent self-criticism, was the Temple of Oheb Shalom [66] which appeared with the following rebuke:

> We, however, have become top heavy with personal contributions of a more-or-less glamorous nature which then fail to find their necessary foil in a dignified, restrained background architecture of a rather impersonal, collective character . . . In our time, architects have left these 'grey' areas largely to the commercial builder to fill up, or they have introduced such a confusing variety of shapes and techniques in one and the same building area that their different structures never attained a common rhythm and close relationship. The modern urge for personal glorification has warped and confused our goals.[18]

In his later years, Gropius often attacked the 'egocentric *prima donna* architect who forces his personal fancy on an intimidated client',[19] without ever specifying exactly who he meant. If one looks around for the objects of these frequent outbursts, they turn out to be none other than most of the students he trained at Harvard – Philip Johnson, Paul Rudolph, I. M. Pei, Ulrich Franzen, Victor Lundy and the prime exponents of American formalism. Perhaps a case can be made out for this formalism,[20] but seen from Gropius's angle the attempt to both practise *and* vilify it can only produce a muddle.

Such a muddle is apparent in the third project to be discussed here, the Baghdad University Complex. The image [59] is remarkably similar to that produced by *prima donna* architects when they venture outside their own culture and try to mix their conventions with those of the past. In this case the result approaches a middle-class, collegiate Alhambra where Moslem ornament and symbols of power are treated with such wooden abandon that they seem like vestigial afterthoughts soon to dry up and disappear for good. The attempt to go half-way with these traditional symbols only ends up as condescension and mockery, as exemplified in the treatment of the Mosque [67]. Traditionally the mosque was at the centre of community life, opening on to a square, a bazaar where

67. **Walter Gropius: Baghdad Mosque.** The bombé shape, the crescent moon and the minaret are all quite attenuated, but the image is so consistently absurd as to have a certain perverse integrity, as in Camp architecture.

trading and other activity occurred, connected perhaps to a library, presided over by a scholar, and very much *not* an isolated symbol. In using the bombé shape, or rather in slicing up this shape like an orange peel, opening it at the sides and putting it out in suburbia, Gropius has denied the traditional form of worship which is centred in the town, and contained rather than open to the outside. And, given the initial assumption that one should use conventional forms, it is hard to find justification for this distortion of traditional usage.

After this account of all the aberrations of Gropius, what balanced portrait of his work emerges? On the positive side, and on the aspects which have led to his repute, there are a few good buildings such as the Fagus Works and Bauhaus and at least two excellent projects – the Chicago Tribune Tower and Total Theatre. But perhaps his really original and lasting contribution was to hire some of the most significant minds in Europe in the twenties, keep them in one place and allow them to do more or less what they wanted. The Bauhaus as a creative, educational institute has been without parallel, and much of the credit must go to Gropius, for he very consciously encouraged individual development, variety and dissent – 'hence the battle of minds, in the open or in secret, as perhaps nowhere else, a constant unrest, compelling the individual almost daily to take a stand on profound problems'[21] – as Schlemmer once again so aptly summarized it.

On the negative side, there is simply the retreat from principle into pragmatism and the willingness to sacrifice all values away in favour of the social totality – or whatever Gropius variously called the whole community or integrated society. On the level of deeper motivation, this probably had its roots in his image of the integrated community, the medieval township, building its collective monument to the glory of an impersonal deity. Gropius, like so many of his generation, longed for this cultural integration and reconciliation and, at least in some senses, achieved it at the Bauhaus for a few brief years. Yet he was not sufficiently critical to distinguish this unified community of dissenters from other forms of collaboration and, with his commitment to relativistic pragmatism, lost the tough clarity and imagination of which he was capable.

Frank Lloyd Wright also conceived of his architecture first as a polemic towards cultural integration, since it would synthesize all objects and elements in the environment into one organic unity:

An organic entity, this modern building, as contrasted with the former insensate aggregation of parts. Surely we have here the higher ideal of unity as a more intimate working out of the expression of one's life in one's environment. One thing instead of many things; a great thing instead of a collection of small ones . . . In organic architecture then, it is quite impossible to consider the building as one thing, its furnishings another and its setting and environment still another. [1910] [**68**]

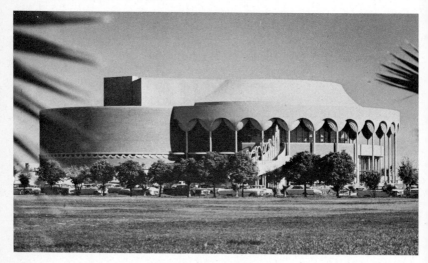

But trying to comprehend Wright's exact meaning of 'organic' is as difficult as trying to understand all his multifarious work in one thought – there is a sad disparity between his overflowing fecundity and the limitations of the human brain which can only grasp one or a few things at a time. Wright's superabundance, like Picasso's, is more natural than human and like an extravagant Alpine landscape he could go on and on endlessly from one pinnacle of magnificence to another in a continual outpouring of beauty that seemed so profuse as to be almost wasteful. For instance, in trying to define his keyword of organic in

68. Frank Lloyd Wright: Grady Gammage Memorial Auditorium, Tempe, Arizona, 1959-66. Applied, decorative motifs of an historicist nature, the kind of unorganic architecture which the early Wright attacked.

the Princeton Lectures (1930), he poured out definition after definition – fifty-one in all – until the concept seemed diluted beyond comprehension. Yet underlying all this profusion, this *embarras de richesse*, were a few inter-related ideas which here will be reduced to a single one, in order to bring out the change in Wright's work. This idea, organic geometry, will be analysed rather than the underlying changes in Wright's character, mostly because the latter have already been so carefully delineated by Norris Kelly Smith.[22]

As is often pointed out, Wright was continuously play-ing with demountable, geometric blocks, Froebel blocks, from the age of seven throughout his childhood. Now one of the incidental properties of these blocks, indeed for this discussion their essential property, is their *undifferentiated unity*: they are at once volume, colour, pattern, silhouette, construction and structure [69]. For instance, there is no difference between piling them on top of each other, the construction, and making them stand up, the structure; it is all done in a single act. Such an intellectually satis-fying property of these blocks must have made a deep and lasting impression on Wright, since when he re-derived this same principle in his own building it became the

69. Frank Lloyd Wright: Froebel Constructions, drawn by Grant Manson.

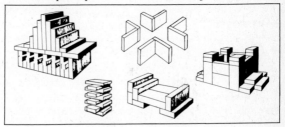

fundamental tenet of his organic architecture and also the prime weapon to use against all other styles, including that of the Beaux-Arts and classicism. However, as is often pointed out, classicism is itself based on primary forms and the superposition of abstract shapes. In what way was Wright's organic architecture different from this?

In the first place, as he said, his geometric ornament was '*of* the surface not *on* the surface', i.e. it usually re-sulted directly from the construction rather than being applied afterwards as a conventional sign. Secondly, his method was more 'democratic' than the classical or International Style because it was open at all ends rather than closed ('like a box on stilts') and it was made up of many geometries ('more suited to human to and fro than the right angle'). Thirdly, Wright insisted that organic architecture grew naturally out of the individual situation and thus its peculiar 'style' expressed personal 'character' rather than the impersonal, dead convention which was adopted without reflection. And finally, as in Sullivan's organic architecture, it did not hide, constrain or coerce the purpose of the building, but rather developed in such a way as to express or make manifest this purpose.

Not surprisingly, all these lessons of the Froebel blocks were summarized in a series of oppositions to the prevailing classical styles and urban ways of life: free and open rather than imposed and closed; a supple tool rather than a dictatorial straitjacket. The tragically absurd condition which Wright, as a romantic, saw very clearly was that means to an end such as style, the machine and law which should serve men had invariably turned into autonomous ends which coerced them. Only organic architecture or the Froebel block, which was undifferentiated means and ends at the same time, would work adequately. Or would it? Suppose that like any other style or mechanical system it had its own contradictions waiting to come out the moment it was adopted uncritically as a panacea, becoming just one more example of absurdity, of a means turned into an end. As is obvious by now, Wright's organic architecture, like any system, contained this contradictory potential and one can see how it slowly came out as Wright became more interested in perpetuating his public career than in working out the intractable problems of function and technique.

Already in the early work there is a hint of this conflict to come. On the one hand, there is the successful relation of the primary geometry with the function, as in the Unity Church interior [70], while on the other hand there are the designs for furniture, sculpture, and statues [71] where the repeated rhythmical forms become Procrustean and force natural shapes and purposes into their mould. While ornament and historical allusion were a constant preoccupation of Wright throughout his life, by the mid twenties they asserted an independence that was anything but

70. Frank Lloyd Wright: Unity Church, Oak Park, Illinois, 1906. Lighting fixture and balcony. The orthogonal geometry happens also to work well in the lighting and structure (a reinforced concrete, two-way grid which lets indirect light through the ceiling).

71. Frank Lloyd Wright: Midway Gardens, Chicago, 1914-18. Already at this time the geometry has become a straightjacket. The actual forms are reminiscent of Viennese *Jugendstil*.

organically related to the rest of the design [72]. The 'Hollyhock House' is representative of this setback both in its whimsical name and overpowering geometry, but that Wright could still relate metaphor and geometry to his larger purpose is apparent in 'Fallen Leaf' and his projects for a summer colony at Lake Tahoe. In these projects the triangular geometries confirm the structure, and the explicit images of teepee, wigwam, and prow of a ship plausibly deepen the overall meaning (actually one

of these designs was for a floating cabin). By the late twenties Wright had reached the height of his powers to reconcile various meanings under a unifying geometry – as shown by the St Marks Tower, which in many ways remains the most expressive skyscraper of the twentieth century. Although never built, it later led to a similar design, the Price Tower, in 1955 [73–5]. What is of particular interest to us here is that Wright is *using multiple geometries*, instead of constraining everything in a single one, and thereby creating a most exciting rhythmic counterpoint as well as a functional building. It is as if finally he had an overwhelming vindication of the organic

72. Frank Lloyd Wright: Hollyhock House, Los Angeles, 1916–20. The hollyhock flower decoration is '*on* the surface not *of* the surface', while the tomb-like Mayan volume has constricted the domestic function within: the music room and library to either side of the living-room are excessively darkened by the lack of windows.

73, 74. Frank Lloyd
Wright: Price Tower,
Bartlesville, Oklahoma,
1953–5. Horizontal and
vertical counterpoint; the
culmination of Wright's
attempts to fuse different
triangular geometries
(30/60°) with the rectangle;
a development that starts in
the mid twenties.

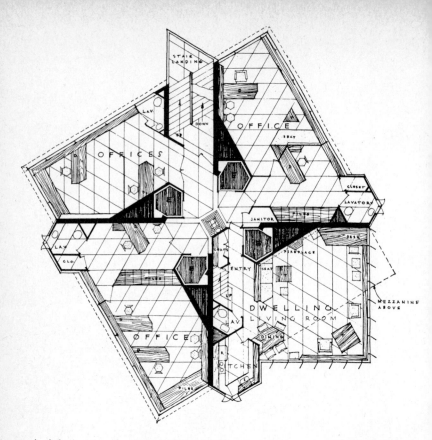

principle, because throughout the multiple geometry suggests and upholds all other meanings . . . except, unfortunately, two: the stamped copper spandrels and the impossibly awkward furniture within [76]. Why did Wright not go to more complex geometries or multiple curves when faced with such supple problems as the human body? Perhaps because in both classical and romantic theory the idea of a 'unified whole' always meant one or a few types of form, a single geometry, rather than the more general property of multivalence, of relatedness. In any case, while having these minor faults, the Price Tower remains a dynamic solution to the vertical building – the sweep to the top is heightened by contrasting horizontal and vertical fins and the faceted prisms of glass, concrete and copper. Although Wright found other

75. **Frank Lloyd Wright:**
Price Tower, plan. The angular geometries are appropriately used for such things as stairways, while the two rectangular geometries interlock to form a double-height living and office space. Each floor is cantilevered from the central mast.

76. Frank Lloyd Wright: Angular furniture in the Price Tower. Wright's unwillingness to accept the curve of the human body was equalled by his disdain for all ready-made artefacts of an industrial civilization. But he had the candour to admit that his own furniture made him, when he sat on it, 'black and blue'!

appropriate uses for his exploration in triangular geometry, such as Taliesin West, 1938, and the Unitarian Church, 1949, nowhere is it more suitable than in a skyscraper – as the original meaning of the word suggests.

In the forties Wright started working on new geometrical patterns such as the circle and hexagon, with considerably less success than in his previous work. Before discussing this, an underrated aspect of his work should be mentioned: the low-cost house. It is generally assumed, not without reason, that Wright built for the more wealthy classes of Americans. In the rhetorical words of the Marxist Utopie Group in Paris: 'Vous avez construit pour une classe particulière, "Mister Wright"?' His rhetorical answer would have been 'Yes, but not because I didn't try to produce low-cost housing, but rather because it was never really accepted.'[23] The only moderately-priced houses that were accepted were his 'Usonian Houses' of the thirties and forties. These were, for the most part, built in that geometry which he was most adept at handling, the rectilinear [77]. Basically, he would start with a

module of construction and then let it repeat in many different rhythmic forms to set up the overall harmony of flowing space, structural wall planes, and the functionally separate areas. In the Usonian Houses the most important area, the hearth, was both the intersection of the two functional wings (sleeping and living) and the point of most visual activity (in terms of light and intersecting planes). Hence there doesn't seem to be any contradiction between geometry and the requirements, but this is not because the rectangle is better suited for building, or for that matter worse as Wright argued, but rather because it has been carefully used until it resolved the various requirements.

77. Frank Lloyd Wright: Typical Usonian House, Okemos, Michigan, 1939. The rectilinear geometry of the construction module creates the rhythm which is taken up in the silhouette and overall volume.

The same is true of the circle which Wright first started using in a tenacious way during the forties. Clearly successful examples of this use include the Johnson Wax Buildings, 1936–9, and the Second Jacobs House, 1948, the partially successful examples include the Guggenheim

78. Frank Lloyd Wright: Johnson Wax Building, Racine, Wisconsin, 1938. Twenty-two foot high columns pinned on brass shoes at the bottom and growing outward at the top, support a ceiling of glistening pyrex tubing.

Museum, 1957–9, while the clearly unsuccessful examples include the Huntington Hartford Play Resort, 1947, the Baghdad Opera House, 1957, and the Marin Civic Center, 1959. As can be seen by these dates, the circle became the last geometry with which Wright was preoccupied, although actually it was first considered as early as 1925.

That Wright could use the circle to structural purpose was shown in the Johnson Wax Building where the tapered columns were supported laterally at the sides and pinned at the bottom [78]. These 'Dendriform shafts' or 'mushroom columns', as they were variously called, actually serve to divide up the large office space and provide a contrast to the brilliant light which shimmers through the

79. **Frank Lloyd Wright: Johnson Wax Building. Pyrex glass tubing** in circular geometry takes up the theme of the columns and corners and the streamlining of the brick.

skylight from above. Without them the space would have been at once too monotonous and too glaring. As for the tower, which was completed later in 1950, it also uses circular geometries in a rational way, this time canti-levering them out from a central trunk to create double-height laboratory spaces within [80]. These areas, again more interesting than the usual flat, open spaces, are both partially revealed and hidden on the exterior, setting up a delightful ambiguity which is furthered by the flattened cylindrical shape that thickens, not thins, towards the top. When justifying this building, which was attacked for its high cost, Wright gave expression to what he called his 'honest arrogance as opposed to false humility' – an arro-gance which was somewhat mitigated by being both clearly acknowledged and slightly mocked:

Reams of paper were covered with drawings. All these were needed to get a flower instead of a weed out of this rampant

80. Frank Lloyd Wright: Johnson Wax Building, Laboratory Tower, 1950. Wright liked his towers to loom out over the viewer, so he tapered them downwards; also they were made with floors cantilevered from a central trunk – on the tree principle. See [75].

industrial system of ours . . . So after all here is the 'flower' now to show what concentrated and coordinated effort (if subordinated to Architecture as great Art) can mean even in a civilization such as ours. The sagacity of Herbert F. Johnson has given to the world this instance of an architect's creation in a field hitherto not invaded by (let us not hesitate to use the word) the great Art of Architecture.[24]

This sort of panache, verging on unironic bombast, allows Wright just to get away with his characteristic message: first of all, conveying the great, individual will-power he always needed in overcoming 'this rampant industrial system', secondly, showing the commitment to the grandiose tradition of the pyramid builders, and thirdly, showing his perennial trust and dependence on the patronage of an enlightened, industrial millionaire. Almost all of his large commissions came from these 'rugged individuals' who, like himself, had great faith in the democracy of the free-enterprise system and had distinguished themselves from the rest of society. They were all, in different ways, rebels and plutocrats who like Wright were obsessed by making a grand gesture that would rise above the average, the herd, the 'mobocracy' (in Wright's words).

Another commission which follows this pattern and is also based on circular geometries is the Solomon R. Guggenheim Museum in New York [81a]. Originally the idea of a circular ramp had been conceived in 1925 for a drive-in planetarium, but here it is abstracted from its original automobile function and used for perambulating art-lovers. A great deal of functionalist criticism has been levelled at Wright for this *a priori* formalism: the ramps impel the viewer continuously downwards, the natural lighting, if used, would have been blinding and the outward cant of the curving walls constricts and interferes with the flat, vertical paintings. Yet even granting these faults, one has to admit that the building works in two very important ways. First, it is one of the most delightful

81a, b. Frank Lloyd Wright: Guggenheim Museum, New York City, 1943–59. Grotesque, primitive curves plunge out on to Fifth Avenue taking up the motifs of the Cadillacs and contrasting with the fretful, rectilinear walls. The image of a concrete pill-box with machine-gun slits is fortuitously appropriate to the place of art in New Yorkers' lives. In the interior, the spectacle of people and paintings against this background makes the 'art-opening' reminiscent of some ancient ritual.

spaces in New York to view people moving and congregating in different groups. Even the sculpture and painting take part in this drama because they can be viewed from afar and against an all-white background [81b]. Secondly, because of its formal and spatial contrast to the rest of the city, the museum takes on an urban importance usually reserved for the city hall or temple – which is not inappropriate to the lives of culturally ambitious New Yorkers. If one denies that a museum should occupy this symbolic place, then one denies the society that worships here – both denials which are of course possible, but neither of which rules out the consistent fit between form and its meaning.

The late projects where Wright loses control of his geometry and allows it to contradict function, material, construction, structure, freedom, etcetera – in short all fifty-one definitions of organic architecture – are usually based on the circle. Hence one is tempted to agree with the usual proverb that it is inherently more difficult to design in curves than straight lines. A circle only has one

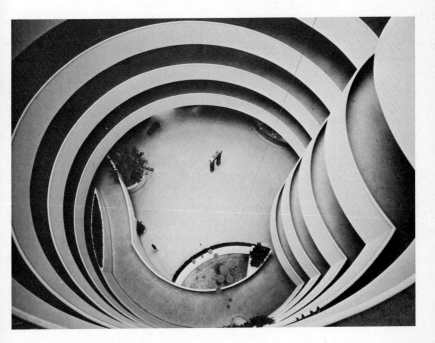

centre and a single, radial dimension and therefore it cannot accommodate itself to changing conditions as well as the rectangle.[25] Yet this explanation seems to be in need of modification, because if one takes the effort to combine curvilinear modules patiently, they can be just as responsive as the straight line: the endless examples of natural forms confirm this. In fact the explanation of Wright's inept handling of the circle has to be sought elsewhere – in his increasing age and credulity toward his own rhetoric and public persona.

By the late fifties, when Wright was in his late eighties, he had managed to surround himself with associates who were willing to accept the most cursory sweep of his pencil as a divine stroke of genius. Various books were written on the magnificent integrity of his character, varying from Ayn Rand's *The Fountain-head* to his son John Lloyd Wright's *My Father Who Is On Earth* [sic] to Mrs Olgivanna Wright's *The Shining Brow*. Criticism from within his *atelier* was never heard, a gigantic portrait of the 'Master' was hung over the door to his office and some projects were even conceived in the dreams of Mrs Wright.[26] The irony of all this was that Wright, who had withstood and even thrived on countless hostile attacks, could not withstand the barrage of overemphatic adulation and he succumbed to an arrogance that was no longer mitigated by self-mockery. The man who had spent the better part of his life attacking the pompous imposition of style as 'grandomania' had himself become a grandomaniac – at least in some of his projects.[27] Rather than analysing all of these, only a representative one will be described.

The Marin County Civic Center is typical of the worst circular projects in many respects. First, as with Mies, a single geometrical unifying element, the circle in this case, has overpowered most of the other meanings. In terms of structure, it has turned what appear to be compression arches, the repeated forms of a Roman aqueduct, into cantilevered slabs which are actually hung in tension [82a]. In terms of 'the nature of materials', it has demanded a smooth, sharp outline more like steel than concrete. In terms of relation to the natural landscape, it makes the volume sit without transition '*on* the earth not *of* the earth'. And finally in terms of image, it has produced

82a, b. **Frank Lloyd Wright: Marin County Civic Center, San Rafael, California, 1959–64.** The only aqueduct in the world where the compression arches are actually held in tension. Two long spines carrying civic functions pivot on the circular library, an inversion of the usual, symbolic emphasis.

a form that is anything but democratic and open, appearing more like an escapist, bureaucratic autocracy leaving the people to fight it out in the city while it plants its copper-minaret-wigwam-totem-pole somewhere safe in suburbia [82b].

By way of summarizing the late aberrations of these two pioneers, one can point out the consequences of this work. Once Gropius and Wright had made the move towards formalism and the critics had either accepted or applauded them, the signal was given for the next generation of architects to try their own hand at the imposition of grandiose geometries – a signal which they responded to with alacrity. While there is nothing inherently wrong with formalism, any more than farce or doggerel, it is unacceptable if one wants a deeper, more 'organic architecture' where all the levels of meaning are interrelated. That this was exactly what both the early Gropius and Wright wanted means that in their youth they would have condemned the work of their old age, if they had a chance to see it. Perhaps this is the fate of most pioneers who live to see their early polemics institutionalized and made commonplace; they end up by believing their latest rhetoric and contradicting their early intentions. Yet that this needn't be the case for all pioneers is shown by the examples of Le Corbusier and Alvar Aalto, two architects who developed their intentions quite far from their early positions, but in ways that never contradicted them on a fundamental level.

4. CHARLES JEANNERET - LE CORBUSIER

83. Sketch made by Le Corbusier when he was both bitterly fighting the authorities and presenting the 'essential joys' of the *Unité d'Habitation*. 'In his existence as dismembered god, Dionysios shows the double nature of a cruel, savage daemon and mild, gentle ruler' (Nietzsche, *The Birth of Tragedy*).

There is a fundamental difficulty, which all critics seem to encounter, in trying to interpret and hence judge the work of Le Corbusier. They do not know exactly what standards to apply – whether rationalist, poetic, both or neither – because all of them work to a point and then fail to be either fitting or inclusive. The most recent example of this critical quagmire is Maurice Besset's *Who Was Le Corbusier?*[1] a book which starts off boldly with the grand question in the title and then by the introduction explicitly gives up any hope of an answer – a course which if not consistent and ambitious is at least wise for its humility.

Le Corbusier himself provided many clues to his own interpretation – such as the continual functional justifications which always accompanied his work – but the problem with these is that, if taken too literally, they end up as *partial* rationalizations. For instance, in much of his writing, Le Corbusier claims to be both a rationalist and a scientist, yet many of his positions are held both dogmatically and uncritically. Or conversely, many people have claimed him to be the best and most successful architect of the first half of the twentieth century, whereas, as will become apparent shortly, he considered his life and work mostly a failure. The contradictions abound and, as is probably obvious by now, their very existence is taken here as of fundamental importance. Put simply, the interpretation is that Le Corbusier started off from a dual position which is represented by the Dr Jekyll-Mr Hyde portrait above [83] or his double identity (part the peasant Jeanneret, part the urbanite Le Corbusier) or his ironic building (part geometric, part biomorphic) or in his tragic persona (part daemonic, part humane). This last conflict, perhaps the most fundamental, is certainly the most important, because it led Le Corbusier to a basic antagonism with society which was completely beyond reconciliation. For instance, even if by some fantastic effort society had accepted all of his *a priori* values from 'the three essential joys' to 'absolute, Homeric silence', he would have quickly invented new ones to hurl at the world, because underlying all of them was the more basic principle that, to paraphrase Hamlet, 'the world is always out of joint, even if it is repaired from time to time'. That such a fundamental, tragic view underlay all others is apparent from two facts: it precedes Le Corbusier's sharp conflicts with society (he starts from a position of antagonism and battle *before* he has been rejected in 1922) and it survives his partial successes by the 1960s. Furthermore, whenever there is a vicious attack on his work or character, he immediately jots them down with the project concerned in order later to throw them back as part of his intended gesture [86]. A more reasonable or politic man would try to bury and forget the conflicts, because they would jeopardize his future commissions. But Charles Jeanneret, with a thoroughness that is obsessive, enumerates each insult that he has suffered – 'lunatic, megalomaniac, criminal', etc. – in such a way as to objectify struggle and evil in the world and, in an ultimate sense, present the martyrdom of Saint Corbusier.

While this last statement may appear as a slight exaggeration and even quite ridiculous, it is nevertheless true that Jeanneret saw his life in terms of sustained conflict even from the beginning. For instance, when only twenty-two years old, he wrote to his teacher L'Eplattenier –

I want to fight with truth itself. It will surely torment me. But I am not looking for quietude or recognition from the world. I will live in sincerity happy to undergo abuse . . . Perhaps reality will dawn cruel one day in the near future . . . These eight months shouted to me 'Logic, truth, honesty, burn what you loved, and adore what you burned' . . . The art of tomorrow is an art based on meditation. Up the concept and forge ahead! . . . It is in solitude that one can struggle with one's ego.[2]

This self-revelation and pronouncement has within it many of the elements of classical, Western tragedy, from the absolute commitment to an ideal ('Logic, truth, honesty') to the presentation of an internal struggle ('in solitude'). If one assumes that Le Corbusier saw himself in these terms then it would be inappropriate, not to say highly dangerous, to judge him in others, as critics have done. The problem is that when Le Corbusier is interpreted as just a rational urbanist or prophet of the machine age, his actions appear more strange and incomprehensible than they really are; whereas if one accepts the tragic persona as essential, then several of the interpretative paradoxes are dispelled.

REASON AND DUALISM

In the very first issue of the review *L'Esprit Nouveau*, October 1920, Le Corbusier and Saugnier claimed that their design and writings would be based on science and 'universal' laws:

The spirit which dominates this review is that which animates scientific research. We are a few designers who believe that art has laws, just as physics and physiology.

Although they started with the intention of *finding* these laws by experiment and observation rather than by deducing them from metaphysical principles, already by the fourth issue of *L'Esprit Nouveau* they had attacked empiricism as 'infinitely impure' and discovered their 'fixed points', their 'universal laws', once and for all. These could be summarized as the natural resonance theory of expression,[3] for they hold that certain forms naturally express certain, constant meanings or sensations. According to Jeanneret and Ozenfant (the real names of Le Corbusier-Saugnier), there are basically just two types of sensation:

1. Primary sensations determined in all human beings by the simple play of forms and primary colours [84] and
2. There are secondary sensations, varying with the individual because they depend upon his cultural or hereditary capital . . . [Furthermore] Primary sensations constitute the bases of the plastic language; these are the *fixed words* of the plastic language; it is a fixed, formal, explicit language determining subjective reactions of an individual order which permit the erection on these raw foundations of a sensitive work, rich in emotion. It does not seem necessary to expatiate at length on this elementary truth that anything of universal value is worth more than anything of merely individual value.[4]

But in making this last point the authors leave their previous commitment to science and experiment and assert a most debatable proposition. If one argues for 'universality' as the Pop artists were also later to do,[5] then it is likely that the Purists' 'secondary sensations' are in fact more universal than their primary ones. A popular advertisement or movie-star is much more likely to release 'identical sensations' in everyone's mind than the Purists' 'billiard ball' with its primary geometry. Furthermore, the next main point that the authors make in their attempt to establish a 'universal language' – that mechanical and natural evolution lead inevitably to these pure forms – is, contrary to their claims, also without scientific justification.

Nevertheless, for our purpose what is of capital importance is that for a time Le Corbusier and Saugnier, not to mention most modern architects, *thought* they were being both rational and scientific in adopting a Purist language. This appeal to reason, function, evolution or all the things that Le Corbusier summarized as 'implacable laws' gave their work a kind of seriousness and moral imperative it would otherwise have lacked – becoming 'mere taste, fashion', etc. – in short the very things they were attacking. There is hardly a project (I can find none) in all of Le Corbusier's work that does not have some rational and

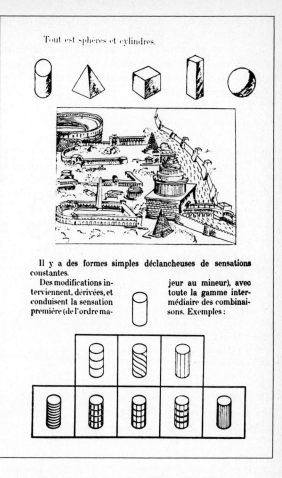

Tout est sphères et cylindres.

Il y a des formes simples déclancheuses de sensations constantes.

Des modifications interviennent, dérivées, et conduisent la sensation première (de l'ordre majeur au mineur), avec toute la gamme intermédiaire des combinaisons. Exemples :

**84. Le Corbusier:
Illustration of Purism
from** *L'Esprit Nouveau.*
Simple forms 'release'
constant primary sensations
which are modified by the
individual's culture and
history, or secondary
sensations.

functional justification. Thus if one reads the *Oeuvre Complète* uncritically, as many critics have, one can come to the conclusion that Le Corbusier was both a functionalist and a scientist – ready to drop a hypothesis the moment it was proved wrong.

That this was not the case is apparent from Le Corbusier's writings: they are all dualistic in a very important sense.[6] It's as if on an intuitive level he realized the old moral problem that one cannot logically jump from an 'is' or 'will soon be' to an 'ought'. But on the actual level with which he was consciously concerned, he realized very well that there is no inevitability that natural or mechanical evolution will necessarily be 'good', 'beautiful', or even in single instances of tools 'progressive'. Thus the logical and, in monistic terms, irrational necessity for human choice as well as natural selection. In fact this aspect of human choice was always smuggled into Le Corbusier's writings in many different ways: in *Vers une architecture* (1923),[7] choice becomes such things as 'the pure creation of the mind', 'regulating lines' and 'the masterly, correct and magnificent play of masses brought together in light'. In *Urbanisme* (1926), choice becomes 'we prefer Bach to Wagner . . . the coliseum endures, engineering rusts' – or we prefer engineering plus plastic imagination to engineering alone. In *La Ville Radieuse* (1934), on the title page the same old dualistic notion of universal technology plus cultural choice comes up again.

Plans are not politics.
Plans are the rational and lyrical monuments
erected in the midst of contingencies.
The contingencies are the environment, regions,
races, cultures, typographies and climate.
There are, besides these, the resources brought by
modern technology. These are universal.
The contingencies should not be evaluated except
with respect to 'man' and his harmony, our harmony.
For us others a biology, a psychology.

Thus, once more, those things which he *thinks* are universal and implacable such as technology and 'primary sensations' should be balanced with those that are subjective and emotional such as choice or 'secondary sensations'. Finally, in *The Poem to the Right Angle* (1955), he reverses a former argument which said that the right angle was universal, a Platonic constant of the rational mind, and now contends that it is a matter of subjective choice.

One has/With a Charcoal/Traced the right angle/
The Sign/Which is the response and guide/The Act/
The Response/The Choice/It is simple and naked/
But seizable/The savants discuss its relativity and rigour/
But of the conscience/In fact it is a sign/
It is the response and guide/The Act/My Response/
My Choice.

In short, to summarize these dualistic positions, we have a direct *contradiction* over substantive issues such as what actually constitutes a 'universal' while there does remain a definite *consistency* as to the general opposition between objective and subjective, implacable technology and individual choice. What did this dualism allow him to do?

First of all, on a tactical level, the appeal to objectivity allowed him to gain credence in an age most gullible to anything scientific. Secondly, the dualistic position allowed Corbusier to undermine the extreme, unitary positions on either side; he could criticize the academy for falling into an irrelevant stability which couldn't deal with modern technology, while at the same time he could fault the functionalists for accepting technology without reservation. In taking the latter position he thus brought down the censure of functionalists like Hannes Meyer, the German members of CIAM and even the Marxists of France who, to his utter amazement, found his formalism 'the expression of the bourgeoisie and capitalism ... !!' He answered these leftist attacks with his characteristic dualism in an open letter to the Czech functionalist Teige.[8] As one might guess, his argument consisted of two approaches.

First of all, he called attention to the irrational element of choice or aesthetic preference even in their position. He pointed out that their slogan 'utility is beauty' or even that 'utility is all' was based on as unprovable and arbitrary a base as his own preference for composition and regulating lines.

If I am a bit wrapped up by the proportions, I find those (apostles of utility) a bit wrapped up by machinism. Otherwise their attitude is very useful.

His second main argument consists in once again affirming his bipolar position by recounting a dispute with Alfred Roth, an exponent of 'utility is beauty' who was working along with Le Corbusier. Roth was apparently stuffing many scrap drawings into a wire waste paper basket of simple, geodesic form. He jumped on the papers until suddenly the basket collapsed into a larger, but chaotic shape (which Le Corbusier illustrates with a sketch).

Everyone guffawed. 'That's frightful,' said Roth. 'Pardon me,' I replied, 'but that basket now contains much more volume than it did before; it is more useful; therefore it is more beautiful. Be consistent in your principles!'

This example is not amusing only because of the circumstances which so fortunately brought it about. I had suddenly re-established an equitable balance in adding: 'the function of beauty is independent of the function of utility; they are two things. That which is displeasing to the mind is waste; because waste is stupid; it is for this reason that utility pleases us. But utility is not beauty.'

From an abstract, theoretical point of view, it did not matter exactly what Le Corbusier opposed to the criterion of utility; as long as there was *something* else, then the relative worth of utility could be gauged. Without this something else, one would have to accept the monistic principle which many have proposed of following utility or technology wherever they lead.[9] And this would be, from the human point of view, absurd, because it implies that men exist in order for there to be technological progress. And yet the converse, humanistic proposition, that 'man is the measure of all things', is from an evolutionary point of view equally presumptuous and dubious. By adopting his dualistic position, Le Corbusier managed to escape the futility of either extreme, but this led him naturally to attack from both sides as well as to the ultimately tragic position of trying to reconcile things which ordinarily remain opposed: beauty and utility, secondary and primary sensations, personal choice and impersonal science.

THE TRAGIC PERSONA

In addition to this dualistic position, there was a particular personality trait which led Le Corbusier into continual conflict with society and ultimately his adopted role as the 'tragic' figure. This was his extreme commitment to certain ideals which he tried to impress on to an unwilling world. Nowhere is this more apparent than in his planning schemes and Ville Radieuse. What we find in these is an application of *peculiar, French reason* to the laws of nature and the functioning of cities. It is *peculiar* because it only extends to certain types of law and not others: 'le soleil, espace et verdure' were considered to be universal constants deduced from a study of cities and men's needs, whereas the street, the community and the political realm, all things which we now recognize as equally objective and necessary, were excluded. Thus reason is being put into the service of personal choice or even dogma. Furthermore, this reasoning was peculiarly *French* because it was based on a Cartesian argument from *a priori* truths. These were to be established as the eighteenth-century architectural theorist Abbé Laugier framed the method: 'If the question is well posed, the solution will be indicated.' Hence when Le Corbusier confronted what he considered to be a Machine Civilization completely out of harmony, he was led to the following kind of French rhetoric and solution:

> A conviction: it is necessary to start at zero; it is necessary to state the question.
> The question: A Machine Civilization out of harmony.
> The solution: The Ville Radieuse.

The most concise example of this rhetoric of reason and also *a priori* values on which it was based is in the preface to his *Ville Radieuse* (1964) with its ending flourish of irony:

> Commentary on the reimpression of the Ville Radieuse: It is necessary to situate this work in time. It furnishes in one block an organism (the Ville Radieuse) capable of sheltering the works of man in a society from now on machinist. Qualifying as the key to a social and economic revolution, this revolution has the force of a mounting flood. This book, drawn up in 1933–34, announces the advent of the three following groups:
> (1) that which satisfies agricultural exploitation (the agricultural unit).
> (2) that which assures the function of linear-industrial cities.
> (3) that which realizes the devolved tasks of a radio-concentric city of exchange.
> All this placed under the magistral shield of the conditions of nature:
> sun
> space
> verdure
> And the mission being devoted to the service of man:
> DWELLING

This passion for classification even went so far as the type of verdure, branches and leaves, e.g., 'six different types of sunshade for India'. But before we dismiss the list as too restricted for any living city, we should note that classification, as a method, always underlay any plan as the justifying schema: it gave functional seriousness to all his work [85, 86]. And it was this commitment to something objective, something that could be verified by all men, that allowed Le Corbusier to have such an extreme commitment to his ideals. Yet in fact the functions were too limited or simply from an urban point of view too irrelevant.[10] For instance, where are the institutions and all the political elements which make up the public

85. Le Corbusier: Ville Radieuse, 1930-38. Four diagrams to the same scale reveal the difference in congestion and the fact that only the top one contains the 'three essential joys': sun, space and verdure.

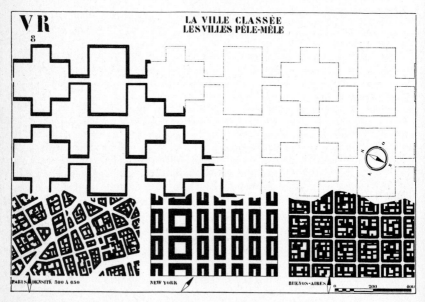

realm? Clearly they deserve another category from the four he lists.

In any case, the really fantastic and daemonic thing about Le Corbusier's urbanism was its pragmatic futility.

86. Le Corbusier: Plan Voisin, Paris, 1925. Cruciform skyscrapers and 'indented dwellings'. For a similar reconstruction of Paris, he was accused of 'A megalomania worse than Ledoux's, a vandalism unique in history, the dreary uniformity and monotony of these skyscrapers . . . have been proved spiritually and materially injurious, a contempt for historic and artistic traditions'. A typical insult which Le Corbusier appended to one of his Paris schemes to present hostility as an objective element.

Even if one discounts half of all Corbusier's claims as exaggeration or just typical French overstatement, he still must have produced the greatest number of unsolicited and unpaid-for plans in the history of architecture. For many plans he would produce up to 150 drawings and he *claims* to have made plans for Paris from 1912 to 1960 without a break! Many of these are laboriously detailed and rendered. They are completely gratuitous and in a pragmatic sense utterly insane. For who but a madman would go on year after year producing urban schemes that were ridiculed, vilified and hardly ever stood the slightest chance of being built? As Le Corbusier said, quoting himself with bitter logic:

> *Town planning expresses the life of an era. Architecture reveals its spirit.* Some men have original ideas and are kicked in the ass for their pains.[11]

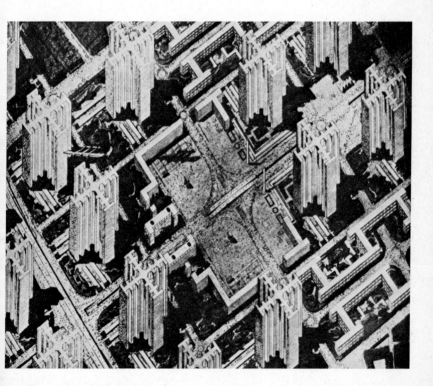

This aspect of spiritual waste was presented by Le Corbusier in the form of a staccato, nasty, unqualified invective hurled at a stupid, petty world.

Mr Lemaresquier points out 'This scheme [League of Nations first prize 1927] has not been drawn in Indian Ink. It breaks the rules. I insist that it should be disqualified' . . . and it was . . . 7 schemes for Algiers rejected, unpaid . . . Plans for Algiers, Stockholm, Moscow, Buenos Aires, Montevideo, Rio de Janeiro, Paris (without a break between 1912–1960), Zurich, Antwerp, Barcelona, New York, Bogota, St Dié, La Rochelle-Pallice, Marseille up to excluding Chandigarh . . . 1932–1935 and 1937, years of misery and abject, blind folly by the profession and officials responsible. But by the autumn of 1939, Adolf Hitler was threatening Paris. The rest is silence. (cf. *Hamlet*).

Unité 1947. Five years of storm, spite, and uproar followed, despicable, ugly . . . Berlin 1957 . . . sensational nonsense! Disloyalty and idiocy combined . . . Chandigarh 1951 is a contribution adjusted to human scale – to human size and dignity – by efforts of a few men of character, worn, chaffed and buffeted by the shocks and frictions of human relations.

In 1956 L–C was asked to accept membership of the Institut de France [*Académie des Beaux Arts*] in Paris: Thank you, never! . . . my name would serve as a banner to conceal the present evolution of the *Ecole des Beaux Arts* toward a superficial modernism.'[12]

Here is at once the final victory and defeat of Le Corbusier. Finally triumphant over the Academy and famous throughout the world, he still never saw his basic morality or universal truths accepted by society. Yet even if his life was a failure on so fundamental a level, still there was the indestructible quality of energy and joy which came through at every point. This insuppressible exuberance and energy would alternate in counterpoint with the disgust and bitterness. In a sense they were connected, since Le Corbusier's extreme depressions could only come from a person who had an equally extreme hope – to be dashed. Presenting this conflict in his buildings became just as important as writing and speaking it, so that one can actually read off what amounts to a self-portrait in the buildings. The photographs of Le Corbusier often show a daemonic, glacial stare behind a wall of black-framed, thick glasses. The face is always intense, uncompromising and at times deeply tragic. So are his buildings.

After the Second World War, there was what was interpreted to be a major shift in Le Corbusier's architecture.
Instead of being the epitome of a Machine Age it was now
thought to be almost primitive: instead of being made up
of right angles and straight lines, it was thought to be
arbitrarily made up of curves and whimsical shapes. Lewis
Mumford, Nikolaus Pevsner, James Stirling and many
others who were closely interpreting the moves of this
pioneer came to these conclusions. The putative shift in
direction was seen to condone a new turn for the modern
movements: the Brazilians took off towards a kind of
modern Baroque [177]; the Japanese developed the 'late
style' of Le Corbusier into a whole national aesthetic
[189]; the Brutalists in England seemingly based a whole
movement on the use of brutal materials 'as found' [152];
the American 'formalists' found their monumental
aesthetic in the Chandigarh work of Le Corbusier [117];
the neo-expressionists found new justification for their
'fantastic architecture' in the exuberant shapes of
Ronchamp [33]; and so on. While all these new directions
could plausibly find encouragement in Le Corbusier's
late work, they are simply wrong in thinking that a major
philosophical shift had occurred. All that had actually happened was that Le Corbusier's 'secondary sensations'
had come to the surface to contrast, ironically, with the
'primary forms'.

If any inversion really did occur it happened in 1928
when both he and Ozenfant, who had split up by that
time, introduced biomorphic forms into their paintings.
From the late twenties on, the amoeboid curve and organic
analogy began to compete in all his projects with the
geometric framework. One can find the same ironic clash
in the relationship between the contingent requirements
of a building and his *a priori* form. In all cases, he makes
this irony, or the presentation of opposed matrices, the
subject of his building.

By the time of the Ronchamp Chapel, the secondary,
amoeboid curves finally break through and dominate the
primary orthogonal geometry just as they dominate his
paintings [87]. This painting, part of the Bull series of the
fifties, portrays many of the actual shapes of Ronchamp

and shows as opposed to the Purist compositions many dynamic objects forced into a unity; and this aggressive content is not repressed as in the twenties but brought to the surface, faced and controlled. Whereas many of the architects wished to suppress behind a Miesian austerity those aspects of man accentuated or visible in the War, Le Corbusier wished the reverse; and here, on a site where many churches had been destroyed, he gave ironic expression to sensuality, aggression and monumentality.

Here is the 'taking possession of ineffable space' which Le Corbusier called the first gesture of living things and the first proof of existence [88]. The sweeping curve of the walls takes in the surrounding landscape, 'the four horizons', provides an enclosure for outdoor service, and quite ironically suppresses the worshipper in the interior space. Essentially, as with all Le Corbusier's work, the specific solution is and should be seen as a variant of the generic, orthogonal system – the cube. Here the rectangular volume has been pushed inwards on three sides, distorted axially to the south as if by a twist of the rectangular structure, and released downward on the ground by a slight slope so that the walls and roof weigh down-

87. The forms of **Ronchamp** can be found in this painting by Le Corbusier, although in many cases they have other specific, iconographic meanings; notice the silhouette of Ronchamp and the back-to-back curves of the entrance right above.

88. Le Corbusier:
Ronchamp, France,
from the south-east. What
Corbusier also calls 'visual
acoustics' amounts to the
embracing of external space
and the domination of
a white form on a green
background.

wards on the worshipper and force his mind in the direction usually thought undesirable by the Church [89]. In fact Le Corbusier's faith in the established Church and dogma seems quite tenuous, as if it would be strengthened by being denied:

The requirements of religion have had little effect on the design; the form was an answer to a psychophysiology of the feelings.

'Joy and meditation' were the primary religious feelings he had in mind; and they were satisfied by the simple family of forms in direct contrast, by the play of light and shadow over the white pebbly plaster, and by its contrast to the dark, rough concrete. Another pair of contrasts was achieved by the ambivalent gesture of the roof – exhilarated and deflated at the same time so that the sceptic and pietist could worship side by side without compromising their faiths.

Indeed they could enter side by side between the towers of the north door, which in their most reverent light were two children looking to the morning and evening sun while the parent watches over them from the south, and

89. Le Corbusier: Ronchamp. Axonometric showing an orthogonal shape which is twisted and cleaved; only the cross on the floor remains from the original geometry; all the forms are actually dimensioned by the Modulor.

which was most carnally a forceful penetration between two muscular curves [87]. Once inside, the dialectic continues with the south wall, a piece of sensuous Swiss cheese blasted away and at the same time a religious device to dramatize the sun and aphorisms painted by Le Corbusier on the glass. Then the gaze is brought to the cross by the slope and the grid of the floor and the directional marker of the dark centre line [90] – all remnants of the orthogonal system which is now overpowered, as is the gaze towards the cross by the bright window of the

90. Le Corbusier: Ronchamp. The floor slopes down to the truncated cross as does the roof, but the eye is taken away to the right by the bright light.

Virgin and the streaming morning sun. Thus the cross (intentionally diminished in size) is just another element in the balanced composition, and the chapel is then a place of worship where the worshippers have to fight the devil in all his most sensual forms while standing up on their feet – since seats for only fifty are provided.

The reason for pointing out this consistent irony is not only because it is typical of Le Corbusier's later work, but also because it has been misinterpreted so strangely as irrational and expressionist.

The American critics, such as Mumford, thought Ronchamp the beginning of a return to the past and plasticity, and some English critics such as James Stirling thought it indicative of the 'Crisis of Rationalism'. Nearly everyone agreed that it presaged a new 'irrationalism' and new departure for Le Corbusier because it didn't appear to have right angles for discipline; and nearly everyone was partially wrong. As Peter Blake pointed out, Le Corbusier was writing his most personal document, *The Poem to the Right Angle*, when he designed Ronchamp: and the orthogonal system is apparent in the earliest models and plans, as is the discipline of the Modulor [89]. Furthermore, the meanings of the building work coherently, which is the only non-ideological definition of 'rationalism', and even further than that, all the elements of this building exist in Le Corbusier's architecture of the twenties. All he has done is turn his architecture inside-out so that the curves and right angles change place.

The only way in which the critics were right to accuse Le Corbusier of irrationality was in the purely conventional sense. By the fifties, the right angle and straight line had come to stand for honest rationality just as the Doric order had in the past, so to deviate from them was to make an antisocial gesture, in the limited sense. While Le Corbusier may not have been particularly concerned with this level of conventional meaning, it is possible that he did intend his later buildings to be read as departures from the 'modern movement', since he felt this tradition had become as dogmatic and restrictive as the Beaux-Arts.[13]

In any case, Le Corbusier pursued his own more personal path and continued to present irony both in content and conflict of geometries. In the High Court of Chandigarh, India [91], as opposed to Ronchamp, the conflict of geometries is resolved on the exterior under the choice of the right angle. The curves, the 'secondary, cultural forms and symbols' are brought under this controlling discipline. Furthermore, as in his Purist days, Le Corbusier's main preoccupation was with essential problem types: the sun, the rain, the winds, cosmic forces, the landscape of mountains to the north, from which he derived the object-types for the High Court. Yet these elements are not suppressed by the Modulor grid but

91. Le Corbusier: Chandigarh, India, Court of Justice, 1956. A complex interplay of different geometries: the small scaled *brise-soleil*, the medium scaled court rooms, the large vertical entrance and finally the sloping walls and the parabolic curves, all in very tight counterpoint The curving out butterfly roof is actually a giant parasol that provides protection from the strong sun and monsoon rains.

92. Le Corbusier: Chandigarh. Section of the two assemblies showing superimposed elements. The hyperbolic shape of the large assembly was suggested by an industrial, cooling tower; a typical form of *bricolage* suitable to this type of composition.

seem to erupt from the curving plane in a medley of colours and forms which confront each other frankly. And they play over a wild landscape, which as in many of his projects has not undergone a possible domestication.

The General Assembly Building at Chandigarh is in many respects the high point of Le Corbusier's use of open planning and what I would call 'compaction composition' [92]. As in a Cubist collage, geometric elements keep their autonomy but are also slammed together in

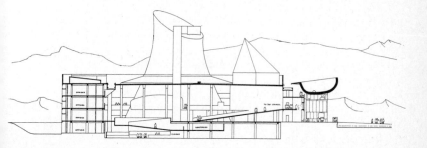

rich interplay. It's rather as if Le Corbusier started first with the individual function-types, picked generic forms for each one and then shook them together hard in a cocktail shaker. Or perhaps the right metaphor and drink is really a fruit punch, because the elements still float around recognizably after all this commotion [93].

Obviously this kind of design is only really feasible where an open plan is possible and much of the space is devoted to circulation and congregation, as here. Otherwise too much space is lost and the noise levels are intolerable. In any case, Le Corbusier has here created the kind of interior space that has preoccupied architects since the days of Egypt and the vast columnar halls at Karnak [94].

While this building is on an heroic scale and the whole capital complex is conceived as an acropolis [95], one can find the pretension of form sustained by the programme. Furthermore, the monumentality is mitigated by the use of 'signs' imprinted in the concrete, the moulded earthworks and the symbol of the open hand [96]. All these elements of human significance provide ironic contrast to the overall, heroic statement and give a personal touch and scale to a governmental centre which is quite rare. The way in which Le Corbusier is led too far by his heroic stance concerns the vast dimensions of the city and

93. Le Corbusier: Chandigarh, south-west façade. 'Compaction composition' works very well on a semantic level as the major elements are clearly identifiable: assembly room under the tower, council chamber under the pyramid, offices behind the *brise-soleil*, and in front, the autonomous entry porch.

94. Le Corbusier: Chandigarh, interior of Assembly Building. Here the 'masterly, correct and magnificent play' of forms is more Piranesian and tempestuous than in the early Purist compositions, but the idea is basically similar.

95 (*below*). **Le Corbusier: Chandigarh,** acropolis planning. The four main public buildings are organized on a series of overlapping diagonal axes. As Le Corbusier said of the Acropolis in *Vers*: 'The whole thing being out of square, provides richly varied vistas of a subtle kind; the different masses of the buildings, being asymmetrically arranged, create an intense rhythm. The whole composition is massive, elastic, living, terribly sharp, keen and dominating.'

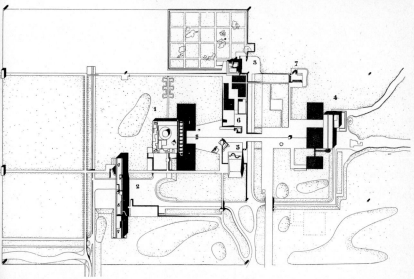

their inadequacy for at least another thirty years, but rather than criticize this we shall look at another project where the same kind of commitment led him astray.

A constant attitude which runs through all Le Corbusier's architecture from the very beginning, when he spent months in solitude sketching the architecture of Europe (six weeks on the Acropolis 'caressing the stones'), is the belief in man's essential loneliness. This belief is best conveyed to him by the Greek view of the cosmos and its architecture which, as an artefact of man, stands in opposition to a hostile universe – 'violent elements, sound-

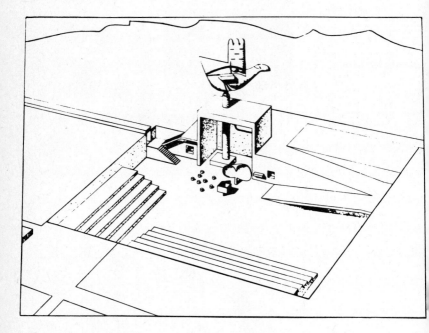

96. Le Corbusier: Chandigarh, sign of the open hand. One of the many elements Le Corbusier has used to suggest human mastery over the bureaucratic process.

ing clear and tragic like a brazen trumpet'. Such an image was always present in his architecture and while it no doubt gave great strength to such works as Ronchamp and Chandigarh, it became a great liability in more urbane projects where activity and warmth were called for. Such a project is the Venice Hospital [97] where Corbusier has rather arbitrarily imposed his 'Homeric solitude' (as he called it) as if the sick only needed isolation:

The form of the patients' rooms represents an entirely new solution: each patient receives an individual cell with no windows to look out of . . . Daylighting remains well distributed as does the room temperature so that the patient can enjoy calm isolation.[14]

But the problem is that people recovering from illness also like to see and hear activity, be in touch with the outside world and re-establish orientation rather than remain enclosed in a giant, horizontal network of diffused lighting and austere form. It's as if Le Corbusier produced this morgue-like atmosphere to confront the patients with

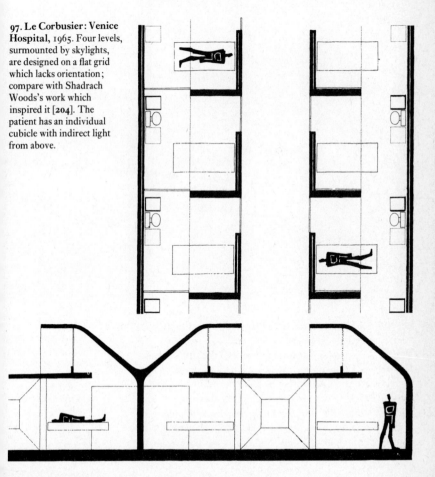

97. Le Corbusier: Venice Hospital, 1965. Four levels, surmounted by skylights, are designed on a flat grid which lacks orientation; compare with Shadrach Woods's work which inspired it [**204**]. The patient has an individual cubicle with indirect light from above.

the all-consuming cosmic element rather than a possible return to life.

But if the imposition of the Parthenon's austerity on a hospital was misconceived, Le Corbusier's last completed work, which also returned to a former metaphor, the ocean liner, was more appropriate. His designs for a combined house/exhibition pavilion return to a basic theme from *Vers Une Architecture*: the house constructed out of bolted-steel plates with the same 'clean and healthy' detailing as the ship. In fact the nautical imagery of Le Corbusier Centre [98] is carried on throughout the build-

ing: the roof umbrellas are sheet metal painted battleship grey, the 'top deck' below it has periscope windows and semicircular doors like ship hatches and the interior with its bolted steel columns, metal decking and open bridges appears like the engine room of an ocean liner [99]. The entrance to the second floor is up a sloping ramp which, except for its concrete material, has the appearance of a gangplank. Finally, the porcelain enamel panels have the neat, clean look of a ship's interior, while their primary colours recall semaphoric flags. All this nautical imagery

98. Le Corbusier: Le Corbusier Centre, Zurich, Switzerland, 1965/8. Two square umbrellas supported at their mid-points shelter two square pavilions; Corbusier has here added one more 'separation' to his repertoire; the roof from the building.

has its primary contrast to the land-based functions within, while without it sets up an even more ironic juxtaposition with the clipped lawns and shady oak-trees. Contrary to the Venice Hospital, nothing seems to have been sacrificed for the sake of the image and contrary to, say, Gropius and Wright, the integrity of imagery has lost none of its former strength and conviction. Indeed with this return to steel building, just at the time of his death, Le Corbusier seems to have been opening up a new and convincing direction in his work which did not refute the integrity of his early youth.

99. Le Corbusier: Le Corbusier Centre, interior with the central staircase and boiler flue. The painted steelwork completes the appearance of a ship's engine room. The steel sections and movable panels are bolted together with 20,000 screws, which makes it one of the most flexible structures to date.

5. ALVAR AALTO AND THE MEANS OF ARCHITECTURAL COMMUNICATION

The smile of the hostess is less a symptom of joy than a conventional sign of welcome and, reading Victorian novels, one may suspect that even the maiden's blush can be somewhat stylized. (E. H. GOMBRICH)

100. Henry Van de Velde: Werkebund Theatre, Cologne, 1914. The impact of an undulating profile supported from below by a homogeneous mass and contrasting against the clear sky above is a constant preoccupation of Aalto; compare to illustrations 104 and 109.

In many respects the personality and work of Aalto are the inverse of Le Corbusier's: relaxed and flowing rather than violent and tempestuous and patient rather than outspoken. Indeed Aalto has said hardly anything of striking interest about his relation to the modern world, whereas Le Corbusier never had to be asked twice for an epigrammatic pronouncement. Hence the rare moments when Aalto did say a little bit were bound to be revealing:

> This wood structure . . . dedicated to Henry Van de Velde, the great pioneer of the architecture of our times, the first to envisage the revolution in the techniques of wood.[1]

If one looks at Van de Velde's Werkebund Theatre one finds oneself suddenly confronted with an architecture that is particularly Aaltoesque [100]: the sharply-etched profile supported visually by an homogeneous mass.

Often with an architect there is a characteristic image, the result of his sketching technique, that summarizes all his work. With Aalto that image is the place where one system touches another – the seats give way to the wall, the wall gives way to the roof, the roof touches the sky. At any place of juncture, one might say that Aalto is obsessed with presenting the full visual contrast and passing this obsession on to the viewer, so that he becomes

167

sensitized to an aspect of the environment which has remained largely subconscious. Often, Aalto singles out an aspect, uses it consistently and dramatically and thereby 'recodes' our visual experience: from now on undulating profiles will never be the same, just as cracks in the wall, cumulus clouds and optical distortions have all been transfigured in the past by great artists.[2] It is a commonplace that artists make us see the world differently by giving us a new conventional language of vision, and Aalto has been particularly appreciated because the architectural language he has evolved has been rich and made use of the full gamut of expressive means, whereas much recent architecture has been simplistic and based on just a single mode of communication.

101. Alvar Aalto: Viipuri, Finland, 1927–35. View of the acoustic ceiling in the lecture theatre which undulates the full length of the room to bring every point audibly 'alive'.

In one sense, Aalto's rich subtlety is the result of a multivalence of meanings where one part of the architecture interrelates with another and thus modifies it. We can see this aspect of multivalence in what is perhaps Aalto's first use of the undulating profile which contrasts two surfaces: the Viipuri lecture theatre [101]. Not only do the visual elements modify each other (the white wall makes the ceiling darker) but so do the functional: i.e. the acoustic requirements which determined the undulating principle were reinforced by the wood-joining technique of parallel slats and the need for an overall, spatial definer. Thus the mutual modification here depends on reinforcement, but it can also work equally well through opposition, as Aalto's Wolfsburg Culture Centre shows. For instance in the main entrance to this building, one finds a relatively dark, low space which has a plethora of conflicting textures and surfaces [102]. The space constricts and vibrates, the columns interfere with direct movement – but all these negative forces are working through opposition as positive circulation cues. The purpose of the entrance hall is to act as a welcoming point and cloakroom but also to keep people moving, and this can be done, among other ways, by vibrant lines and interfering columns. Hence these negative forces serve positively to push one up the stairs to the real heart of the centre, the roof garden and auditoria. Here the same insistent geo-

102. Alvar Aalto: Wolfsburg Cultural Centre, Wolfsburg, Germany, 1959-62. Main entrance with its symphony of jittery geometries which keep one on the move.

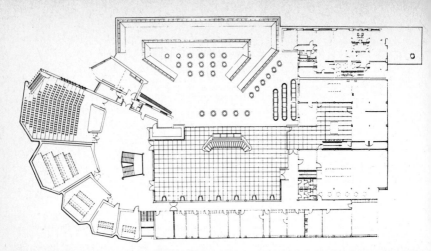

metries, which still buzz over the head, keep one moving to either garden, offices or auditoria where the forms are more relaxed.

The auditoria are, of course, the main purpose of this cultural centre since they are used for adult education as well as entertainment, but they only receive their visual importance because the rather dull offices and under-played club-room accentuate them by hiding themselves. But this is not quite the case. Actually, as the plan makes

103 (*top*). **Alvar Aalto: Wolfsburg Cultural Centre,** plan. To the left the lecture rooms fan out from the basic rectangle, to the right are clubrooms and workshops, while at the top is the library.

104 (*above*). Elevation showing lecture halls above a dark entrance level.

105. Alvar Aalto:
Wolfsburg Cultural
Centre. Aerial view
showing the way the lecture
theatres form an auto-
nomous, inclined plane.

clear [103], the auditoria share centre stage both with the
club-room and the library, and they are all subordinate to
the enclosed space, the roof garden. Thus each one is
allowed to break out of the constricting discipline (the
rectangle) to assert its importance. This is also apparent
in elevation where the discipline of a rectangle is again
broken to articulate importance; although the rise of the
auditoria is within yet another geometric discipline, the
inclined plane [105]. Thus here geometric disciplines are

continually set up only to be significantly violated. As if to underline the importance of the auditoria still further, Aalto has increased the number of columns and changed their monotonous office beat to an erratic syncopation, and finally, to complete their visual supremacy, he has increased the length of the overhang in order to deepen the shadow [104].

INFORMATION THEORY

In effect, while I have so far been overtly describing the way one part of the building modifies another through opposition, I have been covertly describing a reaction to a series of visual cues. One dimension of architectural communication – which Aalto is adept in – consists in nothing else than a series of alternating signals; rough versus smooth, dark versus light and so on. The most general explanation for the way these signals work, information theory, is put forward by Colin Cherry in opposition to expressionist theory, the idea that meanings are inherent both in the viewer and the signals:

106a. Alvar Aalto: Säynätsalo Town Hall, Säynätsalo, Finland, 1950. View from the southeast through the trees showing the high, cantilevered form to the right.
106b. The culmination of diagonal movement, the pitched shape on the axis of the main entrance.

> Signals do not convey information as railroad trucks carry coal. Rather we should say: signals have an information content by virtue of *their potential for making selections*. Signals operate upon the alternatives forming the recipient's doubt. They give power to discriminate amongst or select from these alternatives.[3]

Basically, we may say that 'the alternatives forming the recipient's doubt' are *both* his past knowledge and his immediate present schemata – his interest and purpose. The point that information theory makes clear is that the viewer's experience consists in projecting forward tentative hypotheses and then selecting by observation from among them in a continual sequence of expectation and confirmation or suggestion and frustration.

One can see how Aalto has intended all these provocative signalling devices for the experience of finding the council chamber in the Säynätsalo Town Hall: intended because the project still isn't complete and finding the council chamber is now perhaps too easy. One was meant to approach the Town Hall through a screen of trees and past a series of buildings organized diagonally on a grid

[**106a**]. One thus expects to find at the end of this rise through the trees the most important grid of all, as one does. And further, one expects to find the most important functions to be located around the centre of this grid because it is raised over the shops – as they are. But one's expectancy is slightly confused by the veil of trees and by the unusual form that rises in steps of cantilevers and dominates the whole complex [**106a**].

The probability that this is the council chamber is high because it is the highest point and it is the summation of movement along the diagonal grid; but still there is uncertainty caused by the strange shape which does not seem quite right for a meeting hall. Finally, when one reaches the entrance below the raised plateau, there can be no doubt [**106b**]. Clearly the councillor sits at the deep end of that most important shape, because such a form concentrates the sight and acoustic lines like an amphitheatre. Yet such information is slightly resisted because the pitched shape and its material are still part of other probabilities; the copper pitched roofs and brick that sur-

107. Alvar Aalto: Säynätsalo Town Hall. Main entrance: four more turns have to be made before one enters the council chamber.

108 (*opposite*). **Alvar Aalto Säynätsalo Town Hall.** Struts fan out along the ridge beams and are protected from the extreme temperature.

round one. But the goal is the council chamber and we expect to enter off the main courtyard – and we do and we don't. First we have to turn and go around some more steps through a door [**107**].

Finally, we are in the council chamber, but we aren't. We have to go up some more steps, turn twice and we will enter where the councillor sits under the slope of the roof – but he doesn't. He and the council are oriented at right angles to the orientation of the roof. And the roof, which we expect to be supported by a regular triangular truss, is and isn't [108]. It is the usual triangular truss which is made different (because of extreme Finnish temperature), by placing all the muscle inside the room and not next to the cold skin. In every case, the tyranny of *probability sets up an expectancy which is made democratic by being partially fulfilled – and falsified*. Thus Aalto has consciously set up a series of probabilities only to resist and distort them and, as information theory postulates, the greater the probabilities which are resisted, the more exciting the experience.

If contrast, or a set of alternatives, is necessary to convey information, then it would seem that all visual meanings must be conveyed through alternatives. But this is exactly what expressionists such as the Gestalt psychologists deny. They assert that there are some meanings intrinsic within a form which convey themselves directly, regardless of the context. Thus an angular, jutting line carries the intrinsic meaning of activity and this intrinsic meaning tends to cluster naturally around other meanings such as sharpness, strength, coldness, brightness.[4] In the same way, for the opposite reasons, the flowing, horizontal line naturally tends to mean passivity and naturally tends to the related cluster of enclosure, warmth, sweetness, redness and, not surprisingly, femininity.

Indeed, we do read off psychical meaning directly from a person's appearance. A frown is directly expressive of sadness without our having to be taught that it is because of the inherent perceptual patterns. And the angular, jutting line is directly expressive of strength for the same reasons. But what of a *happy* frown and a *weak* jutting line? Obviously, we can think of a clown's *sad* face which achieves great joy by contrast with his action, just as we can think of many *passive* buildings which are made up of angular, jutting lines. For instance, Aalto's Imatra Church is usually perceived as passive, serene and defensive, yet it is from the outside a compendium of jutting angles [**109**]. Indeed, in one of the most expressive and appropriate critiques of the building, Reyner Banham has said:

... Imatra seems, at first, to turn from the viewer and hide, humping its copper roofs defensively against the sky and lifting cautious windows, like watchful, alligator eyes, above the white substructure in which it seems to burrow.[5]

How can this building turn, hide, hump, lift cautiously like a watchful alligator and then burrow? Especially when it is made up of angular, jutting lines. Something is wrong. Either Banham is writing nonsense or the simple expressionist thesis is in need of complication. The latter seems to be the case, because the windows *do* look like watchful, alligator eyes and the overall church *does* seem to turn from the viewer and hide its copper roofs defensively. But

109. Alvar Aalto: Imatra, Finland, 1957-9. Angular, jutting lines express passivity, in this case because of the other visual signals.

how do we know this? What keeps us from saying that Imatra welcomes the viewer and billows its copper roofs gaily? If we were to assume a simple isomorphism between pattern and expression, then we would have to say that the forms themselves are unwelcoming and defensive – which they well may be. But the point is that these immediate patterns are more correctly confirmed as being what they essentially are *because they are confirmed by other cues* or the structure of other alternatives.

The overall passive form, the function of church, the reinforcing horizontal lines, all confirm the primary meaning of defensiveness, and thus it is appropriate to speak of watchful alligator eyes. The cluster of meanings is coherent and confirms the main expectation. But this is only possible because, in fact, information and expression are working together. Either one alone would leave the interpretation seriously one-sided and vague. The critic who described Imatra without mentioning the social

and acoustic functions which determined the roof would
be as imprecise as the critic who could not read the direct
expression of the forms.

In effect, the combination of information and expression allows the architect to play a richer symphony in
which most meanings are working in a cluster while other
ones are working negatively. It allows Aalto to gain positive results from the negative features as in the Wolfsburg
Centre. Or, in the case of the interior of Imatra, it allows
him to create a space which is an ambiguous blend of joy
and concentration [110]. The rise and decline of the roof
might be said to express these meanings directly. But the
ambiguity is further reinforced by noticing that the altar
and top window are given equal weight. Finally, this ambiguity is confirmed, as we discover that the overall form

110. **Alvar Aalto: Imatra
Church.** View towards the
altar with light from above
and ambiguous relation
of walls to roof and floor.

has been determined functionally, because of acoustics and social divisions [111]. Or has it? The clear answer, confirmed by each classifier and modification, is that the meanings are multivalent. They are meant to be interpreted as ambiguous.

THE AMBIVALENCE OF THE HUMANIST APPROACH

Almost all of Aalto's buildings contain this masterfully complex coding of messages which result in his characteristically subtle language. But what of the messages themselves? He has continuously proposed a form of understated humanism in opposition to the prevailing extremes of a sterile rationalism and bombastic expressionism:

> The horoscope of building art today is of a kind that makes the words negative – and that is not pleasant. Parallelepipeds of glass square and synthetic metals – the inhuman dandy-purism of the cities – have led to a mode of building without return, highly popular in a naïve world. And what is worse, it has had, as a consequence, a change in the opposite direction – an uncritical, clumsy search for a variation theme . . . Grown up children play with curves and tensions which they do not control. It smells of Hollywood.[6]

Contrary to these tendencies, Aalto has produced a relaxed, anthropomorphic architecture. In nearly every project he feels it a duty to point out how he has evolved a form from the considerations of the most humane nature. If it is a funeral chapel, he has divided it up so that no two ceremonies conflict; if it is a large bureaucracy, he breaks down the mass; if it is a mass-produced door knob, he moulds it to the human hand and so on. Even,

179

or perhaps above all, his office is organized along humane lines as one large family of cooperative members:

> No organized teamwork is tolerated in my office. The basis of our work is friendly cooperation and the atmosphere is that of a family. All my collaborators are trained architects, none are mere draughtsmen; thus a practice with no organization, but under my own responsibility, resting on common endeavour, not on discipline.[7]

In short, the ideas of 'mutualism' which are propounded by the anarchists such as Kropotkin, whom Aalto admires. If such a social philosophy is very attractive and intelligent in many respects, it also has its seedy side, especially in the Scandinavian countries where paternalism and social responsibility are oppressive and stifling. Indeed one feels that in some of Aalto's work there is this same kind of overbearing solicitude, that there are no sharp conflicts as everything is smoothed over as serene and saccharine as molasses. The Pensions Bank is a typical case in point [112]. Conceived as a fragmented mass to break up the feeling of bureaucracy, it succeeds all too well in being humane and killing the pensioner with kind-

112. Alvar Aalto: Pensions Bank, Helsinki, Finland, 1952-6. Entrance with bronze doors, copper sheet cladding, red brick and grey concrete base. The official bureaucratic function is broken up into a series of familiar, friendly forms.

ness. The forms are familiar red brick and ribbon-strip windows broken by copper and bronze elements – all carried through with a literal-mindedness that borders on the soporific. Not only does this create boredom of a certain sort, but also it seems irrelevant both to the true nature of such bureaucracies and the larger issues of urban conflict. Perhaps such welfare paternalism works in small, homogeneous countries such as Finland, but its applicability to larger, more plural cities such as New York is questionable. Yet this kind of solicitude comes from a man who, as the rumour has it, could steal out one night with a raiding party and shoot out the advertisements which defaced his Säynätsalo Town Hall. Also he had this to say:

> You could not think about Bernard Shaw without at the same time thinking about him as a fighting man. In their deepest meaning, I think fighting and the highest class of art conform, and in their deepest meaning they belong together.[8]

So on second thoughts, one goes back to his architecture to look again. The question is – are Aalto's humanistic beliefs reductive, conducive to a soft paternalism, or are they recognizable as a serious view towards the complex situation of urban conflict? The answer seems to be mixed. Certainly there is a tendency, since the Paimio Sanitorium (1929), to soft, comforting solicitation; but this is often intensified by rigorous coldness; the totality avoids sentimentality. This reciprocity is apparent in the Imatra Church: at once a secular meeting hall which makes overtures to God through its secularity. That is, by concentrating so much on the functional aspects, such as acoustic curves and division into three social activities, he has managed to make these functional considerations part of another dimension.

At first, one approaches a soft, childlike exterior which conveys little information but sentiment because of its apparent lack of order [113]. No two windows are alike; everything is arbitrary and cute. This arbitrariness does become comprehensible when one sees the other side and begins to understand the building. Once on the inside, one seems to be confronted with a white, Protestant light; clean, clear, rational, social understanding of the necessity of religion without belief itself. But then the light dissolves

from above the whole surface and the roof bends down on to the altar. The acoustic curves become not just a humane function but its imaginative equivalent, a grasping gesture. When one grasps an object, the skin bunches up, pinches and forms a series of twisted folds which acknowledge the act of grasping [114]. This is not the usual statement of belief, or desire to believe, which is evident in most pious church buildings, but something quite different and successful – the imaginative equivalent of a proposition. Whether or not we can fully accept or only partially enjoy this religious gesture is another question altogether, depending, of course, on our own belief.

Thus to summarize Aalto's later work, we may say that it uses the full range of architectural communication, both a systematic presentation of alternating cues, and naturally expressive form. If there is a final doubt as to the ultimate importance of this work, it occurs at the points where it becomes oppressively soft and paternal. That this form of humanism was just one alternative to a rather schematic rationalism and anonymity we will see in the next chapter, which deals with the formalist revolt in America and the 'smell of Hollywood' which Aalto condemned.

113. **Alvar Aalto: Imatra Church.** Entrance side with its seemingly arbitrary forms: pastor's house to the right, exit and canopy for funeral ceremonies to the left.

114. **Alvar Aalto: Imatra Church.** Juncture between windows, sliding door and ventilation equipment is acknowledged by the pinching of the skin.

6. RECENT AMERICAN ARCHITECTURE CAMP - NON CAMP

I am strongly drawn to Camp, and almost as strongly offended by it . . . to name a sensibility, to draw its contours and recount its history, requires a deep sympathy modified by revulsion. (SUSAN SONTAG, *Notes on Camp*, 1964)

115a. Albert Speer: Zeppelinfeld, Nürnberg, Germany, 1934.

115b. Lincoln Cultural Center, New York City. Philip Johnson's building to the left, Wallace Harrison's in front, and Max Ambrovitz's to the right. The objects of Low Camp, from Nazi architecture to American cultural centres, are so ubiquitous in modern societies as to appear normal.

Recent American architecture has had, like the pioneers, a worldwide effect which is beyond dispute. This effect is due as much as anything to an affluence which has resulted in a building boom that has liberated technological and expressive forces unseen before. Whether the result is Las Vegas or the Vehicle Assembly Building at Cape Kennedy, the first large pneumatic building or the perfecting of the curtain wall – American architecture is often there first, because it has the money, energy and pluralism to innovate where other countries cannot. Thus in some respects there is a problem in trying to comprehend or even classify its scope. It is so diverse in form and genesis as to defy simple classification. There is however one aspect of it which is all too clearly comprehensible and that is the official architecture of American corporations and the government. Its resemblance to Fascist architecture of the thirties is, alas, all too great.

One only has to compare Mussolini's Third Rome [21a] with Ed Stone's Perpetual Savings and Loan Association, 1961, or any number of cultural centres appearing across the United States with the architecture of the Third Reich to be convinced of this [115a,b]. Indeed the architect Philip Johnson, writing about the 'Architecture of the

Third Reich' in 1933, could be describing the pervasive attitude for monumental building in America in 1963:

It would be false to speak of the architectural situation in National Socialist Germany. The new state is faced with such tremendous problems of reorganization that a program of art and architecture has not been worked out. Only a few points are certain. First *Die Neue Sachlichkeit* is over. Houses that look like hospitals and factories are taboo . . . Second, architecture will be monumental. That is, instead of bath-houses, *Siedlungen*, employment offices and the like, there will be official railroad stations, memorial museums, monuments. The present regime is more intent on leaving a visible mark of its greatness than in providing sanitary equipment for workers.[1]

Although this summary of Johnson's may not be exactly true of present-day America, it does come uncomfortably close. Furthermore, to extend the comparison, there is the similar neoclassicism, the recurrent style in America of which Louis Sullivan said in 1893: 'This will set back the course of American architecture by fifty years.' If this prophecy were to be true of all American history, then its architecture would be about minus two hundred years old, because as historians have noted,[2] the style reappears regularly on demand, every thirty years.

The causes for the most recent outburst of classicist formalism are, like American architecture itself, diverse. They must be traced, as mentioned before,[3] to the de-politicization of the idealist tradition which occurred in the thirties and the willingness of such architects as Mies, Gropius, Nervi, Ponti, etc. to smooth over differences with the Fascists for pragmatic reasons. But also the causes have to be sought in their old traditional places. The desire of mercantile interests to have a subdued but monumental exterior; the insecurity of these interests when faced with the new or unexpected. All this is familiar ground and without much interest. But what is surprising and different in the American scene is the new attitude, or mental set, which has begun to emerge in certain circles to experience this material without falling into the usual disparagement or rhetoric – the attitude of Camp.

The Camp attitude is essentially a mental set towards all sorts of objects which *fail from a serious* point of view. Instead of condemning these failures, it partially contemplates them and partially enjoys them. It is, as Susan Sontag says in her definitive essay *Notes on Camp*,[4] 'one way of seeing the world as an aesthetic phenomenon'. As such, it tries to outflank all the other stereotyped views of failure which are morbid or moralistic and substitute a sort of cheerful openmindedness. It starts from failure and then asks what is left to enjoy, to salvage. It is realistic, because it accepts monotony, cliché and the habitual gestures of a mass-production society as the norm without trying to change them. It accepts stock response and ersatz without protest, not only because it enjoys both, finding them 'real', but because it seeks to find those usually disregarded moments of interest (the fantastic hidden in the banal). Thus the epitome 'it's so bad that it's good', which accepts the classifications of traditional culture but reverses the verdict.

Usually the term Camp is applied to a fairly restricted and rarefied set of objects such as Tiffany lamps and old Flash Gordon comic strips, but like other concepts such as Baroque or Pop or Kitsch, its use becomes more general and extended as it becomes accepted. In this chapter, I have followed the generalizing tendency applying the term to such new areas as organic architecture, which is excessively metaphorical, and gigantic technology, which is scaleless and often felt to be 'inhumane'. Both kinds of architecture evoke the typical Camp response 'too much' or 'Gosh!', with its innocent, almost naïve willingness to be impressed in a sardonic sort of way. In addition, this overblown kind of architecture fails from a serious point of view since it relies so heavily on a univalent statement of effect – so it does qualify as Camp.

Yet the application of this concept to recent American architecture must not be made as an exclusive classification, as can be seen in the diagram [116]. There are at least six discernible tendencies ranging from the academic to pragmatic which must, and will, be seen in their own terms as well as instances of large, relatively unconscious concepts. The advantage of using Camp to cover some of these tendencies is that it elucidates a large, underlying area of common ground which otherwise appears separated in a confusion of styles. Indeed this confusion, called 'Chaoticism',[5] is itself very much part of the permissively plural Camp attitude.

	Kahn	Venturi	Moore	Giurgola	Belluschi	Cambridge 7	Sert	Esherick	Kallmann	Barnes	Johansen	Breuer	Neutra	Nowicki	Eames	Wachsmann	Fuller	Kiesler	Soleri	Greene	Goff	Wright	Lundy	Gropius	Stubbins	Rudolph	Saarinen	P.Johnson	I.M.Pei	Mies	SOM	Yamasaki	Stone	Harrison
Kahn																																		
Venturi	3																																	
Moore	3	2																																
Giurgola	4	1	1																															
Belluschi	3	4	1	2																														
Cambridge 7	2	2	2	3	3																													
Sert	3	4	2	3	3	2																												
Esherick	3	3	3	4	4	2	1																											
Kallmann	3	5	5	4	6	5	3	4																										
Barnes	3	5	5	6	6	3	3	2	4																									
Johansen	5	7	5	6	6	5	3	4	4	2																								
Breuer	5	5	4	5	3	3	4	4	4	4																								
Neutra	6	4	4	3	4	6	6	7	5	7	7	3																						
Nowicki	4	4	3	4	4	3	3	4	6	4	4	2	5																					
Eames	8	7	7	6	7	6	8	7	9	9	11	7	6	7																				
Wachsmann	9	7	7	6	6	7	7	8	8	10	10	6	5	6	1																			
Fuller	9	9	9	10	8	7	9	8	12	8	10	8	9	6	3	4																		
Kiesler	5	6	6	6	4	5	7	6	10	6	8	8	7	6	7	8	6																	
Soleri	7	7	7	8	6	7	9	8	10	6	8	8	7	8	9	10	8	2																
Greene	7	7	7	8	6	7	9	8	10	6	8	8	7	8	9	10	8	2	0															
Goff	7	7	7	8	6	7	9	8	10	6	8	8	7	8	9	9	8	2	0	0														
Wright	11	9	7	8	6	9	9	10	10	8	6	8	7	9	11	10	10	4	2	2	2													
Lundy	7	9	7	8	6	9	9	10	10	8	6	6	5	6	11	10	10	8	8	8	6													
Gropius	10	8	6	7	5	6	6	7	7	7	3	4	4	8	7	9	9	9	9	9	9	3												
Stubbins	7	7	7	8	5	6	6	7	7	7	5	3	4	5	8	7	9	9	9	9	9	8	3	2										
Rudolph	4	5	6	5	7	8	6	7	5	7	5	7	6	9	12	11	15	11	11	11	9	5	6	6										
Saarinen	8	6	7	6	8	9	9	10	8	10	8	6	5	8	9	8	12	12	12	12	12	10	4	5	5	3								
P.Johnson	7	6	6	5	5	8	8	9	5	9	7	7	4	9	10	9	13	9	9	9	9	7	3	4	4	2	3							
I.M.Pei	9	8	8	7	7	8	8	9	7	9	7	5	3	7	8	7	11	11	11	11	11	8	3	2	2	4	3	2						
Mies	12	12	12	11	11	12	12	13	9	14	11	9	8	10	6	5	9	13	13	13	13	11	7	6	6	9	5	6	4					
SOM	10	8	9	8	8	9	9	10	6	10	8	6	5	8	9	8	12	12	12	12	12	10	4	2	5	4	3	1	3					
Yamasaki	9	7	7	6	6	9	9	10	8	10	8	5	10	9	8	12	8	8	8	6	5	6	3	4	1	3	5	4						
Stone	8	8	6	7	5	8	8	9	9	9	7	7	6	9	10	9	11	7	8	8	8	5	4	4	5	5	4	2	4	6	5	1		
Harrison	9	8	6	7	5	6	6	7	7	7	5	5	6	7	10	9	11	9	8	8	8	7	4	2	3	3	5	2	2	6	3	2	2	

CAMP

The underlying genesis of Camp in architecture may be traced to the movement of formalism which has always enjoyed a certain following in America. The *Beaux-Arts* style, just as the Greek and Gothic revivals, were imported ready-made to America. Likewise the 'International Style' was adopted as a set of formal principles which were cut away from their social and industrial roots in Europe and transplanted to an affluent society where the conditions were more rural and individualistic. Hitchcock and Johnson in 1932 quite explicitly repudiated the extreme functionalism which underlay the International Style in Europe while accepting the aesthetic principles. And later, Johnson again quite candidly denounced the tendency of functionalism to degenerate into sterility, and reasserted the primary value of architecture as art. It is important to see the frame of mind and the situation in which formalism grew. Vincent Scully has said of this situation:

> It [1949] is the date when Philip Johnson began to give his splendid talks which those of us who first heard them regarded almost as the pronouncements of the Devil. He stood up on the platform at Yale University, and he said to a shocked hush across the room, 'I would rather sleep in the nave of Chartres Cathedral with the nearest John two blocks down the street than I would in a Harvard House with back to back bathrooms.' This terrible and even rather frightening pronouncement was the one after which, for the first time, I remember students saying to me, 'He's talking about architecture as an art.' And suddenly I realized that that is what it was all the time.[6]

Thus the growth of formalism was effected by two important sources: a university campus where there was a sophisticated audience that knew the history of the modern movement, and a cultural situation where the existence of architecture as an art was always tenuous. This latter condition has led to many similar assertions and shocks of recognition: architecture is simply an art, and art has little or nothing to do with functionalism, etc. but is always a reduction of things to their 'essentials'. Thus Paul Rudolph, the head of the architectural school at Yale University in the early sixties, has continually asserted the reductive element in architecture, insisting that all art is illusion and all illusion is based on exclusion. The architect, he states, does not solve all the problems, but only seeks to solve and dramatize a few. The paradigm is Mies's 'Less is more'.

One even addresses oneself to certain problems in one building and others in the next. All problems can never be solved. Indeed it is a characteristic of the twentieth century that architects are highly selective in determining which problems they want to solve. Mies, for instance, makes wonderful buildings only because

116. Relation of American architects to each other has been determined through a method called numerical taxonomy. Here the six major schools can be seen (dark shading) as: (1) the Academic School, (2) the Environmentalist School, (3) the Technical (4) Organic, (5) Formalist, and (6) Pragmatic Schools. The first two schools are in general Non Camp (multivalent) whereas the last two are Camp (univalent). See *Architectural Design*, November 1969, p. 582, for a further discussion.

he ignores many aspects of a building. If he solved more problems his buildings would be far less potent. This paradox is heightened by the various commitments to functionalism.[7]

One of these commitments to functionalism was by Rudolph's teacher Gropius, although as we have seen it was not very strong. At any rate it is not surprising that the generation taught by Gropius at Harvard should feel a conflict between art and function because at this time his buildings were very dry and suppressed. Thus a rebellious pupil, Victor Lundy, could say (sharing a reaction with other Harvard formalists such as Pei, Franzen, Johansen):

In my case, I think Harvard almost ruined me. I want my buildings to be exuberant, not safe, lovely, cubular things. Creative architecture comes out of the individual, not out of group design.

And Rudolph could also insist on the primacy of the individual as opposed to the group:

Gropius may be wrong in believing that architecture is a co-operative art. Architects were not meant to design together; it's either all his work, or mine.[8]

So here we have two typical conditions of the formalists: a rebellion against conformity in the name of art, and a university education and audience (particularly Harvard). Both conditions characterize the new sensibility which defiantly claims the right of spontaneous expression leading perhaps to insult. Thus *Time Magazine* could say with mild approval when reviewing Rudolph's trend-setting Art and Architecture Building [**117**]:

He wishes his buildings to end as beautiful ruins . . . 'All sorts of conceits' says Rudolph puckishly pointing out fishbones, sea shells and coral in the concrete, 'are buried in the wall' . . . Gesturing at a flat space he says 'I think I'll put a Grecian nude reclining statue there' . . . the roof terrace where, he says 'all Hell breaks loose'.[9]

This might be called the apotheosis of Middle Camp: the grand gesture, the defiance of convention, honest arrogance, the connection with mass media (Rudolph's face appeared looming out of his building on the cover of *Progressive Architecture* as if he were about to ascend upward at any moment). He was severely chastised and

117. Paul Rudolph: Art and Architecture Building, New Haven, 1963. 'Camp art is often decorative art emphasizing texture, sensuous surface, and style at the expense of content' (Susan Sontag).

praised for this building which had thirty-nine different levels (in the space of seven storeys), impossible working conditions and now, quite recently, has been burned out supposedly as a protest against Yale's restrictive admission and teaching policy. In any case, the building was so forcefully bombastic and such an unequivocal exhibition of the personality cult and star system that it actually worked. That is, when other architects were being less than candid about their underlying motivations, it managed to dramatize in an explicit way the individual's unalloyed pursuit of fame combined with exotic taste (candelabra, orange, pulsating carpets, etc.).

As mentioned, the ultimate Camp statement is that 'it's good because it's awful'. Thus Rudolph's building is not quite High Camp, because it is too good, or rather not bad enough. The point about High Camp work is that it aspires to the condition of greatness, but fails to reach this level rather completely. The resultant gap between pretension and performance is so incredible that the work oscillates back and forth between the interpretative levels of the sublime and ridiculous. For some the work is merely sublime; for others the oscillation is so acute that it actually works imaginatively to produce cathartic laughter and release. Thus from the High Camp standpoint the greatest building is the Cultural Center in Washington [118] by Ed Stone, an early practitioner of the International Style in the United States. To show how accommodating he could be to the client, that is to knock off about forty-five million dollars from the estimate,

118. **Edward Durrell Stone: John F. Kennedy Center, Washington DC, first model, 1964.** 'In naïve, or pure, Camp the essential element is seriousness, a seriousness that fails.' Press report on finished building, 1971: 'The foyer is so gigantic – 630 feet long, six storeys high, with an all-glass wall facing the river – that if Mickey Mantle had belted his longest homer from one end of the room, it wouldn't have hit the opposite wall.' Final cost: 70 million dollars.

Stone changed the shape of the Cultural Center from a doughnut into a rectangle without altering the façade at all: it remained a kind of magazine illustrator's air-brush testimony to the Parthenon. This has the quality of all great art from Stonehenge to St Peter's; it says something to everyone; it reconciles enemies; it appeals to all the faculties of the soul (in exactly opposite ways). Thus the philistine could finally stand shoulder to shoulder with the *avant-garde*, the one crying with his vision of Elysium, the other laughing until tears came to his eyes. In front of such a masterpiece neutrality would not only be cruel, it would be impossible (like neutrality before such films as *The Greatest Story Ever Told* or *Beyond the Valley of the Dolls*).

As Susan Sontag further points out, Camp is a form of 'urban pastoral' which tries to remake the industrial civilization into a dream of nature or any kind of fantasy. Thus Hector Guimard's Paris Metro entrance in which cast iron wriggles like an orchidaceous climber, or the present work of the independent mid-Western architects Greene, Soleri and Goff which also tries to transform the urban civilization through a naturalistic metaphor. Goff's Bavinger House [119a] grows like the spiral of a snail.

119a. Bruce Goff: Bavinger House, Norman, Oklahoma, 1957. This and the following two works are successful and serious examples of imaginative transformation comparable to Art Nouveau. Here the continuous, spiral space is surrounded by sandstone and hung from a steel mast and cables. Goff uses prefabricated elements and organic materials with equal conviction achieving a synthesis through a common geometry and overall image.

Around a central mast all the areas of the house descend from utmost privacy at the top to the public realm below. Greene's houses grow organically by cellular multiplication of the shingle until a curving hide of wood has shaped a sequence of continuous space [119b]. Soleri's Desert

House burrows beneath the ground like a mole to give the image of a return to Mother Earth, even though it appears as a moonscape [119c]. Kiesler, who has explored the possibility of continuous space more than anyone, creates the image of a dripping cave.

But all these images of nature were not actually intended for an urban situation, whereas there are many cases where an architect tried to transform the urban scene through a fantastic metaphor: thus Rudolph's laboratories for the manufacture of pharmaceuticals presents the exterior of a tweedy, Scottish Castle. The white office for the Consolidated Gas Company [120] by Yamasaki, the Japanese-American architect, is topped by a crown of thorns and eternally-burning-blue-gas-flame to suggest both a Gothic spire pushing heavenward and the eternality of Consolidated Gas. Of course one can fault these urban pastorals for inappropriateness: why should a Gas Company look like a Greek Gothic Cathedral (since none has ever existed)? Why should a drug company resemble

119b. **Herbert Greene:** Prairie House, Norman, Oklahoma, 1961. Oscar Wilde: 'To be natural is such a very difficult pose to keep up.'

119c. Paolo Soleri and Mills: Desert House, Cave Creek, Arizona, 1951. One's first reaction to these imaginative transformations is to grasp them by metaphors: a snail, armadillo, moonscape might apply to these three houses.

a tweedy castle? Indeed there is no reason except that all architecture is metaphorical and must by necessity look like something.

What critics find objectionable here is the explicitness and inappropriate content: the easy cliché which is dissociated from the underlying function. But cliché after all is what every metaphor quickly becomes in an instant society where communication overcommunicates; and furthermore there is simply no consensus which could establish propriety, nor technical and functional restraints which could stabilize the norms, nor public myth and philosophy which could sanction the metaphor. The Camp artist accepts this, sends up his critics with the riposte 'there are no rules, anything goes', cheerfully shuffles form regardless of content (with one eye on his audience) and does not try to produce integrated, serious works. He is content to remain in farce, in sin, in short, in Camp. But after all, why should art be a series of Continual Crescendi in the Great Tradition?

Such will always be the answer of the Camp architect who knows (in his candid moments) that his works are not the profound jewels he sells them as. This is the point that must be stressed to avoid confusion: candour. The Camp architect admits at once that whoever he is, it is much more important than whatever he does. Thus criticism is bio-

120: Minoru Yamasaki: Consolidated Gas Building, Detroit, 1964. Gothic fretwork, crown of thorns, the eternal blue flame of consolidated gas, good High Camp. Here is the attempt to transform urban realities into a nostalgic dream of a classical past; the forms are univalent, simple and applied. This is 'failed seriousness' at its best, most horrible. *Yamasaki:* 'An architecture to implement our way of life and reflect it must recognize those human characteristics we cherish most: love, gentility, joy, serenity, beauty and hope, and the dignity and individuality of man. This idea in its essence is the philosophy of humanism in architecture.' *Oscar Wilde:* 'One must have a heart of stone to read the death of Little Nell without laughing.'

graphy, standards are notoriety, symptoms are more interesting than theories, quickness is a virtue, the social gesture is the object, the image cannot be analysed (since it simply dissolves like Cotton Candy) and the news media are exploited and glorified for short bursts. Aubrey Beardsley and Art Nouveau were spurred forward by a new form of communication, by a new graphic means and new urban audience. Art Nouveau, like Camp, was a definite industrial, urban and class phenomenon. In this situation, the mirror is the next most important object after the news media; all statements are self-referential; the first person singular is the most common case. How does my historical image look today?

SAARINEN: The only architecture which interests me is architecture as a fine art. That is what I want to pursue. I hope some of my buildings will have lasting truths. I admit frankly I would like a place in architectural history.

This apparently frank admission has the ironic effect of pointing towards a place in history quite opposite to the one intended, since Saarinen wished to be considered along with the Pioneers. Yet he did manage to produce serious, multivalent works which transcended the dangers of self-assertion: the TWA Building [121] and Dulles Airport. Although topped by a Chinese-pagoda-conning-tower, the Dulles Airport is still a convincing symbol of flight which also actually manages to work because the forms have been resolved both technically and functionally [122a]. We can see that the space has been created as a logical development of circulation and rest [122b]; and the soaring roof is not just a gesture of flight but also

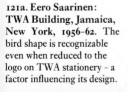

121a. Eero Saarinen: TWA Building, Jamaica, New York, 1956-62. The bird shape is recognizable even when reduced to the logo on TWA stationery – a factor influencing its design.

a sensible enclosure and technical solution. Some of
Saarinen's unsuccessful work, however, is a result of mis-
fired self-consciousness; for instance the Stiles and Morse
Dormitories at Yale reproduce an Italian hill town which
is not gross enough to qualify as High Camp nor integrated
enough to qualify as Non Camp. And this failure must be
connected with Saarinen's obsessive interest in his historical 'place', as if history were some sort of encyclopedia,
or Hall of Fame, or shelf to sit on next to other powders,
cosmetics and ingredients and had nothing to do with
intrinsic worth. One cooks one's place from a limited
recipe.

P. JOHNSON: Mies is such a genius! But I grow old! And bored!
My direction is clear: eclectic tradition. This is not academic
revivalism. There are no Classic orders or Gothic finials. I try to
pick up what I like throughout history. We cannot not know
history.

If it all sounds a little claustrophobic and hermetically
sealed from the everyday world, at least styles can be
manipulated with integrity. One of the reasons for this is

121b. Eero Saarinen:
TWA Building, Jamaica,
New York, 1956-62.

122a, b (*opposite*). Eero
Saarinen: Dulles Airport,
Chantilly, Washington
DC, 1964. Catenary curves
appropriate to the span, a
longitudinal building
organized on circulation,
an appropriate use of steel
glass and concrete – only
the Chinese Pagoda conning
tower is arbitrary. The
multivalence of forms here is
Non Camp and not usual
for Saarinen.

that the everyday world means compromise: it means the tough, commercial world that has to be mastered by speed and pragmatism. Thus Wallace Harrison, a New York architect and expert in skyscraper buildings and the master of the art of the possible, observes:

When you leave the drawing board and start getting your hands dirty, you stop thinking of buildings as a challenge to create absolute art. You're happy to settle for good buildings that get built, in the hope that they will lead to progressively better buildings.[10]

Although this eternal hope of pragmatism is naïve (since compromise just leads to more compromise) it occasionally produces the truly American kind of building: the technically virtuoso. The Alcoa building [123] by Harrison is the perfect expression of transcendental technique and the pragmatic school: light screens of aluminium only an eighth of an inch thick are strengthened by their shape, by triangular facets which cast a shimmering, dissolving light over the gigantic mass. The aluminium sheets were mass-produced, pierced in the centre by a green-glass window, erected and sprayed on the inside for heat and comfort – the whole process being the epitome of American logistics. The image is otherworldly. One has the feeling of being in the Grand Canyon or Wall Street where vast impersonal forces of economy and exploitation have been at work. One also has the same feeling in front of the Lever House, that other masterpiece of transcendental pragmatism by the firm Skidmore, Owings and Merrill [17]. What this large firm has managed to do is to perfect the stereotyped package-deal: the client knows what he's getting from beginning to end – a coolly detailed curtain wall. The attempt has been to produce a clearly recognizable image which will inspire confidence in large corporations. The result is always an interesting prefabricated window wall unit where light and shadow have produced the exterior image while comfort and the unassertive International Style have produced the interior image. This work is rather like elegant canned music, muzak, and the architects make clear their intention to provide background wallpaper and businessman's vernacular. At times the result is brilliantly appropriate, as in the Pepsi-Cola Headquarters which is ice-cool and

123. Harrison and Abramovitz: Alcoa Building, Pittsburgh, 1955. Thin gauged aluminium sheets punched with rounded windows and triangular facets. Technologically sophisticated, the curtain wall became the universal symbol of the corporate look: self-confident, professional and anonymous. It also became the symbol of bureaucracy because of its sociological oversimplification and univalence. This ambiguity is a typical case of Low Camp (contrast [137]).

slick. At times the result is superlatively ridiculous, as in the Bieneke Library where the expensive translucent marble merely looks like endless television sets stacked on one another. Sometimes it can be appropriate but socially dubious: the Air Force Academy so over-asserts regimentation and impersonality that one can understand why there has been continual cheating among the cadets [124].

To say that the work of SOM encourages cheating here sounds at first like a serious charge, but it is not, according to a High Camp reading. In a bureaucratic situation such as big business or big military, there is simply no morality, there is just behaviourism. Everybody steals and cheats the bureaucracy; the bureaucracy predicts this and writes it off beforehand as expected 'leakage'. In many cases where protracted protest and reform have failed to alter this situation and the mechanical 'system' has become greater than any individual's ability or desire to change it, a curious new mood has arisen. Instead of objection or despair, there is inverted, barely ironic, acceptance. The

124. SOM: Air Force Academy, Colorado Springs, 1957-62. Within an environment where everything approaches statistical certainty there is no choice and hence no morality; 2,600 cadets march to the dining hall and sit down in unison, in the most beautiful, Camp, mechanical way.

Camp attitude accepts the fact that often men behave with mechanical certainty and instead of regarding this inflexible determinism as a disaster, chooses to regard it aesthetically: 'How pretty those 2,600 cadets look sitting down to dinner and saying the Lord's Prayer in unison'; 'I want to be a machine.' While the mechanical taking over from the organic has been a subject of humour long before Andy Warhol uttered this last cryptic desire, the situation has moved beyond humour in America because often the *outcome* of the mechanical process is itself uncontrolled. People follow the process wherever it goes with the pragmatic hope that at least they will be successful.

From this pragmatic attitude it follows naturally that anything goes as long as it goes; and what goes fast is fashion. It is not a coincidence that fashion and pragmatism have worked out a happy arrangement: one has to cultivate the quick, daring solution which can only mean changing the façade. Thus:

> In a few quick strokes on the back of a brown manila envelope, Stone set down the plan and elevation for the new Embassy, a building destined to become one of the most exciting structures in Modern Architecture.

One can almost feel the electric excitement rip off the page: 'new grill work by Ed Stone changes course of Modern Architecture'. This description from an ex-editor of *Time Magazine* shows the optimistic mood of fast change and exciting news flash. If one is really to project into Camp architecture one has to catch the essence of this mood, has to recreate the emotion of social gesture running amok, the quick violent change of mass opinion, the stereotype of violent mood, the overpowering urge to cheer with the voice of one crowd in a Dionysiac frenzy of optimism. One has to project into the clichés that roll off Madison Avenue and the critics' lips: 'skin and bones, buttery-hatch, playboy, ballet school, neo-hysterical, grill frills, existentialist, eclectic, chaoticism, fashion school, formal school', etcetera.[11] All these are quickly forgotten and swept into the dustbin. Eternal optimism encourages fast production and fast production encourages change and growth. One must cultivate naïvety and forgetfulness because the memory of fashion cycles has to be shortlived if the process is to go on. In fact comparison with the past and a critical temper upset the process at once.

There thus develops underneath this grinning optimism a strong pessimism: nothing can be changed, we are all determined by the process, it will end in disaster. Camp is eternally hopeful and yet eternally apocalyptic: a large credibility gap; no one listens to ideals any more; everyone exploits the public domain, it will end in the hydrogen bomb, says Lewis Mumford, continuously.

There thus also develops a certain heroic involvement by those who both embrace and criticize the process. The 'Chaoticism' which all the Camp architects agree is *the* style (i.e. everystyle) demands a personal sacrifice and suffering. The pressures are crushing, but continual confusion is bittersweet:

> This [library for Clark University] is my first modern building [1966]. By that I mean it is the first that is attuned to contemporary thinking in science, in philosophy, in the arts. I regard my earlier works as Renaissance buildings by comparison . . . I believe that no architect can produce buildings which are valid unless he is sensitive to the prevailing conditions and experiences of his time . . . Our time is one of uncertainty . . . Einstein's theory of relativity . . . [12]

This building [125] reflects the very consistent movement of Chaoticism which Johansen, Rudolph and Johnson were leading in the middle sixties. But Johansen sold himself short when he debunked his former buildings and attitudes. He came closer than any other architect of this movement to explicitly understanding the relation of the personal act to a behaviourist society. In an article in *Perspecta 7* (the Yale journal which like *Time* is another outlet for the movement) he explicitly stated the necessity for the individual to act against the social average, the necessity for personal sacrifice to establish the public domain. But the public domain is exactly what didn't exist in American architecture in spite of the occasional attempts by Johansen and others to create it. The reason lay in the inherent pluralism where every group ended up by exploiting the public to further its own ends.

Lacking a believable or even credible political base, it was not surprising that the public domain continued to look like Lincoln Center [115b] or all the other pseudo-classical cultural centres across America [118]. The

125a, b. John M. Johansen: Clark University Library, Worcester, Massachusetts, 1966–9. Justified with the philosophy of uncertainty, relativity, existentialism, collective unconscious, Archigram and the Boston City Hall, this building erupts out of its central, controlled organization, a good example of 'Chaoticism', the eclecticism of Camp.

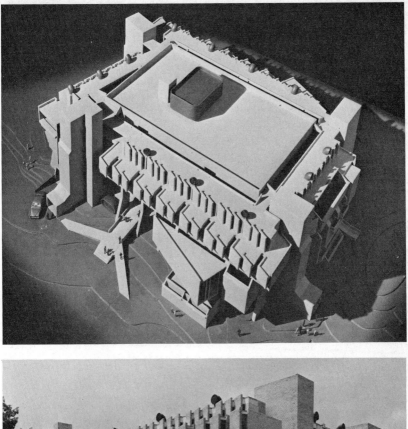

reason was simply that when a large amount of hetero-geneous groups couldn't agree on a positive, new direction for the endeavour, they had to fall back on the style which was most familiar and least divisive: classicism. This was just as true in the building of Washington D.C. as it was in the Chicago Exposition of 1893. And even when such new attempts as Lincoln Center were declared a 'disaster' by everyone involved (from drama critics to city planners to acousticians and plumbers), it was still copied with equanimity because of its monumental clas-sical look.

In the face of such unremitting omni-incompetence it is not surprising that a sardonic attitude has grown and that many feel that protest is emotionally and rhetorically bankrupt. They claim or by their action imply that the situation is inevitable, and if it is inevitable then it is no longer tragic or sad or even pathetic. Rather it is just one more amoral datum, like an 'act of nature', which can be regarded neutrally as an aesthetic game.

This honest amorality is exactly what gives Philip Johnson his integrity. He more than any other architect has been true to fashion, an affluent society and city life. His background is instructive: an education in the clas-sics at Harvard; then a term with the Museum of Modern Art where he wrote *The International Style* with Hitch-cock and then defended Nazi monumentality from a neo-Nazi position (see quote above); then his return to Harvard to get a degree in architecture under Walter Gropius; then his book on Mies, and finally his Miesian work, the famous house with all glass walls [126].

This work was consciously designed to exaggerate the principles of modern architecture to a provocative extreme: the effect was contemplated and perfect. Not the inter-penetration of space, but a totally see-through house; not a machine-made office, but a machine-made cottage; not asymmetry alone, but combined with symmetry. A trans-parent mirror was placed on a carefully manicured lawn of green. The building was provided by Johnson with an '*explication de texte*' so that the Modern Movement could follow all the allusions (among the twenty-seven were – Le Corbusier, Van Doesburg, Malevitch, Mies, Ledoux and Schinkel). These historical programme notes published in the *Architectural Review* were helpful for a full archi-

126. Philip Johnson:
Glass House, New
Canaan, Connecticut, for
Philip Johnson reviewed by
Philip Johnson and finally
published in *Philip Johnson*
(by Hitchcock and Philip
Johnson), 1949.

tectural experience, but the real significance of the house
was as a social gesture.[13] All of a sudden architectural
journalism had become part of the object. Marshall
McLuhan, Tom Wolfe and Robert Rauschenburg were
pre-empted here. The social celebration of architecture
through photographs was suddenly as significant as the
building. Soon Rauschenburg could 'paint a portrait' by
merely saying: 'This is a portrait of Iris Clert, if I say so.'
But Johnson was the first to realize the implications of a
sophisticated audience and new means of communication
for the architectural tradition.

His next two significant buildings, the Wiley house and
the Boissonnas house took the combination of historical
and Miesian allusions even further. The Wiley house was
an open steel image (albeit built in wood) over a closed,
rusticated base (albeit Corbusian rather than Renaissance); and the Boissonnas house developed an additive
space concept that looks back to Mies's grid at IIT [**153**]
and the new space conception of Kahn.

Other than these essentially Miesian works, the rest of
Johnson's architecture is entirely Camp – a demonstration
of his impeccably perverse taste and motivated by histori-

cist allusions. Hence the entrance to the Roofless Church which recalls those of so many Nazi Villas [**127**], or the Nebraska Art Gallery whose classicist columns were first built and tested in Italy for the 'play of shadows' (sic), or

the New York State Theatre which resembles Fascist work of the thirties [**115b**], or the Kline Center at Yale with its 'Athenian Temenos' and so on. Although these works are striking in image while being univalent (a condition for Camp), the particular contribution of Johnson lies more in his candid approach than his building. For his candid self-disclosure shows a limited but at least frank way open to the urban future. It is worth quoting an interview between Susan Sontag and Johnson on the future city morality (i.e. amorality):

ss: ... I think, I think in New York your aesthetic sense is in a curious, very modern way more developed than anywhere else. If you are experiencing things morally one is in a state of continual indignation, and horror, but [they laugh] but if one has a very modern kind of –

pj: Do you suppose that will change the sense of morals, the fact that we can't use morals as a means of judging this city

127. Philip Johnson: New Harmony Church, New Harmony, Indiana, 1960. The entrance to the temenos of this church is self-consciously historicist and probably intentionally reminiscent of Nazi architecture. *Johnson:* 'There is only one absolute today and that is change. There are no rules, surely no certainties in any of the arts. There is only a feeling of wonderful freedom, of endless possibilities to investigate, of endless past years of historically great building to enjoy.'

because we couldn't stand it? And that we're changing our whole moral system to suit the fact that we're living in a ridiculous way?

ss: Well I think we are learning the limitations of, of moral experience of things. I think it's possible to be aesthetic . . .

pj: . . . I mean your moral approach is the Mumford one that you're speaking about.

ss: Yes.

pj: Patrick Geddes, the greatest good, and we must be good and do these things. That criterion leads you into what we have today, so we've retreated, or maybe advanced, our generation – if I can lift you up.

ss: Oh it's nice of you [they laugh].

pj: To merely, to enjoy things as they are – we see entirely different beauty from what Eddie Mumford could possibly see.

ss: Well, I think, I see for myself that I just now see things in a kind of split level way . . . both morally and . . .

pj: What good does it do you to believe in good things?

ss: Because I . . .

pj: It's feudal and futile. I think it much better to be (?) nihilistic and forget it all. I mean, I know I'm attacked by my moral friends, er, but really don't they shake themselves up over nothing?

ss: Well people do things.

pj: Do they?

ss: Do accomplish things.

pj: Do they? What have they done in New York City since the start? You read all the reports the other day in the paper – the chief man said you might as well spend your time writing to Santa Claus as to talk about any possibilities of city planning in this city, and incidentally the English that are so good about morals and city planning, and have all these London County Councils and things they are so proud of, have ruined their city in the name of morality. Even worse than New York in this hopeless chaos . . .

And then later, on the question of artistic morality:

pj: Pop art is a comment.

ss: That's the value.

pj: Is a comment on a comment on a comment. This is disturbing in its intellectual overtones – it's not very pretty.

After examining various Pop paintings in Johnson's collection:

pj: . . . Can we look at architecture, or do we always have to look at painting?

ss: No, no, we can look at everything, because it all fits together.

PJ: . . . [pointing to works] I'm a plagiarist man – you see, you must take everything from everybody – you see this is copied from Corbusier, that's copied from Byzantine Churches – this is taken from Jaipur India. This is, I don't know, maybe this is original. It's an underground house. We have some ponies grazing on the roofs, you see as it comes down to the water, but . . . But it just shows you that at this very same time you're doing one thing, you flip moods, you do something entirely different, quite opposite and quite at the same time.

SS: But this is the very essence of modernity [PJ: Sure] in all the arts. I mean you see it even in somebody like Picasso [PJ: Yes, Picasso is rather . . .] he's the first person who understood the principle of artistic plagiarism. [Goes to flowers]

SS: Yes – and these are real, real –

PJ: Real flowers – real, *fake* flowers.

SS: Real, fake flowers, of course.

PJ: You see the level of fakeness, that's real [telephone rings] three dimensional [voice says hello] imitation, yes of an advertised meaning, and it's those various levels of reality that make it all so fascinating . . .[14]

Andy Warhol's painting of the Campbell Soup Can is of course the paradigm of this imaginative oscillation between levels of reality. When we look at this Campbell Soup Can [**128**] we notice on a literal level that it is an elegant rectangle placed exactly where it should be according to all the classical harmonies. On the iconographic level however, the subject matter is an insult: tomato soup affronts divine proportion. On the next level, as we oscillate between pleasure and anger, we notice that it is not just a Campbell Soup Can but rather a photograph of a photograph of a painting of a mass-produced object (not even the real object). In other words it is thrice removed from reality; in Platonic terms then a triple lie. The photograph (mass-produced, hence valueless)[15] of an art object (unique, valuable) of a mass-produced soup can (valueless). It remains for the painting to be mass-produced for that to be devalued and hence revalued. This consistent reversal of all accepted categories actually works imaginatively to transform the work of fancy into a sublime experience. That is as long as we follow the experience beyond the primary insult and understand the insult (the failure to appreciate Camp results from not knowing on which level to be insulted). In this frenetic oscillation Camp makes an imaginative virtue of the detached fancy.

128. Andy Warhol:
Campbell Soup Can,
1964.

One should insist on this detachment as the prime characteristic of the new sensibility. It is close to the scientific attitude and opposed to the moral because it manipulates content in an abstract way just as the scientist does. As Sontag points out: 'Camp is the consistently aesthetic experience of the world. It incarnates a victory of "style over content", "aesthetics over morality", "irony over tragedy".' If this is true, if Camp is like science in being completely amoral, then the Camp object must be univalent, that is the work of the intellect and fancy. But furthermore if it is amoral, then it will tend to be both pragmatic and fatalistic with regard to trends, and thus destructive of the public domain which depends on both personal sacrifice and morality. Hence while the Camp architect can be honest to the private sphere and create objects which are vital and striking (because personal) he cannot create a lasting public work which endures beyond his own career unless this permanence is guaranteed by others. His work must express his own personal fame, and although fame means by definition public notoriety, it is still essentially private because it is always some*one's* fame. To create a lasting public work, the Non Camp architect must believe in and act for a social reality that transcends his own history: hence Louis Kahn's continual acts of faith which begin to create that reality.

CAMP – NON CAMP

Before discussing the Non Camp American architects, it is necessary to mention some transitional figures who are both serious and moral and yet still, at times, univalent. I mean those architects who have a moral commitment to technology and the social ideals of the twenties. The technical ideal is pursued by Buckminster Fuller, Konrad Wachsmann, Charles Eames and Myron Goldsmith and the social by Richard Neutra, Marcel Breuer and Matthew Nowicki. All these architects have made significant con-tributions to those ideas developed in the Bauhaus. Actually Fuller has refuted the Bauhaus ideas by taking them on a literal level and taking them much further than Gropius ever intended. Thus he has designed a mass pro-ducible house (the Wichita House [129]) that can be flown in and placed anywhere because of its light weight and the fact that all the services are pre-moulded and pre-installed. The image recalls the curves and metallic sleek-ness of an airplane, which is not unnatural since the house was to be produced by the same methods and factory that produced warplanes. And the image is fresh because it is the result of an intensive re-study of all the traditional requirements of living in a house. But it is still univalent

129. Buckminster Fuller: Wichita House, Kansas, 1946. Maximum performance per pound of Fuller produced such memorable queries as 'Madam, do you know what your house weighs?' This house weighed 6,000 pounds and was transported in the vertical cylinder to the left.

(as are his domes) because the social values implied are one-dimensional and based on a behaviourist sociology.[16] There is never any idea of the way houses might form a larger group nor of the way political institutions operate in an urban fabric. In fact there is no social and public realm at all. Presumably the reason for this is that Fuller looks on politics as essentially subjective, irrelevant and corrupt, since whenever he speaks about the political realm it is to point out these negative qualities.

Charles Eames, on the West Coast, has managed to incorporate the same technical image that Fuller only allows to appear, but Eames is intent on finding the social use of technology. His 'Case Study House' [**130a**] is the rare masterful use of technology having implications on a domestic, urban scale because he has allowed the technique to become the background and gain meaning through juxtaposition with the objects it holds.

The Smithsons from England have pointed out the Eames' attitude towards 'collected objects', an attitude which brings out their 'prettiness'; 'a love of the object photographed, a kind of reverence for the object's integrity.

The Eames-aesthetic is to do with object integrity', that is to say with a quasi-religious, quasi-bourgeois attitude towards possessions. Call it 'object-obsession', the point is that everything the Eames gather in their house is

130a. **Charles and Ray Eames: Eames House, Los Angeles, 1949.** Steel decking, steel walls, steel joists and steel framed windows from a catalogue. This building, 'off the peg', became a paradigm for many visiting English designers such as the Smithsons and James Stirling.

patiently placed and felt to be significant. Thus the open-webbed joists are equal to the bowl of fruit, the exposed metal decking is adequate to the eucalyptus trees, the off-the-peg industrial sash is as significant as the displayed flowers. Although the industrial form serves as a background to the human foreground, both are of equal, emotional weight [**130b**].

The result however is not like the bourgeois drawing room nor the composed still-life, nor even a cubist collage. It is more like an additive collection: a museum display which can grow or shrink without disturbing any overall composition. This open aesthetic, reinforced by the catalogue parts of which the house is constructed, suggests a casual relation towards possessions; perhaps familiar rather than obsessive.

In any case, the Eames' steel-framed house comes very much in that West Coast tradition of Neutra and Soriano and is followed by the later essays in transcendental steel

130 b. Charles and Ray Eames: Eames House, interior. The 'Eames aesthetic', the answer to Le Corbusier's 'Purist aesthetic'. Instead of dislocating industrial and human objects in a cubist collage, the Eameses compose them in a rectilinear system, just as they might appear on the front page of a newspaper.

of Koenig and Ellwood. All of these Westerners exploit the potential that Mies had discovered earlier: open planning, precise detailing, accuracy, neatness and the light quality of steel and glass. A continuous perfection which is possible only with a sophisticated technology that can avoid crudeness. Koenig, speaking of this necessary sophistication, says 'steel is only as good as its detailing . . . In order to make exposed steel acceptable in the living room it must be so well detailed that the joining connections are imperceptible.' And this was only possible after arc-welding had been developed, and all connections could disappear in a smooth continuity of synthetic materials.

Thus this West Coast work has always had an unreal, absolute look to it, as if it had just been extruded from some Platonic kitchen where dirt and age had been eternally expunged. The ideal is to flick open a plate glass door and step effortlessly either into a marble framed pool,

131. Pierre Koenig: Case Study House 22, Hollywood Hills, 1959.

exfoliating forest, clear desert or cantilevered balcony – the last surveying endless miles of lower Los Angeles [131]. In every case an absolute, triumphant technology is juxtaposed to a lesser nature: raw or human.

In summary, there have been two main contributions of the technical school and technology to American architecture: on the one hand, an advanced technology has allowed architects a more free range of expression because it has lessened utilitarian constraints and thereby increased the opportunity to manipulate the form and space in any way the architect wishes. And, on the other hand, where this increase in liberty is denied for reasons of efficiency and ascetic restraint, it has produced a remarkable kind of parametric architecture [132a, b], where the brilliant form is a by-product of functional decisions.[17] The fruits of this are not only an original and striking image, but also a basic trend of 'doing more with less', an increase in efficiency. If there is any deficiency in this approach, it lies in assuming that an increase in technical efficiency is necessarily accompanied by an improvement in the quality of life. It is this confusion of means with ends that has led this school to judge social institutions

132 a, b (*opposite*). **Vehicle Assembly Building, 1964, Cape Kennedy, Florida, and SOM: Solar Telescope, Kitts Peak, Arizona, 1965.** Both external forms are simple and forceful, the result of a few parameters, whereas the internal forms are multiple and complex showing the more typical expression of the cybernetic age. The external form of the solar telescope was determined by three constraints (exact angle, complete stability and complete coolness) for which technological virtuosity was demanded. Hence the absolute and uncompromising expression.

of men as mere utilitarian objects to be kept only in so far as they are useful. That men's consciousness is a deliberate construction to be developed through the proffering of ideals is a question which does not arise. It is only for such architects as Louis Kahn, for whom belief is the *sine qua non* of action, that men's ideals and their effect on the public domain really matter.

NON CAMP

Before discussing Louis Kahn, the sensibility and ideas of the Non Camp architect have to be outlined, because there is enough common overlap of attitudes and ideas to speak of the Non Camp sensibility as if it existed as one thing. Whereas the Camp architect is morally cool (the result of an overheated urban society) the Non Camp architect is morally hot (the result of a connection with an underheated rural or academic place). To further the analogy one might say that Camp is force grown in a hot-house and that Non Camp grows slowly according to its own laws, the laws of the imagination, which produce, unlike a hot-house, a flower which smells. The Camp flower is pretty, but the Non Camp flower is sturdy and actually gives off an odour.

Whether this odour is delicious and full or musty and rancid will depend on the individual case since the academies tend to produce both smells in equal quantity. The former is caused by the freedom to develop one's ideas and beliefs slowly and to the full, whereas the latter is caused by a removal from larger issues into the confines of a closed discussion. One of the ideas which has been partially developed by the Non Camp architects is the relation between the public and private realms, or the city as an articulate frame for human action.

For instance, the work of the Philadelphia architect and writer Robert Venturi is directly complementary in intention. The exteriors of his buildings reflect the external public forces, whether Pop Art or urban space, while the interior reflects the individual circumstance:

I tend to design from the outside in as well as the inside out. The necessary tensions help make architecture. Since the inside is different from the outside, the point of change which is the wall is

133a, b. Robert Venturi: Chestnut Hill House, Pennsylvania, 1965. The façade has a public function with its own validity quite apart from the inside, the private realm. This contradiction between public and private shows a selfconscious return to rhetoric and the responsibilities of articulate, social discourse.

an architectural event. Architecture occurs at the meeting of interior and exterior forces of use and space. These interior and environmental forces are both general and particular, generic and circumstantial. Architecture, as the wall between the inside and outside, becomes the spatial record of this resolution and its drama.[18]

His house for his mother Mrs Robert Venturi contains this duality. The public front [133a] is symmetrical, relatively simple and general and has a symbolic arch denoting the entrance. The interior however reflects the complexity of what he and Kahn call the individual circumstance [133b]. Here it amounts to a distortion of circulation space to keep it at a minimum and the assertion of each function's identity out of the rectilinear frame.

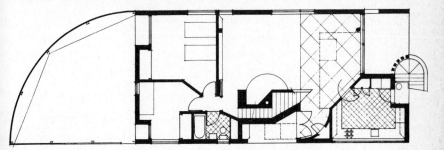

133c. **Robert Venturi:**
Chestnut Hill House.
Stairway distorts one way to
acknowledge the entrance,
the other way to recognize
the chimney.

Thus each room is allowed to speak its social function by starting a dialogue with each adjoining function, e.g. the living room acknowledges the kitchen, the kitchen the flow of the entrance and so on. Social meaning in this context is thus not a question of the appropriateness of particular forms but rather their mutual relation.

Venturi has developed his ideas of 'Complexity and Contradiction in Architecture' in a manifesto of that name published in 1966. This book is in some respects an inversion of Le Corbusier's *Vers une architecture* of 1923, except that it eschews any arguments from a technical base and conducts the discussion on the levels of architectural history and personal taste:[19]

I like complexity and contradiction in architecture . . .
I like elements which are hybrid rather than pure . . .
I am for messy vitality over obvious unity . . .
I prefer 'both-and' to 'either-or' . . .

The subjectivity of these statements is disarmingly
frank. Venturi, however, underpins his preferences in two
ways. First he cites countless fresh examples of the kind of
irony and ambiguity he enjoys, and second, he touches
on the psychological advantages of a complex and ironic
view towards reality over a simple outlook. He then draws
the parallel of this to an inclusive, complex architecture:

> But an architecture of complexity and contradiction has a
> special obligation toward the whole; its truth must be in its
> totality or its implications of totality. It must embody the difficult
> unity of inclusion rather than the easy unity of exclusion. More
> is not less.

Venturi's gentle manifesto' has had an extraordinary
impact in architectural circles, perhaps because he is
virtually the only practising architect who has written an
extended, comprehensible polemic. In any case, his arguments for an 'inclusive architecture' which can use any
elements whatever (whether they be Las Vegas billboard
[134] or classical arches) have effectively challenged the

134. Robert Venturi:
Football Hall of Fame,
1968. The use of a
scoreboard as a large device
in scale with the external
parking lot and contrasting
with internal, museum space
behind.

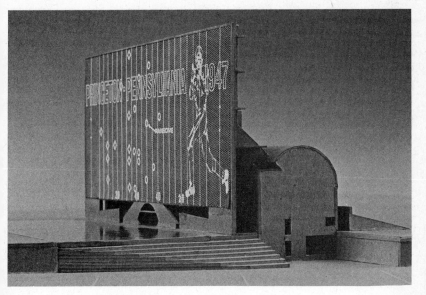

prevailing exclusivist arguments for purity and restriction. Venturi sets out in his buildings to expand the possible repertoire of available references to those a pluralist society uses as a matter of course [135]. In a sense his polemic is directed against the idea of an historicist sensibility which wants to restrict the available metaphors to those which are only current or technologically up to date.[20] The idea is that in the age of travel and tourism, the age of the 'museum without walls', this restriction is no longer relevant and furthermore that in any large city with its plurality of sub-cultures, such limitation is highly paternalistic.

Charles Moore, an architect from the West Coast who succeeded Paul Rudolph as the head of Yale University's architectural school, has developed many of Venturi's ideas concerning the displacement of scale ('Supergraphics') and the use of cut-out screens to suggest greater

135. **Robert Venturi: Lieb House, Long Beach Island, New Jersey, 1966–9.** This house uses ordinary elements in a distorted and fresh way. The house number is five feet high, the usual siding is painted dark at the base, light at the top; a circular window is cut into the stairway where it is needed, etc.

136. Charles Moore and
William Turnbull:
Faculty Club interior,
University of California,
1968. The overwrought use
of neon banners in a baronial
hall mocks the clubbies'
pretension, while the relaxed
use of 'readily available
techniques' is more
straightforward.

space [136]. His Faculty Club for the University of
California is both a straightforward use of vernacular
elements and an esoteric game in art history. Thus the
dining room of the club makes use of neon banners and
stuffed animal heads to both accept and mock the traditional ideas of a baronial hall, while the references to
Sir John Soane, Theo Van Doesburg, Spanish Colonial
Architecture and the shack-style add a certain frisson for
the architectural pundit.[21]

It is partially this allusiveness and the incorporation of
fashionable elements into architecture which has mistakenly led many people to classify Venturi and Moore as
the Camp architects above all. But this is classification by
thematic matter and as wrongheaded as assuming that
Stravinsky is a Pop composer because he used popular
material in his work. In fact both Venturi and Moore
have very explicit beliefs on which their architecture

rests which transcend the justification by cycles of taste alone. For instance, Moore and Lyndon have written:

> ... that the first purpose of architecture is territorial, that the architect sets out the stimuli with which the observer creates an image of 'place' ... To build such places, often on a low budget, we like to, and must, build simply with readily available techniques.[22]

While these intentions of place-making are orthodox among recent architects, Charles Moore has extended their use to a more relaxed acceptance of 'readily available techniques' and thus his architecture has a certain easy width of reference it would otherwise lack: i.e. it is openly friendly to the local inhabitants and their usage without being condescending or cliché. It accepts local material such as corrugated sheeting, wood battens and industrial

137. Sert, Jackson, Gourley and Associates: Boston University Tower, 1965. The vertical city articulating rather than suppressing the complex content as in the usual curtain wall (compare [123]). Here the dimensions were finally fixed through proportional rectangles and '*tracés régulateurs*'.

light fixtures to articulate a communal space through convention.

Another way of achieving the same public articulation, again without bombast, is shown by the work of José Luis Sert, a Spanish architect who emigrated to the United States, a member of the CIAM, and a successor to Gropius as the head of Harvard's architectural school. His architecture extends the approach of Le Corbusier, more particularly the Algiers skyscraper project of the latter which articulates urban functions within an overall frame. Sert's Boston University tower [137] is really the first building to follow the implications laid down by Le Corbusier in 1938. Here the general elements of the surface (the wall, the mullion, the sunscreen) are used in such a way as to articulate the specific functions within (denoting auditorium, office and communal space). The

138. Sert, Jackson, Gourley and Associates: Holyoke Center, Cambridge, Massachusetts, 1963. Through slight variations of form, the mass is broken down and the vertical city is shown to have the same diversity and grain as the horizontal.

point is that if the vertical city is to be as comprehensible and rich as the horizontal city it must be capable of signifying the same distinctions, even if they are the wrong, or false distinctions. Because an articulate surface is always more universal than a blank surface for the mere fact that we can read different meanings into relations, whereas we cannot read them into a blank. Thus as we become more familiar with the Boston University scheme, we slowly learn what the multiple relations may signify. The same is true of Sert's Health Centre [138] which also relates a multitude of urban functions. The health deck (where the patients rest) is clearly articulated on the fourth floor behind the sunscreens, the seminar rooms are articulated at the top of the building by changing the rhythm and the health service is articulated at the bottom by the same method. But these functions only gain articulation by being just enough different from the background of offices to be perceived. They are not too different, which would destroy the perception. This building then is not just a lesson in subdued prose, but also a very subtle lesson in urban scale, the primary social intention of Sert. Through the interior of the building is a pedestrian street which connects Harvard Yard with the Harvard Houses and also serves as a shopping street. The effect of this is twofold: the small shops on the outside are always between the pedestrian and the tall blocks, and on the inside they form a comprehensible space of non-academic functions. Thus scale is achieved through size and content (i.e. human scale is simply that which is comprehensible or has relations which can be grasped).

That scale consists in social meaning rather than any particular size or unit of measure can be seen in Kallmann, McKinnell and Knowles Boston City Hall, which is gigantic in size without being overscaled or incomprehensible [139a]. These architects started the design process with the preconcept of a 'megastructure', that is a gigantic system of all the repetitive constants in a large building (structure, mechanical equipment, circulation). From this fixed structure they then hung the various functions which occur in a City Hall: the offices at the top, the council chamber projected below in a different rhythm, and the mayor's office at a prime point on the side. As with Le Corbusier's work, one function gains meaning by

139a. Kallmann, McKinnell and Knowles: Boston City Hall, 1964-9. Articulation within a megastructure: the rhythmic counterpoint and syncopation are used to clarify the different functions. The corner detail [**139b**] shows concrete elements which act in a multivalent way as structure, mechanical ducts, mullions and rhythmical articulation all at once.

biting into another function and taking its place. Thus the office rhythm is abruptly stopped by the introduction of the Council Chamber in a way which recalls Le Corbusier's visual dynamics at Chandigarh. Kallmann, an East Coast architect influenced by Kahn and Le Corbusier, had discussed this approach to design, to 'Action Architecture', a few years before he designed the building but the same principle seems to be operating: the generation of form through the repetition and development of an idea:

> Keeping the imagination within the framework of a built-in principle of composition and typology, it yet permits the spatial phrasing to be freely dynamic. This serious play, undirected as to outcome but controlled in keyed sequences of manipulation, is a technique used in the experimental sciences and in the major arts. The Miesian dictum 'God is in the details' is followed to its proper conclusion. The detail and its topological potential becomes the generator.[23]

The idea, or preconception here, is thus a generating form or detail [**139b**].

What Kallmann is doing then is close to the work process of Louis Kahn: starting with a conclusion and then working back towards a beginning. It is the exact reverse of the process which Gropius and others had preached of washing one's mind of all preconception and starting from scratch with a clean slate. What Kahn starts with and tries to achieve is a preconception, a 'preform'. He tries to realize at once the essence of a building (what he calls 'the Form'). Only when this is firmly grasped in all its archaic strangeness can individual 'circumstances', 'the Design', be allowed to enter and distort the Form. Thus this process also differs from the preconception of the Camp architect in two significant ways: instead of being the preconception of a past idea it is the preconception of a present essence and instead of refusing to admit circumstance, it allows the contingent to distort the essence. By keeping the Form (or preform) archaic, Kahn thus always keeps his belief in it. It is never destroyed by circumstance, by the endless practical exigencies that destroy other architecture and conviction. It thus has the mark of all individual work which insists: 'belief is the *sine qua non* of excellence'.

> I really felt very religiously attached to this idea of belief because I realized that many things are done only with the reality of the means employed, with no belief behind it. The whole

reality isn't there without the reality of belief. When men do large re-development projects, there's no belief behind them. The means are available, even the design devices that make them look beautiful, but there's nothing that you feel is somehow a light which shines on the emergence of a new institution of man, which makes him feel a refreshed will to live. This comes from meaning being answerable to a belief. Such feeling must be in the back of it, not just to make something which is pleasant instead of something which is dull: that is no great achievement. Everything the architect does is first of all answerable to an institution of man before it becomes a building. You don't know what the building is, really, unless you have a belief behind the building, a belief in its identity and in the way of life of man.[24]

Then Kahn distinguishes a belief in any one particular value from the generic realm of belief which is common to all men and which transcends any one man's particular circumstance. To this realm the architect also owes his action precisely because it transcends his own personal career and establishes the identity of the public institution:

The institutions are the houses of the inspirations. Schools, libraries, laboratories, gymnasia. The architect considers the inspiration before he can accept the dictates of a space desired. He asks himself what is the nature of one that distinguishes itself from another. When he senses the difference, he is in touch with its form. Form inspires design.[25]

One other quote throws light on Kahn's particular equation of belief = Form = inspiration = institution:

Reflect then on the meaning of school, institution. The institution is the authority from whom we get their requirements of areas. A school, or a specific design is what the institution expects of us. But School, the spirit school, the essence of the existence will, is what the architect should convey in his design . . . what School wants to be.[26]

Thus we have the complementary aspect of all Kahn's work: both Form and Design, belief and *a* belief, inspiration and circumstance, existence, will and facts of a programme. This is having it both ways with a vengeance. Kahn is both Camp and Non Camp, wilfully personal and public. And thus he is open to attack from two sides: for trying to idealize that which is ephemeral such as mechanical equipment and for making disfunctional that

which is important such as laboratory space.[27] When this occurs as in his Medical Research Building [140] the result only just fails to convince. One is disturbed at finding the ideal form devoted to removing gas and the ephemeral, disfunctional structure devoted to 'served' space for laboratory experiments. With a little more effort devoted to the circumstance of lighting a laboratory and a little less effort spent on keeping the preform intact, he could have achieved a reconciliation that was truly 'believable'. As it is, the result is more a symbol than an example of multivalent form.

Kahn's first entirely successful reconciliation of Form and Design where the space, structure and function were thought through to the point of actually working was the Jewish Community Center at Trenton, 1955. Unfor-

140: Louis Kahn: Medical Research Building, Philadelphia, 1961-8. The brick towers appear to support the laboratories whereas in fact they are either stairways or service ducts. The windows allow too much glare and the internal structure does not facilitate functional variation. Despite these flaws this building became a key example of 'exposed services' during the sixties.

tunately this project was never built and we can only judge its worth by a model and a single bath house which was built. The Bath House [141] shows the preform of four squares (less important) surrounding a central square, which is also made more significant by being topped by a pyramidal roof. The preform is thus two squares, the smaller one for entrance or storage space and

141. Louis Kahn: Trenton Bath House, Trenton, New Jersey, 1958.

the larger one for communal or 'served' space. 'Servant and served', the two kinds of space which ironically reversed their appropriate positions in the Medical Building, are here, four years earlier, more acceptable.

In the Salk Institute project Kahn has achieved a different kind of relation between servant and served, private and public, by wrapping a circle around the square ('wrapping ruins around buildings') and by dividing the project into three types of public relation: the private living area located to the west following the slope; the semi-private area for research laboratories located at the pivotal point to the east [142]; and the public meeting house isolated in the north west across from the private area. Thus this tripartite relation forces the scientist to go through the research area to reach either other area, but

231

it also forces him to acknowledge the subordinate independence of living and community.

On another level, Kahn has here created a more satisfactory relation between form, structure and space than he achieved in the Medical Research Building, because here the 'servant' spaces are subordinate to the 'served' laboratory space and integrated with the structure, the entrance and the exhaust stacks, thus achieving a resolution between meanings which implies a continuous relation. This can be seen in an axonometric drawing [143] where the overall pencil outline defines each additive part in its relation to the whole. The method is additive and expresses 'how it is done'.

If we were to train ourselves to draw as we build, from the bottom up, when we do, stopping our pencil to make a mark at the joints of pouring or erecting, ornament would grow out of our love for the expression of method.

'Love for the expression of method' seems to animate all Kahn's work and almost take over from other concerns. The constant danger of Platonism (whether of method or

142. **Louis Kahn: Salk Institute Laboratories, La Jolla, California, 1965.** The scientists' study towers in concrete and wood are angled to catch the breeze and sea view.

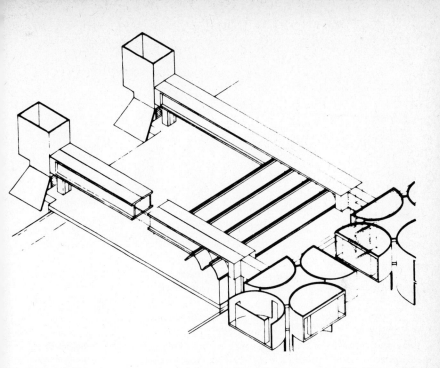

143. Louis Kahn: Axonometric of Servant and Served. This early drawing of the fabric shows the service stacks to the left (with their cant for the stairway), the main nine-foot service ducts and the individual study rooms to the right.

ideal form) is that it will devalue the contingent and force a schism between metaphor and reality – a schism which the nineteenth century and Camp have already perfected as a supreme principle of schizophrenia. The schism is only somewhat evident in Kahn's case. The Medical Building was not sufficiently open to the contingent and in the Salk Institute changing the preform of a folded plate into a more realistic flat, vierendel truss amounted to a small religious conversion (as Kahn has described it). Nevertheless, Kahn did manage to allow the contingent to modify the preform, without sacrificing the basic principle behind it, as he also did in his very successful Unitarian Church at Rochester [**144**]. On first approaching this building, the overall impression we have is of massive hoods carrying on an equal discussion back and forth between four points. Whatever angle we see this church from, the anthropomorphic shapes seem to be dominating the whole, asking each other questions:

. . . it occurred to me that the sanctuary is merely the center of questions and that the school – which was constantly emphasized

– was that which raises the question . . . and I felt that that which raised the question and that which was the sense of question – the spirit of question – were inseparable.[28]

Thus the preform is 'the question': a square sanctuary in the centre, surrounded by an ambulatory and surrounded again by a school and work rooms. This preform was evident in Kahn's first sketch which was merely a circle surrounding a square with a question mark in the centre. Then he tried to challenge this preform by splitting up the project into two: the church and subordinate parts. But finally, one by one, the parts came back to their original surrounding positions because they were all functionally interrelated and tied to the sanctuary by common purpose. At this point, Kahn started working on the preform of light, until it defined the space and structure. He went through the cyclical process of 'Form and Design' until the structure was integrated with the space, marked the entrance points and combined with the light hoods to define the four extremities of the sanctuary [145]. On the exterior, light again became the generator for Form and Design. Because Kahn felt that direct light would cause glare and obscure the transition between inner and outer space, he designed a series of buttresses which would shield the windows from direct light and allow it to reflect indirectly on the side of the wall. Between these buttresses (which are stepped back) he placed window seats so that one could sit in an enclosed space

144. Louis Kahn: First Unitarian Church, Rochester, New York, 1964. High window hoods define the four points of the central sanctuary which is in turn surrounded by smaller classrooms and then again by the band of vertical light breakers.

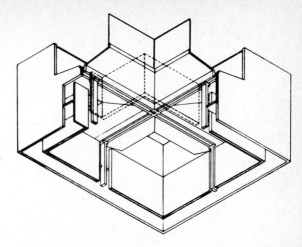

145. Louis Kahn: Axonometric of light hoods. The structure, space and light are resolved through the cybernetic process of 'Form and Design' and the meanings are interrelated into a multivalent whole.

and see the soft light fall upon the reveal. When pressed for another reason, he admitted: 'the idea is to develop really quite frankly a silhouette' – which accounts for the stark horizontals which seem to push against the sky.

More than any other design of Kahn's this church embodies a strong relation between space, structure and light, and here too the relation between servant and served is acceptable. In short, the particular forms have a great degree of generality while still fulfilling their specific use, thus again implying a continuity between the prosaic and religious demand.

Finally to conclude this account of Kahn and recent American architecture, one must end with a question which is perhaps best conveyed by an unfinished project of Kahn's – the Dacca Assembly Building in Bangla Desh [**146**]. Here is the same kind of central communal

146a. Louis Kahn: Dacca Assembly Building, Bangla Desh, 1962-. Fundamentalism or megalomania?

146b, c, d. Louis Kahn: Dacca Assembly Building, offices and passageways, Bangla Desh, 1962–. The circular, masonry geometry is conceived on a Roman scale – this area was called by Kahn the 'Citadel of the Assembly'.

space surrounded by an ambulatory and work rooms (with again their light-breakers) that exists in the Unitarian Church. The individual forms, particularly the triangular cut-outs which recall Mycenae, are emphatically hieratic, not to say monumental. The whole project is carried through with a finality and consistency which at once speak of Kahn's unshakeable conviction – really his fundamentalist belief. But the question is whether this fundamentalism is enough?[29] On the one hand it leads to a kind of overdependence on monumental masonry at the expense of a more flexible and cheap form of technology so that the project threatens to become a 'wrap around ruin' before it is even finished (especially

since the liberation of Bangla Desh). But on the other hand, it definitely conveys that sincerity of belief which is fundamental to the establishment of a public realm – a literal necessity in this case of an assembly building. Thus to the Camp statement of Oscar Wilde that 'in matters of grave importance, style, not sincerity is the vital thing' – it gives the Non Camp answer of Stravinsky 'in matters of grave importance, sincerity is the *sine qua non* which guarantees nothing'. In short, the fundamentalist belief may not rescue other inadequacies but at least here, as opposed to so many other American cultural centres, it provides the necessary base for any more successful an attempt.

7. RECENT BRITISH ARCHITECTURE: POP-NON POP

Tout a changé dans l'ordre physique; et tout doit changer
dans l'ordre moral et politique.   (ROBESPIERRE)

If one were to pigeon-hole the scene of recent British
architecture in a single metaphor it would have to be
'battlefield', and 'scarred battlefield' at that, for it is
saturated with the shellholes of polemic. It is full of old
battle lines marked 'New Empiricism/New Brutalism',
'one-off/repeatable', 'Art/Social Service', 'Indeterminate/
symbolic' and, in the late sixties, Pop/Non Pop. Each
label (or insult according to the enemy) marks the place
and time where a battle was fought or where a flag was
stuck marking out new territory. The architect proceeds
as the *avant-garde* does in any battle, as a provocateur. He
saps the edges of taste, undermines the conventional
boundaries, assaults the thresholds of respectability and
shocks the psychic stability of the past by introducing the
new, the strange, the exotic and erotic. His battle tactics
may even extend towards nudity of one sort or another
[147]. Yet this provocation is not simply an end in itself
as it often is with the Camp and Dolce Vita architects.
Rather, it is combined with a technical ultra-sophistication
to break down accepted conventions and generate change.
Hence, unlike the cyclical situation in America, where
patterns tend to recur every generation, the architectural
movement in England really is a movement in the strong
sense of the word. It is a coherent development from one
position to another, a sequence of ideas and forms which
are developed intentionally. Thus beneath the surface
agitation, the polemical war cries, there is a more serious
struggle going on: creative evolution in a sense. For

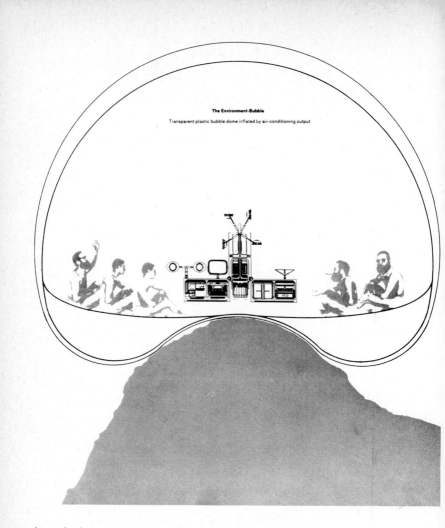

The Environment-Bubble

Transparent plastic bubble dome inflated by air-conditioning output

through the extreme movement from one position to another, ideas are clarified and tested. They are continually modified within a tradition or problem-situation, and this critical dialectic always produces progress of a sort.

To cite three examples which will be discussed below, there is first of all the problem of change and expendability which has been continually sharpened to the point where its effect on buildings and cities is now becoming clear. Secondly, along with this has developed the first radical critique of design philosophy since Le Corbusier's *Vers une architecture* – I mean both systematic design and

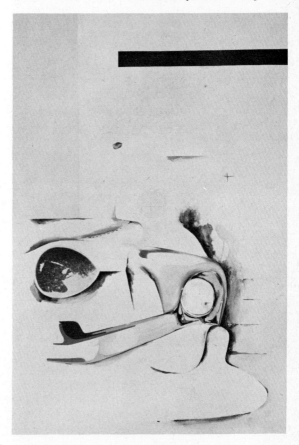

147a, b. Reyner Banham and François Dallegret in their Un-house, 1965, and Richard Hamilton, *Hommage à Chrysler Corp.*, 1957. Eroticism and sophisticated technology, two primary preoccupations of the avant-garde. *Hamilton:* 'pieces are taken from Chrysler's Plymouth and Imperial ads . . . The sex symbol is, as so often happens in the ads, engaged in a display of affection for the vehicle. She is constructed from two main elements – the Exquisite Form Bra diagram and Voluptua's lips.'

the work done by the Pop theorists, more particularly Banham. Finally, the last example also concerns a new development in design which was also clarified through constant use and criticism: the axonometric technique. This latter technique has been used by a group of British architects to demonstrate how a building is put together and how it works. It is also used to handle three-dimensional design which could not have been coordinated in any other way. In the hands of a particular architect, James Stirling, it has led to a new mode of architecture known throughout the world. If all this sounds optimistic and forceful however, the general background against which it all occurred was anything but.

NON-POP

COMPROMISE AND THE TOWNSCAPERS

The mood in which England conducted its post-war skirmishes was first of all set by the devastation of one third of the City of London and the lack of money, skills and materials, and secondly, by an attitude which could best be characterized as realistic, sentimental and liberal. How a tough-minded realism could combine with a lachrymose sentimentality to produce such works as the Festival of Britain [148] or the New Towns is at first hard to see until one remembers the sticky glue of liberalism. For liberalism, the Welfare State, the dreams of helping others often in spite of their wishes, leads to a position of rigorous

148. Robert Matthew and others in the LCC Architects Department: Royal Festival Hall, London, 1951. On the exterior, 'nautical whimsy', the flattened gesture of the roof, the Corbusian patterns, the revealing cartouche of the Queen. This was the exhibition which brought Modern Architecture to the British public.

compromise. This was most publicly proclaimed (as were most of the positions outlined here) in the pages of the *Architectural Review*, the journal which had done so much to support modern architecture in the thirties. In a rhetorical call to arms termed 'Programme for the City of London', the authors stated as early as June 1945 what was to remain the main party line for the next ten years: 'constructive compromise is what the *genus locii* calls for, not *tabula rasa*'. The position was accompanied by a series of what were later to be called 'townscape sketches', which left no doubt as to what the position implied: a sleek and picturesque integration of surface effects from any and every source.

Lewis Mumford also condoned another key idea at about the same time, defending Abercrombie's 1944 plan for the decentralization of London. This was to be achieved by creating a series of New Towns, together with a vast public housing policy. A National Planning Authority was set up 'to secure a reasonable balance of industrial development throughout the country'. What it meant in practical terms was (1) the creation of over twenty New Towns with the self-supporting industries, (2) the creation of over half a million new dwelling units in the next five years, and (3) a shift of architectural practice from small private firms to larger, public authorities. Finally some of the social ideals of the early modern movement were coming to fruition. But other ideals were not. For what this meant in terms of the politics of architecture was that individualism, expression and 'Art' were to be denied in the name of the Welfare State, economy and 'Social Service'. Both the Labour and Conservative Parties were united on this score and in these terms.[1] As a Conservative Minister, Duncan Sandys, said to the RIBA: 'We desire as much as anyone to maintain diversity of design and scope for the individual talents of architects. But first things must come first. The houses must go up and nothing must stand in the way.'

The politics of architecture were conducted under the basic dichotomy 'Art or Social Service' (as one of the Fabian pamphlets put it), showing that it had to be one thing or the other. One need not concern oneself with the truth or otherwise of such a dichotomy, since its practical truth will be borne out according to what people believe

149. Foster Associates: Computer Technology Ltd. Office, London, 1970. A typical British team firm devoted to architecture as an elegant service rather than necessarily as building. Inflatable office, blown up in fifty-five minutes, which carries the short-term services: the steel booms carry fluorescent tubes which bounce the light off the skin and act as support – in case the inflatable deflates.

and how they act. And in England the architectural debate was continuously formuated in such polarities from Duncan Sandys right after the War to Cedric Price twenty years later (when he advocated servicing rather than architecture) [149].

In fact, public housing and architecture as a social service were two ideals that extended very deeply into the English grain going back well into the nineteenth century. And they produced, after the War, what is commonly regarded as 'the finest housing and some of the finest schools in all Europe'. This remark of Kidder-Smith refers mainly to the work of the LCC (the London County Council), more particularly part of their Roehampton scheme, but it also refers to the government support of industrialized building which made that area more highly developed than in any other country.[2] So one has what amounts to a classic, potentially tragic or comic, conflict. On the one hand, the best and greatest amount of housing and on the other hand, its undeniably mediocre appearance and social timidity.

These latter qualities were apparent in almost all the housing and most conspicuously in the New Towns. If the English architect could point with pride towards the fact that his country was the first to initiate such Garden Cities and New Towns, he was also forced to admit that it was the first to make mistakes in this area: they were obviously lacking in the life and density of the old cities – and worse – their social uniformity made the epithet 'social ghetto' inevitable.

Indeed in many respects the Garden City and the satellite New Town are virtually indistinguishable: particularly in their salubrious imagery. Both are reactions to the Town Planning metaphor of 'disease, cancer, apocalypse, death' which have plagued planning circles since Patrick Geddes. Both react to these metaphors with counter-images of cleanliness, and cosiness.

150. LCC Architects Department: Alton East Housing, Roehampton, London, 1953-6. Example of 'people's detailing' which became so widespread during the fifties as to constitute the orthodoxy and hence the ground for all subsequent revolution.

This last quality can be seen in the 'People's Detailing', the English version of 'Social Realism' or Marxist aesthetics, that became mandatory at the LCC in the early fifties: pitched roofs, bricky materials, ticky-tacky, cute lattice-work, little nooks and crannies, picturesque profiles all snuggled within a cardboard-like rectitude [150].

This and its variants became the major mode of building in England and hence the common background for all subsequent revolution. Essentially, it was justified by the 'Townscape Philosophy' put forward by the *Architectural Review*. What this amounted to was a picturesque aesthetic and an updating of Camillo Sitte's nineteenth-century *Town Planning According to Artistic Principles*. Sitte had proposed that the architect should compose the city like a Beethoven symphony; it should become a great, dramatic experience to walk through a sequence of urban spaces pulsating in scale on either side, mixing new with old, monuments with parks, all unfolding on a series of axes and contained vistas into exploding crescendi. City space would be contained, not fragmented.

Some members of the *Architectural Review* renewed many of these Viennese ideas, but pared them down to the exigencies of the Welfare State. What were strong formal routes became arbitrary, meandering alleyways composed of 'street furniture'. Although the intention of providing a tangible city coherence was positive, the effect was arbitrary and cute, and, to revert to the military metaphor, was attacked as such.[3] The basic objection was that the Townscape Philosophy was only interested in surface effects, in curing symptoms, not causes, of urban blight. In any case, the philosophy became the major orthodoxy and mode of design. First of all, Hugh Casson gave visual embodiment to these ideas, in a series of townscape sketches already mentioned. Then Gordon Cullen further developed the technique in 1948 and together with 'Ivor de Wolfe' (a pseudonym for one of the *Review*'s editors) they developed a full 'Townscape Philosophy'. This philosophy combined the old, English respect for the picturesque, for accepting the 'given' properties of any situation and making the best of them, with an empirical approach that 'judges every case on its merits', like good-English-Common-Law. In fact even the 'Case Book Method' of Common Law was used; that is, as the editors proclaimed, 'precedents (not principles)'. A series of on-the-spot examples of townscape were to be collected into a working scrapbook which would then be distributed to regional designers and Local Authorities. It could all be summarized in two quotes: 'revolt against the old bore Plato' and 'Be thyself . . . let's have more character . . .

i.e. significant differentiation' (the last request appealing to Darwinian evolution).

The *Architectural Review* also put forward a series of related positions in such titles as 'The New Empiricism' (referring to the pragmatic, deadpan approach then current in Sweden) and 'The New Humanism' (not actually a title, but a reworking of the former). Perhaps it is stretching a point, but a similar attitude could even be found in their other positions: 'The Functional Tradition' and 'Picturesque Theory',[4] for they all put emphasis on the vernacular and the eighteenth-century dictum 'consult the genius of the place in all'.

This complete nexus of attitudes culminated in the final, liberal response to urban mess, called 'Outrage'. And this 'Outrage' (the subject of a whole *Architectural Review* issue, June 1955) was then elevated to the level of a recurrent column. For the next thirteen years Ian Nairn's column slugged away at 'Subtopia' and those images of 'barbarian' civilization. Little did he realize that while he was churning out this continual rage in a series of barbed photos (such a mood sustained for thirteen years is quite a feat), the nascent Pop theorists were busy changing the captions. This was possible as early as 1950 when all the icons of mess were attacked in one issue, 'The Mess That is Man-Made America'. All the proto-pop icons of billboards and car-dumps were there and explicit; all that was needed was a new attitude, a new caption. As so often in history, the relation between form and content flips when it becomes too explicit.

But to return to the underlying attitude, post-war Britain was on the whole despairing, realistic and liberal. The latter two moods could combine to produce such things as system building and the Hertfordshire Schools. These in fact were built as early experiments in prefabrication; the intention was to pool many educational interests and to perfect a building method that was inexpensive, quick and in need of a small labour force. The schools that resulted were planned on a flexible grid that allowed picturesque massing, multiple materials and again cosy street furniture; in short the values of townscape. However, the attitude of despair combined with a common-sense realism produced such quasi-Gothic gestures as Coventry Cathedral by Basil Spence – a compromise of traditional and modern requirements that became all the more bizarre when juxtaposed to the strong Smithson design for this building.

But compromise (not synthesis) was built into the realist's position. He had to appeal to an impoverished country which had never accepted the modern movement in any of its forms; he had to get things done with little money, hope or principle. This difficulty, this ambivalence, was brought to consciousness by one of the *Review*'s editors, J. M. Richards, when he wrote looking both ways that:

> Few men are innovators, and while it is vital not to inhibit those who are, it is equally vital to provide the others with a standard by which they can be guided; hence the need for a canon, for a contemporary vernacular, even for clichés.[5]

This defence of clichés was an answer to Frank Lloyd Wright's attack on cliché, and there are two things to note because most of the following positions are in reaction to it. First, the point that one provides non-innovators with a standard and does not inhibit innovators underscores the attention to the common man and the indifference towards excellence which was a common response of most Welfare States; second, the characterization of a contemporary vernacular as a cliché, a language which will be supported from the top down and which is already dead. Given this attitude, it was not surprising that the Pop-theorists inverted cliché: they decided to enjoy rather than suffer it.

Nevertheless it was suffered. The standard, the canon, the contemporary vernacular became a watered down International Style reminiscent of what Wright had called 'deflowered classicism'; that is, a well-behaved, cheap version of Le Corbusier's Purism. It could be seen in such large-scale housing developments as Churchill Gardens, or any of the New Towns, at Fitzhugh Estate, Brandon Estate, Elmington Estate, Silwood Estate and nearly every other scheme of the LCC late in the fifties.

It permeated the St Paul's area, it threatened to 'integrate' Piccadilly, it stepped over the impoverished Stepney and Poplar areas, spread to the Shell Building, 'harmonized' Bowater House, 'regularized' the State House, 'unified' the Barbican, etc. The justification was always clear; firmness, commodity and a tight budget.

The need for a standard architecture. The victory was all but complete. There was a common vernacular which everyone could immediately recognize as 'modern' and take for granted. There was a consistent background against which to revolt. And one of the strongest revolts was to come from within the liberal tradition: Sussex University, the Roman Catholic Cathedral at Liverpool, the New Hall for Girls at Cambridge [151], all took off

151. Chamberlin Powell and Bonn: New Hall for girls at Cambridge, 1966. These New Imagists rebelled against their previous vernacular with an outburst of symbolism on to which the girls quickly and affectionately cottoned with the nickname, 'the great tit'. Other images include an orange peel Byzantine dome, Ronchamp stair towers on the corners and a megalithic entrance.

from the restrained International Style with cream-puff abandon. Finally, warmth and imagery were back with a vengeance in the new, improved, contemporary vernacular.

THE NEW PALLADIANS

Yet the real revolt had already occurred twenty years earlier and before the party line was established, and again in the pages of the *Architectural Review*. The first voice was that of Colin Rowe, the historian and student of Rudolf Wittkower at the Warburg Institute. This institute of art or really cultural history was transferred to

England just before the war; it was made up of German scholars who considered art and history in theoretical and quasi-scientific terms; thus something unique for England at the time. One of its leaders, Rudolf Wittkower, had been working for thirty years on his *Architectural Principles in the Age of Humanism*, a book that was soon, and quite unintentionally, to influence the idealist tradition. What Wittkower sought to prove was that Renaissance architecture was primarily symbolic and not abstract. He did this by quoting at length the intentions of architects and clients in Italy; particularly those of Palladio and those concerned with mathematical systems of proportion. Thus when Colin Rowe published his article 'The Mathematics of the Ideal Villa' in 1947, those who had been following the emergent Neo-Platonism, that is those close to the Warburg, were not surprised. Here was New Palladianism fully born right from the top of Corbusier's head. In one of those striking historical comparisons (which are always possible when forms are multivalent), Colin Rowe showed a similar proportional system in a Palladian and Corbusian villa. Going beyond this numerical similarity, Rowe then showed that both villas were deeply embedded within the European tradition. They both evoked a Virgilian dream of living above yet distinct from nature (hence 'Ideal') as well as within an eternal order (hence 'Mathematics').

The effect of this and Rowe's following article 'Mannerism and Modern Architecture' was to give the younger generation of architects the metaphor of the past, of history, of references, as a viable generator of present form. The alternative was quite distinct from townscape or the New Empiricism. In fact it could have been called the New Academicism, except that the title would be too derogatory in view of the rigour and life of the movement, and except for the fact that another title was soon to be coined for a related phenomenon: the New Brutalism (see below).

As this last new 'ism' suggests, the title was partially a barbed joke flicked at the prevailing liberals with the trenchant prefix 'brutal' added for sting. But also it was an acknowledgement that movements, architectural and otherwise, could all be summarized and pigeonholed by a label. It was a recognition of the politics of architecture.

Yet it took a few years to crystallize in the minds of the Smithsons, and when it finally did, their connections with the academic rationalists were becoming tenuous.

Nevertheless, in spite of this, the New Brutalism was definitely in the academic tradition of calculated 'movements'. This is clear from the Smithsons' first building, Hunstanton School [152], which is full of historical

152. Alison and Peter Smithson: Hunstanton School, Hunstanton, 1949–54. The formal ordering is academic, both Palladian and Miesian, but the underlying attitude is ascetic and literalist: bricks are bricks, steel is steel and never a metaphor shall they become. Except Brutalist.

references. Yet the deeper characteristics were quite original in tone. All the materials were used 'as found' without trying to become metaphors for other materials. In this sense Brutalism was never more than a dramatization of honest literalism: it argued that things taken in themselves are more honest and evocative than any anthropomorphic meanings which may have become attached. In short the metaphor of literalism. However, Hunstanton did also have explicit reference to past works, to the Miesian idiom of frame and infill and to the Palladian order of rectilinear formality. It was this latter allusion which was most apparent to the rationalists.

They could read the building as an object-lesson in controlled, bi-axial symmetry; it had a consistent order worthy both of the Roman Forum and the Venetian Campagna – small wonder that it was attacked for being an impossible school for children and (implicitly) a reminder of 'the old bore Plato'. The point was, as in Mies's work, that the client should rise to his architect and become a more disciplined, sober adult. That this discipline and sobriety were valued in Mies, especially by the academics and to a fanatical degree, is apparent in some of the other scholarly discussion of the time.

THE ACADEMIC PLATONISTS

For instance in 1951, at the Architectural Association, then the temple of reverent Miesolatry, the three academics Llewelyn-Davies, John Weeks and Leslie Martin put forth a philosophy of 'endlessness' inspired by a Mondrian painting and a Miesian corner [153a,b]. Their

argument was, on a literal level, pure balderdash – although forgivable because of the religious conviction with which it was presented and the insignificance of its occasion. What had occasioned their philosophy of endlessness was a Miesian corner which supposedly

> . . . goes unnoticed when we look at the building as a whole. It is the very opposite of the emphasized rusticated corner of the Renaissance, and is almost refined into non-existence. By stepping it back behind the wall faces, by breaking the angle up into

153a, b. **Mies van der Rohe: Alumni Memorial Hall, Chicago, 1947.** The corners of this building are full visual stops, yet the reverse was argued by Llewelyn-Davies who proffered an 'endless' architecture appropriate to mass production. Compare to text.

numerous angles and planes, the corner has been dissolved away. Thus, and this is the real reason for doing it, the continuity of both walls is preserved. Neither is allowed to pass beyond the other so as to stop its imaginary infinite prolongation.

If this prolongation was here much more imaginary than real, it did later lead to several real schemes in the endless tradition: notably a hospital by Llewelyn-Davies and Weeks which was justified because the architects had made a minimum of fixed decisions: i.e. had created an 'indeterminate' structure which could be shuffled and changed with apparent ease [154].

This philosophy of indeterminacy was taken up later by several anti-academics as will be mentioned below, but at this stage in the fifties it was seen to be the natural result of the mass production process. It was assumed that mass production led to infinite repeatability (endlessness), and that uncertain or changing use patterns led to flexibility (indeterminacy). Thus the façade of the Northwick Park Hospital was justified because it had been determined just by the structural loads to be carried and not by any particular geometry. The only fixed parameters were the mullion and beam system and its indefinite extension. Thus an open aesthetic of repetition was clarified and remained one of the possible ways of handling change, while the Smithsons were developing the next, dialectical step in their House of the Future (see below). Perhaps one could fault the actual design for a monotony and for failing to signify those more permanent elements, but it definitely did make a contribution to the 'problem-situation' of change.

Another example which grew from this academic tradition was the Hostel for Caius College [155], which was

also justified because it could be extended without disruption and because it was flexible. Yet the same building could equally well be explained by other pursuits then current at Cambridge in the late fifties. There was a group in touch with Colin Rowe interested in the way Cartesian space led to certain possibilities of form: either a building could be centroidal, in which case all its surface would tend to be the same, or it could be linear, in which case there would be a natural change of surface on each axis. And there was another group headed by Leslie Martin and Lionel March which was experimenting with a series of fresnel squares on the relation of built form to land use. Now curiously enough this building, which was designed before any of this work came to fruition in the sixties, managed to illustrate all these developments at once without being an explicit example of any of them. It was almost

155. Leslie Martin, Colin St John Wilson and Patrick Hodgkinson: Hostel for Caius College, Cambridge, 1962. Perhaps the epitome of the academic 'Platonists', this building could be justified for its reverent handling of materials, its hieratic quality, its controlled sequencing of space. In the politics of architecture however, it became one of the objects of Cedric Price's censure, 'just the middle ages with 13-amp power points'.

a series of fresnel squares and a combination linear-centroidal building. I mention these oddities, because it is the rare case in England where practice actually preceded and clarified theory (supposedly the common case).

Still another example of this dialectic occurred within the academies and also tended to be supported by a form of Platonism. This was the method of design variously called 'logical, parametric, systematic, or cybernetic'. While it will be more fully discussed in Chapter 8 as Parametric Design, its aesthetic and moral preconceptions should be mentioned here since they tie in very closely with the academic Platonists. The moral preferences of rationalist designers such as Christopher Alexander, Thomas Maldonado and Bruce Archer favoured clarity, precision, thoroughness and self-effacement while the aesthetics invariably reflected the geometrical patterns found in nature: the snow-flake, soap bubble or bone-joint beloved by D'Arcy Thompson. In fact one could even speak of an architectural analogy to such natural form – BUILT FORM (as it often appears) that was regarded with a high seriousness verging on the mystical.

NON POP – POP

PARALLEL OF LIFE AND ART

There is of course another viable attitude to take towards process and form: less idealist and more casual. This was developed in reaction to the New Palladianism mentioned above, out of the movement known as 'action painting' and after an exhibition on 'Growth and Form' (with its echo of D'Arcy Thompson's book on that subject). It came to explicit formulation in an exhibition called Parallel of Life and Art held at the Institute of Contemporary Arts in 1953. The protagonists, the Smithsons, Paolozzi and Henderson, assembled over a hundred images of 'Life' which they presented in a common, gritty textured form of photography, 'Art'. Actually the 'Parallel' which they were drawing consisted of a common assumption: an attitude which was impossible to define beforehand but which was very apparent after the exhibit. Drawing from the action painting of Pollock, it could be characterized as more open and free to immediate sensation: the images all had a compulsive violence as if they had just been torn from a context for their immediate impact. Beyond this obsessive quality was their direct approach to science. Most of them presented an image of some scientific or technological truth: for instance number 100: 'A benign tumour made up of proliferated cells X53 (microphoto); 119 Section of Thrombosed Pulmonary'. There is no attempt to humanize the image of science, no attempt to anthropomorphize the truth. What is consistently sought is the undomesticated view of the present research: the visual equivalent of cosmological truth as it was then known. What this turned out to be was a series of gritty coarse-grained photos that translated everything into a scaleless biomorphic texture: 'Brutalism' was almost defined as the straightforward image of science.

To avoid doubt, the Smithsons introduced their exhibit into the New Palladian tradition at the Architectural Association with the capital lettered pronouncement 'WE ARE NOT HERE TO TALK ABOUT SYMMETRY AND PROPORTION'.[6] The break was clean: instead of a Platonic architecture with some conceptual scale there was to be an architectural equivalent to the present cosmology of endless and continual space. Instead of a Virgilian dream of urbanity, there was to be a direct, realist approach to existing city situations.

THE NEW BRUTALISM

What grew out of Parallel of Life and Art was sort of a halfway house between Non Pop and Pop, the New Brutalism. It is possible to discuss this movement emphasizing both its moderate and futurist sides, as Banham has done in a book on the subject subtitled with the significant query 'Ethic or Aesthetic?' The more moderate aspects of this movement will be treated here; leaving the futurist aspects for discussion under Pop. The reason is simply that when the movement was futurist, it was really more a small part of something else: the Independent Group at the ICA and the Pop theorists there. Otherwise, as the protestations of the Smithsons make clear, the New Brutalism was always a direct approach to present problems:

> Any discussion of Brutalism will miss the point if it does not take into account Brutalism's attempt to be objective about 'reality' – the cultural objectives of society, its urges, its techniques and so on. Brutalism tries to face up to a mass-production society, and drag a rough poetry out of the confused and powerful forces which are at work.[7]

What this meant could be seen by the two Smithson projects already mentioned, or by their Golden Lane Competition entry (1952). What appears from this project is the 'direct' image of Brutalism, the visual equivalent of a mass-production society [156]. But what the Smithsons

156. Peter and Alison Smithson: Golden Lane Competition, 1952. Bombed-out site with movie hero Gérard Philipe superimposed. This bare technosophistication can be traced back to the Russian schemes of the twenties and forward to Park Hill, Sheffield, and the work of Cedric Price. In this project, the Smithsons put forward the idea of urban re-identification: human associations should determine the formal elements.

explicitly projected was something else: a new version of the CIAM idea, the street in the air, or as the Smithsons renamed it, the street deck. They also took the concept beyond the CIAM as well as changed the name, for what they provided was an open, wide deck that really could contain a viable street life: a 'deck' not a 'corridor'. The idea was to recreate the present street life above ground level forming a series of urban 'places' open to the air and accessible by the kitchen of each house – that bastion of London's East End Society from which 'mum' directs the scene.

Introducing this figure of working-class society is appropriate because at this point in the fifties sociology and ecology were becoming important architectural issues. At meetings of CIAM, the Smithsons and other activists were putting forward the idea of a new urbanism based on particular sociological determinants. They proffered such ideas as 'identity, place, cluster' in opposition to the CIAM ideas which emphasized the universal. They juxtaposed an existing city fabric to the general city approach. They studied the East End, read sociological tracts and built for a 'particular time and place'. One result of this new commitment, although not by the Smithsons, was the East End scheme of Denys Lasdun. His Bethnal Green Cluster, as the Smithsons' 'cluster', was meant to give identity and location to a large development.

Another Brutalist scheme which did take a realistic and accommodating position towards 'the way of life' of the inhabitants was the Park Hill scheme at Sheffield, 1961. Here the architects make use of the Smithsons' deck idea to create a lively city street in the air (although not as lively as it might have been because of the absence of stores, pubs, etc.). The architects have also made use of other Brutalist principles such as an informal, topological grouping which follows the system of movement [157]. The continuous building just snakes around the site in order to trap space and find good orientation: it is not the

157. Lynn, Smith and Nicklin under Wormersley: Park Hill, Sheffield, 1961. Materials used 'as found', a formal organization according to the topology, realistic towards the existing way of life, street identity; all the principles of Brutalism are illustrated.

result of any Platonic organization other than a flat sky-line. Furthermore, the materials are direct and straight-forward (used as found); the façade is a literal result of what happens within (no attempt at composition), and the existing way of life is faced up to and accommodated. In short, the building illustrates every one of the Smithsons' principles without having being designed by them. In this sense it is typical of the Brutalist movement as a whole: worldwide and only half acknowledged.

BRITISH BUILDINGS

One of the reasons for this is that Brutalism was so ob-viously related to Le Corbusier's late work that what might have been acknowledged to it often went to the French master. There were his two buildings which used *beton brut* in a ruthlessly straightforward way, the Unité and Maisons Jaoul. Furthermore there was his epigram which epitomized a whole area of Brutalism: *'L'Architec-ture, c'est, avec des matières brutes, établir des rapports émouvants'*. As if these two uses of the adjective *brut* were not enough, there was the further problem that he had already pre-empted almost every architectural position, for instance using industrial objects 'as found'. As Alison Smithson said, speaking in effect for a whole generation:

... when you open a new volume of the *Œuvre Complète* you find that he has had all your best ideas already, has done what you were about to do next.[8]

Such a sentiment could be expressed by just about every architect practising in the fifties, so pervasive was Corbusier's influence.

In England, this influence was not only acknowledged, it was proclaimed with open gratitude: the Roehampton slabs for instance were described as 'an act of homage to Le Corbusier'. And his touch could also be seen in such widely different work as that coming from Llewelyn-Davies and Basil Spence. Indeed all the buildings illus-trated in a collection called *British Buildings 1960-64* owed something to the master. There was the Hostel for Caius College already mentioned, the Forest Gate High School by Colquhoun and Miller, the Royal College of

Art, the Wolfson Institute, the Imperial College Hostel and the Economist building by the Smithsons – each institute, each name, resonating with an attention to social and symbolic meaning which they all in fact achieved.

Thus, in addition to Le Corbusier, what underlay these schemes and united them in the book was their awareness of architecture as social and intellectual discourse. They all fit into their environment. They all speak a restrained language of Corbusian form. They all take a position on the social *status quo*, and they are all in the book dedicated to Colin Rowe. The dedication which appeared in the beginning of the book caused some consternation because it was never explained or made explicit. In fact, some of the architects did not know they were influenced by Rowe or that their buildings were examples of architectural discourse, because this was never spelled out. Indeed, there were so many small influences at work, that none of them were large or conscious enough to be rallied around or turned into a manifesto. The closest these architects came to a polemical movement at this time was the continual passage through the flat of Thomas ('Sam') Stevens where they received intellectual amplification, or their Saturday mornings over beer at the York Minster pub, where they exchanged it. This ambivalent position was recognized by Sam Stevens when he wrote in 'The Third Force in British Architecture':

. . . how far we fall short today, in achieving any such public architectural conversation: think of Oxford Street, or think indeed of the rebuilding of any great city . . . There is no more reason why architecture, a public art, should lie under the intolerable necessity of being an arid dispute between contestants all talking at once, in mutual abuse and invective, than that conversation should become a diatribe . . . Hence our present impasse.[9]

JAMES STIRLING OR FUNCTION MADE MANIFEST

One of the members of this group, however, did achieve a very developed and original position and became, in my view, the best architect of his generation. The influence of Rowe, Brutalism, Corbusier and Liverpool, incommensurable as they were, nevertheless combined in the psyche of James Stirling into a very powerful rhetoric of building, uncommon to the British sense of restraint. The compromise which has often characterized English architecture, from St Paul's Cathedral to the Festival of Britain, was piqued if not routed. For the first time since the Palm House at Kew or the Crystal Palace, Britain had a designer who could handle glass with virility; for the first time since Mackintosh, an architect who could combine glass with a moulded masonry and send them rebounding around the façade; and for the first time since Hawksmoor an architect who could pile masonry on top of itself, one masterful conceit following another into the clouds.

Ah, one might protest, but he has not the social vision of a Morris or Ruskin, the refinement of a Jones or Yevele, the taste of an Adam, the imagination of a Soane and the wit of Vanbrugh. Quite so, but like each one of these men he is the locus of a new sensibility. And that sensibility is above all tough, mannered and highly intelligent. Perhaps the apotheosis of the functional sensibility. Not that his buildings work extraordinarily well, but (more important) they look and make the inhabitant feel as if they did: i.e. they are the 'essence' or representation of function. The expression of function, as Sullivan called it, or function made apparent and clear, as Aquinas would have it.

All of this was achieved against much opposition and discouragement, many lost competitions and rejected housing schemes, because as Stirling pointed out, too much good-English-taste had a habit of knocking off its talent in the name of aesthetics:

> We used the forms of this village extension on individual houses in an attempt to get aesthetic approval. At this time I was trying to start a practice with six private houses, four of which were rejected as being aesthetically sub-standard . . . At this stage we suffered badly from the aesthetic opinion of architects who had the authority to reject and throw out schemes . . .[10]

Stirling's break from the custodians of provincialia came with a commission obtained through the father of one of his students at the Architectural Association. He was asked to design a low-cost group of flats that would be competitive with the relatively cheap 'Span' housing. As a result of this offer, he left the private firm he was working for, formed a partnership with James Gowan, and together with him designed Ham Common (1956), a semi-Brutalist, semi-Palladian scheme that was immediately recognized for its power and logic. At the same time as he was designing Ham Common, he was busy analysing the new turn of Corbusier and the modern movement. Two articles appeared in the *Architectural Review* which discussed this turn. There was a shift from an urban, technological commitment to a rural, peasant architecture; 'From Garches to Jaoul'; from the machine aesthetic to Brutalism, from Utopia to a Provençal farmhouse right in Paris.

Although this article suggested a pessimism about the loss of Utopian drive, it also suggested an optimism about the possibilities of vernacular building and making the best use of existing techniques. Stirling, as other architects of this time, saw the possibilities inherent in 'The Functional Tradition' with its straightforward use of ready-made parts. But it was not just a question of Liverpool Warehouses and 'bull-nosed sills', the nostalgia of Worktown (although this was important in their Preston Housing) - it was also a question of pragmatic 'one-up-manship', skimming the trade magazines for new industrial products which they could use in an unforeseen way.

The basic idea was ingenious stealing to save money, the use of systems building out of context ('perhaps there is hope for CLASP if used out of context'). In their Preston Housing, a standard plumbing trap is lifted straight from its sewerage role, turned on its side and then re-used as a rainwater spout. In the same scheme, standard Worktown details are used, such as the bull-nosed sill, splayed setback and engineering brick. Partially, it is justified as maintaining the spirit of the city; but also, as can be seen by the rest of their work, it is an attempt to beat the bloodyminded at their own game of cutting costs. And the architects' success at this endeavour must have appealed to many businessmen and contributed a great deal to their continuing acquisition of commissions.

In spite of this reasonably new '*adhocist*' method, the real contribution of Stirling and Gowan to the international scene did not occur until 1959 when they designed two schemes, one of which was built. The unbuilt scheme, that for Selwyn College at Cambridge, was the first in a new mode of building. It was basically a new skin architecture with an undulating surface that could wrap around and articulate any function. This new mode was formulated from essentially three sources: from the student experiments (the beginning of Pop, then going on where Stirling and Gowan were teaching), from the use of standard industrial parts already mentioned and from the use of the axonometric technique which was then becoming an accepted method of design. Yet it was not until their next scheme, the Leicester Engineering Building [158a–e], that they developed their idiom in its complete maturity. Instead of drawing in perspective, they switched to a bird's-eye view which could analyse and dissect the whole project showing its underlying anatomy. This method of drawing really is a method of designing for it allows the architect to work out the space, structure, geometry, function and detail altogether and without distortion. It was a necessary tool for the Constructivists to analyse their meccano-like joinery; in the hands of Stirling and Gowan the tool became such a magic wand that it made the one Platonic viewpoint, the only verifiable position, the wing of a plane [159]. For those architectural buffs who could not afford this necessary vantage point, the buildings were merely dynamic.

For instance, the climb through the Leicester Engineering Building is a sequence of asymmetrical volumes separated by diminishing sheets of glass [158]. The water

158a, b. Stirling and Gowan: Views of Leicester Engineering Building, Leicester, 1964. Industrial '*adhocism*'. The extract unit, the lighting fixtures, the glazing and engineering brick are all standard parts which are resolved together through the axonometric technique.

tower looms at the top, capping off the expanse of glass which is also stopped below by the jutting cant of the lecture theatre. Thus strongly profiled bricks enclose facets of glass at both ends. But at the back, the glass continues to the edge and is only turned at 45 degrees to block out direct sunlight (for workshops below). Otherwise the geometry is mostly at 90 degrees to economize the circulation. But it is through this duality of two geometric systems that the architects achieve the dynamic juxtapositions. Glass planes extend over corners, cross over spatial areas in a wholly new way, sliding back and across in a rational but vertiginous way, heightening the feeling of ambiguity and movement. Glass skylights in 45-degree troughs, saw-toothed edges break across the sea of glass like an approaching wave and then recede into so many 'icy glass-bergs' to sit upon the horizon. One notices the similarity to the Leicester cityscape. An industrial town of glass and brick finds, instead of the nautical whimsy and People's Detailing, its own poetic equivalent. Finally Britain has an architecture equal to its post-industrial age.

The following projects of Stirling, a few of which were built, worked out some of the remaining possibilities inherent in his method of articulation. The Cambridge University History Faculty [160] took the same basic method and materials a bit further to achieve a more complex integration of space – i.e. views up through the spaces are more dynamic because they have been jammed

158c, d, e. Stirling and Gowan: Views of Leicester Engineering Building, Leicester, 1964. The lecture theatres jut out on either side of the entrance. The use of industrial objects is similar to that of the Constructivists.

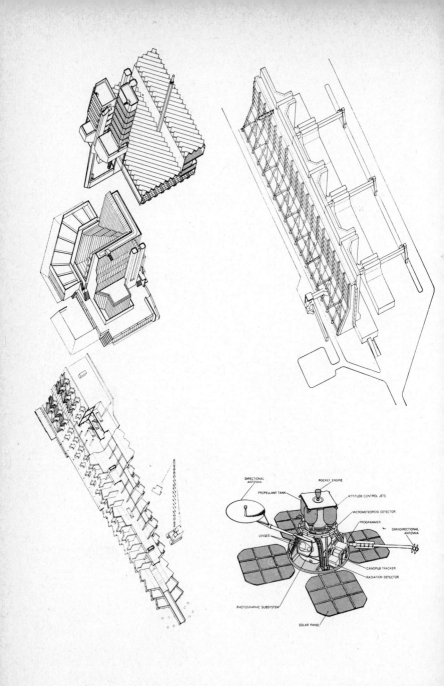

DIRECTIONAL
ANTENNA

ROCKET ENGINE

PROPELLANT TANK

ATTITUDE CONTROL JETS

MICROMETEOROID DETECTOR

PROGRAMMER

OMNIDIRECTIONAL
ANTENNA

LENSES

CANOPUS TRACKER

RADIATION DETECTOR

PHOTOGRAPHIC SUBSYSTEM

SOLAR PANEL

159 (*opposite*). **James Stirling: Four axonometrics and a lunar spacecraft.** Stirling's work is rooted in his technique of draughting; the method leads to the form. Without such a technique, sophisticated constructions would be impossible. A whole aesthetic and way of life comes from the logic and articulation possible with such a method (incidentally, used by all the architects in *British Building*). Counterclockwise from top left: Leicester Engineering Building, Cambridge University History Faculty, St Andrews University Hostel, Mariner 5, Dorman Long.

160a, b. James Stirling: Cambridge University History Faculty, finished 1968. Again the use of off-the-peg parts. Below the standard extract unit can be seen splayed from its sides like a bug on display – actually a method of reducing the vibration and noise. Above, the glazed, tapering section follows the sensible iceberg principle of having more activity on the bottom.

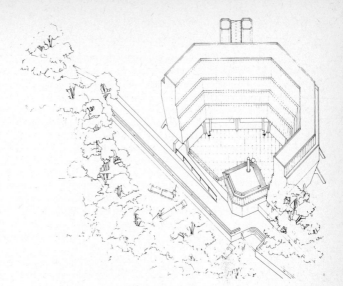

161a, b, c, d. James Stirling: Florey Building. Oxford, 1966–71. The stadium-like section of this undergraduate hostel is partly due to the brilliant view and relation between enclosing bedrooms and enclosed common rooms.

together under one skin instead of separated. Next, in his St Andrews scheme, the skin is further articulated by facing each unit with a different diagonal pattern in order to assert the significance of each room [19]. Next, in the Dorman Long project, [159] the articulation achieves a new emphasis as the structure is separated both from the skin and space (to advertise the potential of steel). If one were to characterize this architecture in a single phrase, it would be like the perspective of the Lunar Spacecraft [159], complex functions made manifest.

Finally, his Florey Building at Oxford summarizes much of this previous work [161]. It has the sharp visual contrasts of Leicester, the shimmering prismatic glass versus bright red tile. It has the sloping section and circulation discipline of Cambridge, the exposed exhaust stacks and elevator towers of all his projects and that uncanny fragmented geometry – here five eighths of an octagon which is stretched around the public rooms and gives a strong sense of enclosure. The forms, while not directly derivative, remind one more of those which clothed the heroic functions of post-revolutionary Russia, than they connote musings of Oxford undergraduate life.

In fact underlying this architecture is a basic pessimism as to the legitimacy of the functions themselves:

> ... I think architecture at the moment [1965] is rather static because I think architects are cynical about the society which they have got. It seems to me that in the 'twenties and 'thirties Corb, the Constructivists, Futurists, and others, had an intense vision of society ... which gave them a consistent plastic inventiveness, something which is lacking now. A new culture will, in time, become apparent, quite unlike what we know now. Maybe an entirely interior one. It won't be anything to do with Bloomsbury Square or piazzas or anything like that.[11]

Thus Stirling stays in his perceptive disillusion within the traditions of architecture and finds it impossible to envisage the form and content of a future society. He may be the best architect that Britain has produced, but 'who cares about architecture?'.

POP

IG BREAKING THE THRESHOLDS

The rhetorical answer to the last rhetorical question is 'not those who care about other aspects of culture' (small c). For them the traditional distinctions which separate each field are less important than the totality of man's relations to his products. It does not matter whether the products are firm or soft, visible or invisible, traditional or modern; as the Independent Group (IG), a group of artists and writers who invented Pop Art at the Institute of Contemporary Arts in London, in the fifties, said 'it's all information', or as Archigram and Andy Warhol say 'it's all the same'. What these two quotes have in common is not just their radical levelling of distinctions, but more important, their insistence on the possibility of anything, if not everything. (Everything is not possible but anything is.) Within this opening of possibilities is another important rediscovery: the relation between form and content is mostly conventional and therefore *always* open to dislocation. In short, whatever happens in cultural history could be different; there is little natural meaning in form; and since the connections between form and content are largely arbitrary, they can be changed at any point. The Pop artists rediscovered this possibility and in a sense rammed it home with all its potential brutality. Whatever is learned, repeated and codified on the brain to the point of a stock response becomes a potential subject for Pop to restructure. The form is taken out of its fixed position, the position which by necessity everyone spends his life trying to determine,[12] and is relocated. The resulting dislocation destroys habitual distinctions, inviolable codes, reasonable categories. For this the Pop movement has often been termed 'infantile, barbaric, regressive', which is only a partially true appreciation, because what is invariably happening is a new levelling of an old and laboriously maintained distinction. Yet this anti-sensitivity is not all destructive. In fact, it can be positively creative in its aggressive optimism and good cheer.

Whereas most humanists and liberals of the Welfare State in the fifties could be counted on to find America's popular culture a 'mess', 'subtopia' and generally an 'outrage', the new sensibility was determined to 'admire' it for its 'inventiveness' and find it 'serious'.[13] As already mentioned, the Pop theorists merely took the photos in the 1950 *Architectural Review* devoted to the 'mess that is man-made America' (form) and changed the captions (content). They did not actually do anything so explicit or simple as that, but that is what it amounted to. Rather, they slowly became aware of a new, casual attitude towards popular culture; something which they shared and could enjoy without embarrassment. This positive acceptance, this sheer enjoyment, is perhaps the most fundamental quality of the new sensibility and one that is most often missed in description. Lawrence Alloway, founder and caretaker of the concept 'Pop', described how it grew in the meetings of the Independent Group:

The IG missed a year and then was reconvened in winter 1954-5 by John McHale and myself on the theme of popular culture. This topic was arrived at as the result of a snowballing conversation in London which involved Paolozzi, the Smithsons, Henderson, Reyner Banham, Hamilton, McHale and myself. We discovered that we had in common a vernacular culture that persisted beyond any special interest of skills in art, architecture, design or art criticism that any of us might possess. The area of contact was mass-produced urban culture: movies, advertisement, science fiction, Pop music. We felt none of the dislike of commercial culture standard among most intellectuals, but accepted it as a fact, discussed it in detail, and consumed it enthusiastically . . .

Hollywood, Detroit and Madison Avenue were, in terms of our interests, producing the best popular culture. Thus expendable art was proposed as no less serious than permanent art; an aesthetics of expendability (the word was, I think, introduced by Banham) aggressively countered idealist and absolutist art theories. Subjects of the IG in the 1954-5 season included: Banham on car styling (Detroit and sex symbolism); the Smithsons on the real dreams of ads versus architectural ideals; Richard Hamilton on consumer goods; and Frank Cordell on popular music (he actually made it). In one way or another, the first phase of Pop Art in London grew out of the IG . . . Meetings were always very small, and by the end of the season we all knew one another's ideas so well that one of the last meetings turned into a family party with everybody going to the cinema instead.[14]

Presumably to see Marilyn Monroe in *Some Like It Hot*. The point is, as Warhol never tires of explaining to his unbelieving public: 'Pop Art is liking things'. The straightforward acceptance of the heretofore untouchable. The 'things' which Pop artists chose to 'like' were very special in the sense that they were, at once, more immediately gratifying and sophisticated, sensual and technical, so that, effectively, they moved the two thresholds of acceptability both up and down at the same time. This double movement (summed up in Alloway's phrase 'mechanomorphic eroticism'), the careful realignment between form and content, is probably common to the politics of any movement and the shift of taste in any civilization. In Pop's case, it led to such unbeatable send-ups as 'I want to be a machine' and 'Someday everybody will probably be thinking alike'.

EXPENDABILITY OR THE THROW-AWAY AESTHETIC

Although these continual protestations may echo with a sound of 'the power of positive thinking', or an unbelievably-cool, Bogart-like insouciance, they do point to a genuine enjoyment of 'things' that most intellectuals of this period happened to hate. The prime among these as Banham has pointed out is expendability: 'It is this that really galls fine art people about the Pop arts; printed words are the sacred tablet of their culture . . . The addition of the word expendable to the vocabulary of criticism was essential before Pop art could be faced honestly.'[15]

This addition, as already mentioned by Alloway, was what Banham had done in an article variously titled 'Borax, or the Thousand Horse-Power Mink' (for the IG), 'The Throw-Away Aesthetic' (for *Industrial Design*) and 'The Machine Aesthetic' (for the *Architectural Review*). Each change in title indicated a *slight* shift in content to suit the audience. But basically the message was the same and amounted to two interrelated things: a popular aesthetic which was also an expendable or throw-away aesthetic.

This essay and its mutants, more than any other essay of the Pop theorists, tries to face up to the implications of a mass culture. Its major tenet, expendability, is not only attacked by the traditional humanists but by the very 'Daddy' of Pop painting, Richard Hamilton, who finds it the one malicious principle of popular culture. It is abhorred, naturally, by the New Palladians and Platonics and ultimately this abhorrence has to go all the way back through Western Culture to Plato, whose absolute horror of change was the very animus of his philosophy.[16]

So Banham is consciously probing at the sensitive roots both of design philosophy and his traditional culture. What he says is interesting. 'We may now advance as a working hypothesis for a design philosophy this proposition: the aesthetics of consumer goods are those of the popular arts.' That is to say an aesthetic which will be 'used up' as fast as the product and quickly forgotten; an aesthetic which is based on the popular images of power, sex and other forms of social emulation, and an aesthetic which above all is popular, which will sell, which is always just one step ahead of the common dream – 'on the frontier of the dream that money can only just buy'.

This last phrase with its echoes from the fashion world was in fact a constant preoccupation of the Independent Group. Toni del Renzio had given a quip-studded talk to this group which clarified this nature of fashion merchandising. What it amounted to was this:

Depending on the skill of the fashion editor to assess the real and the mythical, the nascent and induced needs of the reader, this process can secure for the chosen garments sales unattainable

273

by other means. This skill is exactly the gauging of the force of the tendency to be typical, the defining of trends, the capturing of the next step, the double game of procuring and answering, unvoiced wants, the confidence trick of significance, the acceptable and meaningful coding.[17]

In other words, according to information and Pop theory, what is most 'universal' to most men is a delicate combination of the 'typical' and the 'next step'. This kind of universality was clarified at meetings of the IG in its discussions on mass communication and information theory, but it was specifically Banham who drove home its relevance to modern architecture.

For what it meant was that the attempt by the Pioneers, by Corbusier and Gropius, to get to a 'universal' style was misconceived. Instead of such a style being based on psychophysical constants as Corbusier had argued in 'Purism' (1921), a 'universal' style which would be understood by almost everyone (and this *is* what Corbusier was arguing for) would have to be based on convention. The conclusion is radical. It reverses exactly the supposition of the twenties, the International Style with its basis in Gestalt psychology. It contends that the learned codes, the conventions – in short whatever is current, 'in the air' and repeated often enough – form the near universal substratum and not the instinctual codes that Corbusier had postulated – which are relatively powerless. Banham twists in the point, at once destroying all the technical and psychological arguments for the International Style, for the Machine Aesthetic. Instead of 'simple' forms being produced by the machine as the Pioneers had argued, usually 'complex' ones are: the Buick V-8 rather than the Bugatti; instead of engineers working towards these shapes 'objectively' as Gropius had argued, they are subject to all sorts of marketing pressure; instead of their work naturally producing 'ideal standards' as Corbusier had argued, their prototype is always a compromise between possible production and possible further development – in short a pragmatic norm stabilized for the moment. One by one all the arguments of Loos, Corbusier, Gropius, Pevsner and Giedion came crashing to the ground: at least in so far as they were naturalist arguments (which is to say very far). For if man and the machine were left to their inherent 'nature', they would produce complex, changing, ornamental symbols of power that were always just one step ahead of the people and not any eternal, simple shapes of 'natural selection'. It was this latter neo-academic prejudice which was fouling the nest of product criticism, that was getting in the way of a style suited to mass production and mass culture.

The relevance of this argument for architecture had already been partially shown in at least two schemes of the Smithsons: their Sheffield University project based on

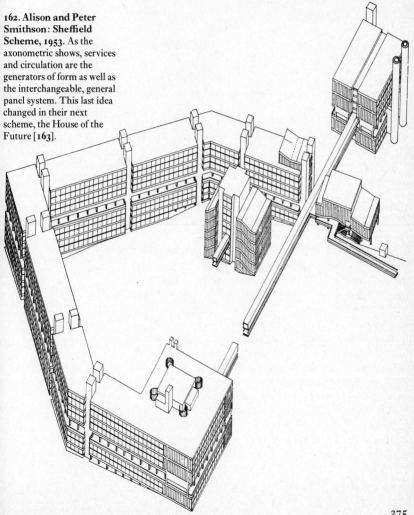

162. Alison and Peter Smithson: Sheffield Scheme, 1953. As the axonometric shows, services and circulation are the generators of form as well as the interchangeable, general panel system. This last idea changed in their next scheme, the House of the Future [163].

163. Peter and Alison Smithson: House of the Future, 1956. A new step in expendability: every form is different in each house, but repeated in the next. This principle, taken from the auto-industry, was given even more validity in the sixties when, as McLuhan said, moulds can be changed as fast as forms can be produced. This photograph shows in the foreground the living-room with raisable table and other gadgets. Behind this can be seen the patio, bathroom and dressing area.

the 'aesthetics of change' [162] and their House of the Future based on advertising and the automobile industry [163].

The Sheffield scheme (1953) introduced, or rather established, three qualities of expendability. It showed that a changing complex of this size must be organized on a circulation 'route', since this is the form most dominant and likely to remain so. It showed that the form must be open-ended and aformal in order to allow change which does not disturb the whole. And it showed that the structure and panels must be sufficiently *general and repetitive* in order to be changed with internal change. It was this last principle of expendability which proved to be itself expendable in their next scheme, the House of the Future (1956). The reason was, as the Detroit engineers had shown, that no two parts have to be alike, such as the hood and fender, if one produces enough repetitive cars.

In short, opposed to the universal joint repeated within the single unit (Gropius) was the particularized joint repeated over many units (Ford). This immediately leads to the House of the Future which is individualized to the extent that no single pattern occurs more than once within the unit. In this case, the pattern consists of a light, smooth, plastic shell divided by dark joints much as the car is moulded and divided. The house could thus be cleaned as easily as the outside of a car inasmuch as all the joints were curved and open to the 'electrostatic dust collector'. Furthermore, to continue the car analogy, a chrome strip streamlined the exterior and an annual model change was contemplated. There were also the car accessories or 'extras': the mobile service trolley dispensing favours like a benevolent robot, the pogo chair which could fold and stack, the mobile cooking articles which could be 'wander-plugged', and the built-in storage cubicles which divided the areas *en suite* and closed out the household clutter with the flick of a concertina shutter. If the whole concept sounded a bit like an advertisement it was meant to, for, like Banham, the Smithsons were then also answering the Pioneers:

> Gropius wrote a book on grain silos,
> Le Corbusier one on aeroplanes,
> And Charlotte Periand brought a new object to the office every morning;
> But today we collect ads.

'But Today We Collect Ads' was the title of a polemic they were publishing at this time with the intent of confronting what they considered the most powerful force: 'Mass production advertising is establishing our whole pattern of life – principles, aims, morals, aspirations and standard of living.' In spite of this professed intention, however, it was the rest of the IG and not the Smithsons who were to get the measure of advertising.

The first steps towards this, as mentioned, were the series of papers which the IG itself presented on popular culture. Concurrent with these was an exhibit at the ICA organized by Richard Hamilton, 'Man, Machine and Motion'. As the title suggests, there is a fairly intimate connection between these three things: machines are often the result of man's fantasies about the impossible and technology.

The aeroplane, which evolved with the illogical wastefulness of biological evolution, was born of a myth. It was a fantasy for centuries before any man flew. Even now, in the interstellar spaces, the myth, the fiction, is again ahead (from *Catalogue*, 1955).

This exhibition documented the continual interplay between the 'wish-dreams of science fiction' and the technical progress of 'science-fact' showing that while the former usually preceded the latter, the latter with its intractable requirements distorted the former. Nevertheless, man's fantasies were a major impetus for technological development and it was this fact which became the fundamental principle of the Pop movement.

Richard Hamilton was again the one to emphasize this point with the first real, that is to say programmatic, Pop painting: *Homage à Chrysler Corp.* (1957) [**147**]. What Hamilton did, very consciously, was to assemble a list of all the Pop icons current at the time and then compose them into an associational whole of 'mechanomorphic eroticism'. He elucidated this painting in the pages of *Architectural Design*, the only magazine having proto-Pop sympathies at the time:

> The main motif, the vehicle, breaks down into an anthology of presentation techniques . . . pieces are taken from Chrysler's Plymouth and Imperial ads, there is some General Motors material and a bit of Pontiac. The total effect of Bug-Eyed Monster was encouraged in a patronizing sort of way. The sex symbol is, as so often happens in the ads, engaged in a display of affection for the vehicle. She is constructed from two main elements – the Exquisite Form Bra diagram and Voluptua's lips . . .[18]

But if Hamilton was very conscientious about including all the right popular images, the actual painting was quite accidental because it was the result of an unanswered letter to the Smithsons.[19]

About this time, September 1956, the Smithsons were starting their slow exit from the Pop movement in an exhibition prophetically entitled TIT or 'This is Tomorrow' (the usual combination of erogenous zones and the future). Their contribution was a collection of homely '*objets trouvés*' which were displayed in a manner almost identical with an archaeological site – corrugated aluminium, garden shed and even a sand pit.

But while the Smithsons were marching back to the past over their previous House of the Future, Hamilton was taking it a step further in an exhibit which could have been entitled the 'Environment of the Future'. It was basically a collage of appealing images taken from the street and hung in a way to (itself) form an environment.

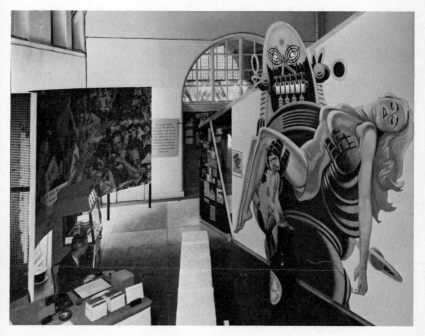

164. Richard Hamilton: *This Is Tomorrow*, 1956, robot collage. John Voelcker designed a vertiginous structure for this part of the exhibit, while John McHale, who had just returned from America with the first large collection of glossies, supplied many of the images. The environmental nature of this exhibit is also apparent in the juke-box and advertisements.

The images ranged from a 17-foot robot carrying an about-to-be-ravaged, certainly-fainted, curvaceous blonde to a gigantic beer bottle, indiscreetly placed below her [164]. All of these images were presented in a multi-layered symbol-thicket which had closest affinities to a tackboard with its many pin-ups. The comparison is not altogether idle since the tackboard had become at that time a chief form of memory and display and in fact was itself a major agent underlying the exhibition of Alloway, del Renzio and Holroyd. Their contribution was 'intended as a lesson in "how to read a tackboard", a tackboard being a convenient method of organizing the modern visual continuum according to each individual's decision'. The subject they displayed was basically 'information theory';

279

in other words the theory of shared experience which was a necessary idea before Pop art could be conceived as sharing in a 'visual continuum' to fine art.

The first acknowledgement that these ideas had become architecturally relevant occurred, again, in the pages of the *Architectural Review*, in another review of the American scene, this time called instead of 'Man-Made America' – 'Machine-Made America'. Also instead of the account being one of failure, it was a 'success story', the story of a new contemporary vernacular, the curtain wall which was then 'transforming the urban Environment of America, replacing masonry and mass with glittering glass and diagrammatic transparency'. But again, as John McHale pointed out in his marginalia, the real relevance of the American scene was the way technology tied up with popular dreams 'that money can only just buy' to produce a consumer's style that was equally high in expendability and hot imagery. He found that the same 'Good to look at, pleasant to hold' plastic curves could be found right across the gamut of American products from Kentucky rifles and duelling pistols (*sic*) to the rear end of the 'Flight Sweep Year Chrysler '57'. It was, as Banham had noted, current consumer preference which determined product design and not any Platonic categories; it was a full-blown, emphatic style banking on the assets of competitive sex and as quickly perishable as the obsolescing product it wrapped.

THE ARCHIGRAM NEXUS

Between 1957 and 1961 there was a short hiatus in the Pop architectural movement which paralleled that in the art world; a gathering of breath for the definitive campaign. During this time a younger group of architects was building up strength in the schools and LCC. One could even say that this was the beginning of another political shift in architecture with students emerging for the first time as a major polemical force, out-producing their elders in wit and creativity while adopting their tactics of broadsheet and exhibition. First of all, there was a group at the Regent Street Polytechnic headed by John Outram and manned by Michael Webb with his particular weapon

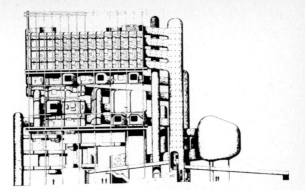

165a, b. **Michael Webb: Furniture Manufacturers Building, 1959.** 'Bowellist' project, or 'tubism', inside a rectilinear frame. The overriding theme of *Archigram I* was organic movement similar both to 1920s Expressionism and the then currently debated Ronchamp.

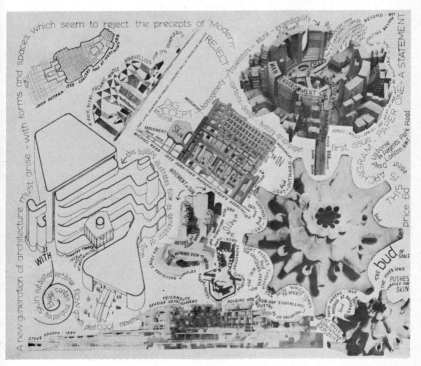

called 'Bowellism' – because the flowing tubes and stomach-like lumps resembled that part of the anatomy [**165a**]. This group was somewhat under the influence of their teachers Stirling and Howell and others, but the influence was definitely two-way: 'Howellism', a sister of

'Bowellism', gave quick birth to many buildings based on pedestrian flow and 'the erupted skin' (i.e. the splayed panel system meant to mould and reflect light).

Connected with this was another student group at the AA and Nottingham which in turn later connected up with still other schools such as Bristol and the Bartlett. The second of these groups, led by Peter Cook, taped the free-flowing student projects into a gushing whole of which the following is representative: 'This building illustrates flow as a generator of form'. Lastly, there was a third group at the LCC which was currently designing the South Bank Art Centre, based again on the combined flow of people and warm/cold air. The first two groups came together and pooled their common interests in the first issue of *Archigram* (1961) [**165b**]. This broadsheet amounted to an architectural telegram (hence the name) of all the current issues jammed together in one information-studded image. The common thread which could be extracted by painfully close perusal was: 'flow and movement'.

Thus it was not surprising that these two groups teamed up with the third at the LCC and produced *Archigram II* based on 'expendability and change'. These two 'preoccupations' as Archigram called its current interests (as opposed to 'ideals') indicated a shift in the direction of the preceding Pop movement. Indeed, Cedric Price contributed a few post-Banhamite notes on the 'expendable aesthetic' and Michael Webb produced the first real architectural equivalent of Hamilton's mechanomorphic eroticism – that is his 'Sin Centre' for Leicester Square. The kind of activities that Webb imagined for this entertainment centre hardly merited the prefix 'Sin', but the feeling of the building or its physiognomy did call up very specific associations [**166a, b**]. It was sparsely clad in an all see-through glass façade, and the floors glistened in high-gloss metallic-chrome like so many rubber-wrapped nubilities while the long hose-like mechanical equipment snaked in, over and around all possible areas without a blush of modesty – inquiring, unsuppressible tentacles. In fact, many of the visual metaphors which Archigram was to inject into the architectural language could also be seen: the angular space frame, the grasping tubes from which are slung one continuous, open skin.

166a b. **Michael Webb:
Sin Centre, 1962.**
Geodesic skin, tentacle
air-ducts, space frame;
many of the visual
metaphors which Archigram
introduced later into
architectural parlance (see
[**171**]).

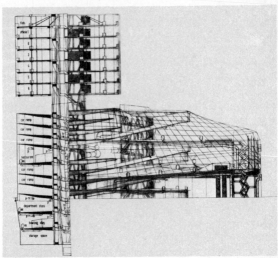

Although all of these forms had existed before, they had not existed together in such emphatic contrast, in such an *ad hoc* manner, except for the Bird Cage of Cedric Price, which was being finished at about the same time [**167**]. Yet it would be entirely wrong to assert that Price was metaphorizing architecture here. In fact he was doing the reverse, stripping it of all the associations until a kind of 'degree-zero' was reached. He objected that 'the over-hot imagery of present day English architecture puts a brave face on an empty head' – perhaps a cut at Archigram's hotted up imagery but more likely a shot at the Townscapers. In any case, his Bird Cage (1961) was the first of many visionary projects which tried to do away with enclosure, monumentality, stasis and even imagery. Price thus became the most extreme member of the *avant-garde*. He later decided to jettison *all* the traditional categories of architecture that even Brutalism had held on to, such as identity and place. He put forward an idea of 'servicing' instead of architecture; he placed primary value on all structures capable of quick change and response; he envisaged a kind of non-building activity which would liberate man from all the constraints and

167 (*opposite*). **Cedric Price with Lord Snowdon and Frank Newby: Bird Cage, London, 1961-2.** All structure, services and air; not since the Constructivist work of the twenties has such non-architectural work been seen.

168. Cedric Price: Potteries Thinkbelt, 1966. Reading from bottom to top, in a series of sandwiched zones: railroad transfer, test bed zone, flexible faculty zone, general trading zone, social exchange zone, accommodation towers. This vast regional scheme has many affinities with the Constructivist Leonidov's work of the twenties.

categories of the past; in short, he sensed the idea of absolute freedom and thus put one finger on the underlying student pulse of the sixties.[20] The other finger was on the exposed nerve ends of the architectural mainstream. In any number of witty epigrams he could at once summarize both: make the mainstream look like a mud puddle and complete freedom like the lifesaver which could ford it. This combination of wit and morality again moved the two thresholds to a new extreme position.

His Fun Palace became a mixture of complete do-it-yourself-pleasure-land plus support system. On the one hand, all leisure time activities which could be imagined were imagined – from star gazing to political rallies – and on the other hand, the only visual 'thing' which could be fixed upon was a collection of parts, a kit of mechanical components. Architecture had thus dissolved into a series of ephemeral pleasures and technical gadgets. Starting with the Brutalist idea of '*une architecture autre*',[21] the idea of pure servicing, it had shed its traditional trappings of form and space and was now on its way to becoming the

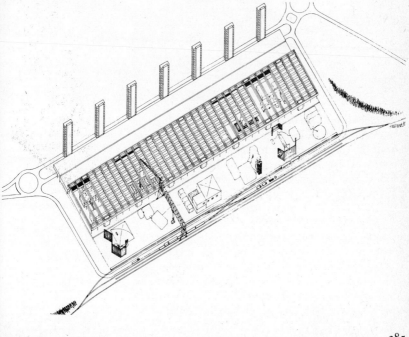

un-house of Banham, the non-city of Webber, the non-architecture of Archigram, or the next, non-building of Price, the Thinkbelt [168].

In this project, as the name implies, Price contended that thinking or education should be put on the same level as mass production with its linear belt. Price is unequivocal about this as he starts with an attack on the mainstream and the Standard Average Humanist:

> Higher education and further education should become a major industrial undertaking, not a service run by gentlemen for the few.[22]

What Price imagines as his educational Thinkbelt is in fact a large industry itself with up to 40,000 'learners', that is, itinerant teachers and students. This industry is located in the Potteries, that exploited area of the West Midlands which is often merely poverty plus slag-heaps [169]. And

each Thinkbelt would be located at specific, key points in this area, being, unlike the present universities, a living part of the community which emphasized the liberating pursuits of science and technology (liberating for the Potteries that is). Furthermore, it would be located beside railway tracks and be made up of changeable parts all serviced by gantry cranes. The idea of the railroad location was to get second use out of a nearly defunct instrument; the idea of changeable parts was to provide the least constraints on a changing educational pattern. It is this idea of avoiding a fixed social pattern which really appeals to Price and underlies his idea of liberation. Liberation means for him 'liberation from' – i.e. 'no one will be strait-jacked into a fixed community', because either

169. **Cedric Price: Potteries Thinkbelt, 1966.** 'Hanley Site: battery, sprawl and capsule housing' among the slag-heaps. While intentionally avoiding imagery, Price has managed to produce the strongest image yet, with its obvious overtones; the content of the Thinkbelt is an equally radical mixture.

they can get into a rail-bus and move out, or because the student community has merged with manufacturing, or because it has ceased altogether and become just 'sprawl'. Yes, the living accommodation is, among other unlikely things, 'sprawl': 'There will be four main types of housing: crate, sprawl, battery and capsule . . . The new Thinkbelt housing areas produce, in effect, suburban sprawl among the existing towns.'

But this is not the last jibe at liberal opinion, far from it. Other favourite chestnuts are thrown around and crushed one by one: 'fix' (Smithsons), 'image of the city' (Lynch), 'symbols of identity, place and activity' (Team Ten), 'Balanced Community' (New Towns) . . . and so on are all ridiculed for their rigidity. In such an explosion of controlled sarcasm one almost forgets the purpose of Price's flexibility, which is to 'provide the progress of ordered social change'. He wants education to become a national service; he wants it integrated with manufacturing in such a way that each will support the other – no doubt a possible trend of the future and a humane one at that. But for Price, if education is to become a service, then it 'must be provided with the same lack of peculiarity as the supply of drinking water or free teeth'. Or, in his other memorable words, it must become a regularized service called 'life conditioning'. Now 'life conditioning' is, in so far as it implies 'behavioural conditioning', the very antithesis of classical education because it entails the fact that everyone becomes conditioned and reconciled to a process – as Skinner has so ably demonstrated. Call it intelligent 'brainwashing' – what is 'conditioned' are a set of norms, skills and ideas which are not questioned or debated. Thus with this apparent, final inversion of humanist values, Price approaches the role of the Wildean critic. Paradox after paradox rolls from above the starch of his ubiquitous white collar as he defends the rights of the working man to be at the same time absolutely free *and* conditioned! For by 'life conditioning', Price probably means simply some liberating service like 'air-conditioning' which will make one cooler as one goes about one's business, yet also, as George Baird has pointed out, an unconscious component of the values built into the conditioning.[23]

Not since the bitter-sweet insults of Oscar Wilde have the poor had such an intelligent, upside-down defender.

Unfortunately, as with Wilde, some of the proposals are so brilliant that they are in little danger of being immediately put into effect by their author (like the one of creating a link between education and manufacturing), while others are so dubious as to seem quite likely (like education as conditioning). As if to underline these paradoxes, Price has tried so ruthlessly hard to avoid any built-in values or image that he has probably created the most powerful and disturbing image to date (with its obvious associations of a concentration camp) [**169**].

However, one of the points which tends to become obscure in all the debate over the Thinkbelt is that some of its extreme values (like 'imbalance, sprawl', etc.) are proposed with the acknowledgement of a balanced and conservative society and should only be seen against this background. It's rather a question of 'baiting' a conservative Welfare State than knocking it to pieces; trying to change it through critical laughter rather than revolution. For this reason, and since often the extremists such as Banham and Price are apolitical, such activists as the student revolutionists and neo-Marxists criticize their position continuously. For instance, the continual *critique* of Archigram is that it is apolitical: it accepts the basic technology and premises of a consumer society.[24]

But the reason for this, as with the Pop artists, is that the immediacy and feeling for life is said to be more important than any doctrine or system: imagination is considered prior to logic, or the 'Living City' [**170**] is more important than any dead abstractions which can be, and are, made about it. In an exhibition called the Living City, Archigram demonstrated the immediacy in urban products which had been predictably termed moribund and infantile by the older generation. They collected images from any part of the city – the accepted Pop iconography of spaceman, superman, robotman and woman – but presented them in a way and with a message that was new to architecture. The city was seen not as architecture (hardware), but as people and their 'situations' (software). It was these infinitely variable and fleeting situations which gave the real life to the city: in this sense 'the home, the whole city and the frozen pea pack are all the same'. Not only are they all expendable, but they are all products which interact with man on the same level, *the situation*.

THE PASSING PRESENCE

ELEPHONE
letter box
phone booth SITUATION as is GLOOP 7
man
clip on bin
trash cart
City of Westminster

170: Archigram: Living City Exhibition, 1963. 'The Situation', showing how various activities are brought together to create either an event or a system which is greater than the part summation; this concept of multivalence relates to Fuller's idea of synergy and Alexander's idea of a city system.

Although Archigram did not produce any radical departure in this exhibition, what it did achieve was an expanded definition of what the architect could consider as his provenance – the products interacting in and producing any situation.

Contrary to expectation, Archigram did not move the next step after this to 'beyond architecture', as it was to do later, but rather moved in a sense 'back to architecture' and produced a series of monumental objects (one hesitates in calling them buildings since most of them moved, grew, flew, walked, burrowed or just sank under the water). It was in this period, between 1963–5, that the extraordinary inventiveness and imagery of Archigram came to world attention. Cities were designed that looked like computers and molehills [**171a**], that crawled on the shoots of a telescope like Paolozzi's Bug-Eyed Monsters [**171b**], that bobbed under the sea like so many skewered balloons, that sprouted – swock! – out of the sea like a

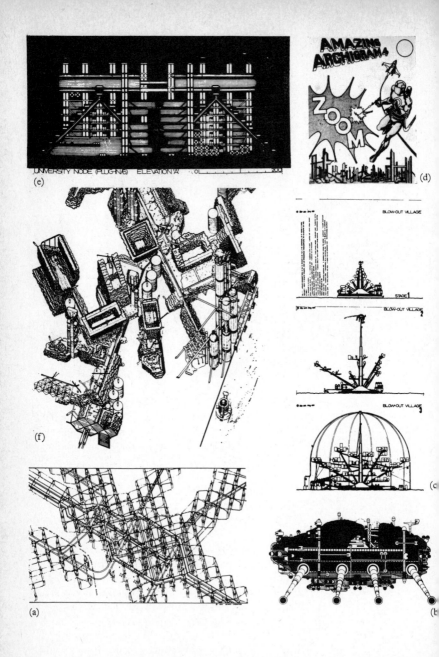

UNIVERSITY NODE (PLUG-IN6) ELEVATION 'A'

(e)

AMAZING
ARCHIGRAM 4

ZOOM

(d)

BLOW-OUT VILLAGE

STAGE 1

BLOW-OUT VILLAGE 2

BLOW-OUT VILLAGE

(c)

(f)

(a)

(b)

Tom Wolfian, hydraulic umbrella [**171c**], that zoomed down from the clouds flashing 'Destroy-Man! Kill-All-Humans', a space-comic-robot-zaap [**171d**], that clicked into place along pneumatic tubes, a plug-in plastic layer cake [**171e**], that gurgled and spluttered over the old city like creeping, cancerous, testubular, friendly Daleks [**171f**]. In fact none of this was new; at least not in the sense that a space capsule is new. Because what Archigram was essentially doing was consciously borrowing (stealing) images from any and every possible source and then turning them into urban forms: a method of *ad hoc* addition where the theft remains clear for everyone to admire. Only the whole, only the metaphor was new while the parts remained familiar objects from the past.

It was this mixture of old and new, particularly in Plug-in City, which proved so effective. Because, as Banham pointed out, it finally gave the world the visual equivalent of how it was to enjoy playing with an expendable, moving, locomotive city with its kit of parts.

The strength of Archigram's appeal stems from many things, including youthful enthusiasm in a field (city planning) which is increasingly the preserve of middle-aged caution. But chiefly it offers an image-starved world a new vision of the city of the future, a city of components on racks, components in stacks, components plugged into networks and grids, a city of components being swung into place by cranes.[25]

Finally after ten years, modern architecture had found its throwaway aesthetic.

Half the world gasped in horror. Sigfried Giedion, the grand old historian of the previous generation, fired off a missile condemning Archigram in the name of Le Corbusier who had just died,[26] and Doxiadis, another proponent of 'universal' architecture, complained:

The worst example of all [dystopias], however, appeared at a London 1963 exhibition where a walking city was shown, with all buildings conceived as steel tanks moving mechanically and certainly crushing, as tanks do, nature and any person outside them. The example is appalling, not only because it represents an inhuman conception of the city of the future by a small group of people, but because it received wide publicity without, as far as I know, any corresponding protest.[27]

Even much of the younger generation gagged at the image of those over-glutted monsters moving across the

East River as if they were about to swallow the rest of New York [171b]. Cries of 'Fascism, war machine, totalitarian', etc. were heard when this scheme was presented at the student conference at Folkestone. And finally, as if to prove things had gone too far, previous to this 'the Smithsons and Eduardo Paolozzi and people like that [called] rather necrophiliac revivalist meetings of the Independent Group to try and clear their names of being responsible for the present Pop art movement in England'.[28]

In fact, the Smithsons, with a consistency rare for them, launched a series of slightly-veiled attacks on the whole Archigram movement. They put forward the idea of a 'normalized', quiet aesthetic which got 'mechanicals under control', 'concealed' behind an 'Eames aesthetic' of 'good taste' (*sic*). All this should be 'without rhetoric' because now we are in a period where 'mechanicals' are usual and where 'mass production and the social arguments of past modern architecture are irrelevant!' Really what it amounted to was a 'special sort of anonymity of styling (a conclusion no one would have dared even think about in 1952)' – except of course the *Review* editors and everyone practising the International Style (which was then enjoying its greatest popularity). This seems extraordinary on face value: the Smithsons renouncing their 'But Today We Collect Ads' for a return to propriety and 'An Essay on the Doric'![29] Until one remembers that in the politics of modern architecture, whenever one person occupies a new, polemical position, it changes the positions of all the rest: the Smithsons had been outflanked on their left-tending extremism and had to occupy the reverse field in order to be heard. The way fashion was supported by information theory was brought home to the Smithsons now, in a very concrete and vivid way.

ARCHITECTURE IS DEAD

Meanwhile, Archigram was itself off on a new tack way 'Beyond Architecture', as the seventh issue in 1966 was called. Gone were all the enclosures and monumental service ducts and back again were the products of Living City. This Archigram and the next to appear in 1968 were designed as what would have been called a 'bag-o-pop-goodies' in the fifties or 'popular-pak' in the sixties, that is a collection of ideas and photos tucked into a folder for mailing, or just throwing away after consumption [172].

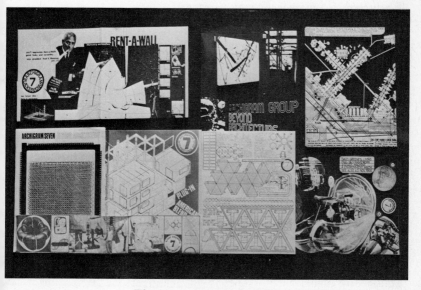

172. **Archigram 7, 1966.** Popular Pak layout. The death of hardware and the rebirth of software: 'There may be no buildings at all in Archigram 8.' **Archigram 8, 1968**: 'So we have no buildings here.'

The idea behind this is of course greater than just the specific gesture and amounts to a rejection of architecture, form and building in the name of software, content and servicing. As such the idea has a long genealogy which extends back to the caveman warming his hands in front of the camp fire, surrounded by his unpretentiously clothed family (software) and definitely outside of his cave (architecture) and the idea extends forward to such abstract mystics as St Bernard who could worship their imageless ineffabilities (content) without any constricting icons (form). But recently, in the twentieth century, this iconoclastic tradition has taken a completely secular turn and been tied to social and even political issues. In the twenties, for instance, a design in masonry with anything approaching an external colonnade would immediately bring the consistent epithets 'formalist, establishment, Beaux Arts', from a certain quarter. A similar nexus of ideas underlies the recent rejection of architecture in Britain. Thus Cedric Price's comment about the masonry colonnade of Caius College: 'just the Middle Ages plus 13-amp power points' [155].

In opposition to this stasis, Banham, Price and Archigram have put forward a new series of ideas which support dialectical creation and, hopefully, more personal freedom. The basic idea is to construct an environment which is so flexible as to be immediately responsive to the individual's wish:

What we want, clearly, is a miniaturized, mobile, cooking, refrigerating, sewage-disposing, VHF and three-channel-televiewing, trunk-dialling, dry-cleaning and martini-dispensing services robot with fitted ash-trays and book rest, that will follow us around the house riding on a cushion of air like an interplanetary hoover.[30]

In short, the Aladdin's Lamp which modern technology has made possible. This idea of a servicing robot which is sensitized to immediate wish fulfilment has a long American history culminating, in one sense, in the executive suite where all photo-electric doors open and close at the bat of an eyelash, and in another sense, in Buckminster Fuller's 'standard of living package' where all the necessities of life are immediately serviced. The idea also extends from the outboard motor (an attachable service) to the inboard motor (a built-in service) to the millions of self sufficient motors (all the appliances any housewife expects to have, from the mouligrater to the garburator).

Appropriately, the kind of software that Archigram projected in their 'Survival Kit' (a selection of products thought necessary for survival in the Living City) was similar in kind to the ideal American consumer: all disposable items of current interest from the recent *Playboy* to the latest hi-fi selection. The next step was made again by Banham who took the idea out of the house and put it back into the woods:

When your house contains such a complex of piping, flues, ducts, wires, lights, inlets, outlets, ovens, sinks, refuse disposers, hi-fi reverberators, antennae, conduits, freezers, heaters – when it contains so many services that the hardware could stand up by itself without any assistance from the house, why have a house to hold it up?[31]

Indeed why? In his article on the 'un-house', Banham projects the ideal image of the noble savage returned to nature, unfettered by his enclosure, unrestricted by his 'cultural wardrobe', even unconstrained by clothes; the only culture allowed is that which can be transferred through the transistorized tubes of the mechanical, standard of living altar [**147a**].

> But a properly set-up standard of living package, breathing out warm air along the ground (instead of sucking in cold along the ground like a camp fire), radiating soft light and Dionne Warwick in heart-warming stereo, with well-aged protein turning in a infra-red glow in the rotisserie, and the ice-maker discreetly coughing cubes into glasses on the swing-out bar – this could do something for a woodland glade or creek-side rock that *Playboy* could never do for its penthouse . . . From within your 30 ft hemisphere of warm dry lebensraum you could have spectacular ringside views of the wind felling trees, snow swirling through the glade, the forest fire coming over the hill or Constance Chatterley running swiftly to you know who through the downpour.[32]

The idea may be rather concupiscent for the city, where the movements of Lady Constance would be too closely observed, but such an un-house is obviously a country possibility as the great plethora of tents, campers and trailers make clear. Moreover, the means have existed for years. As Banham pointed out in the sequel to this article – appropriately titled 'The Great Gizmo'[33] – the great unsung genius of American ingenuity is the portable gadget: that unique piece of equipment which can be ordered by catalogue, sent through the mail (instructions enclosed) and easily used to transform 'some undifferentiated set of circumstances to a condition nearer human desires'. A main advantage of the portable gadget is that it is semi-autonomous (like an outboard motor or camera) and at best disposable, or at worst movable, so that it can leave the invaded wilderness semi-intact after civilization has marched through (as opposed to present artefactual deposits like cities or summer resorts which in some sense constrain future freedom).

It was the problem of urban as opposed to rural freedom which Archigram next tried to solve in its 'Control and Choice Living' of 1967 [**173**]. Basically, the problem was to find those 'systems, organizations and techniques that permit the emancipation and general good life of the individual' within 'a high density location'. The solution was a minimal set of fixed elements which increased in

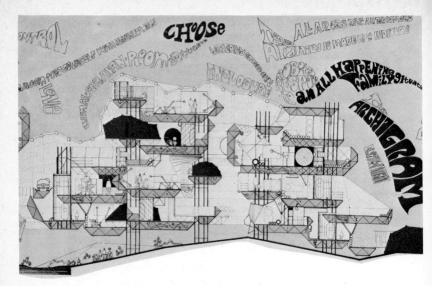

flexibility from the relatively permanent pylons to the completely flexible 'air-habs'. The latter invention was a combination un-house and blow-up satellite (that is an air-inflatable satellite). But the more interesting invention of this project was its miniaturization of the plug-in unit into smaller more flexible parts. Instead of being a whole capsule, it was now a series of 'conditions' which could be changed: wall, skin, roof, services, robot and even the electric car were merely 'conditions' open to the individual's wish. He could dial out a room or if this were

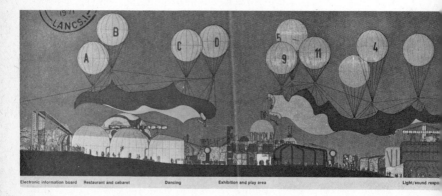

Electronic information board   Restaurant and cabaret   Dancing   Exhibition and play area   Light/sound respo

not desired drive the electric car into it and sprout out a room within a room. In effect, the services robot is now decentralized to include every part of the house.

Finally the same idea was applied to a different scale, the 'Moment Village' and 'Instant City' which could be anywhere 'on the whole surface of the world'. All that was needed was the servicing mechanism and some vehicle of locomotion, to turn everyone, who wanted the freedom, into an instant 'nomad' or turn a week-end retreat, such as 'Woodstock Nation', into a small city of half a million [174]. The point is similar to McLuhan's: in an imploded world where the same information can reach every point with equal ease, then all points are the same and the world is one, great, happy, tribal village with everyone reintegrating his sensibility (previously flattened by too many years of print). This is supposedly most true of those consumer societies where the same products are distributed. The particular freedom in this case consists in the freedom to choose between products. No longer is production the problem because there are less and less production constraints: what is difficult, takes time, talent, training and sensibility is consumption, or as the poet of *Archigram*, David Greene, has it:

> It's all the same. The joint between God-nodes and you, eat-nodes and you is the same. Theoretically, one node could service the lot. There's no need to move. Cool it baby! Be comfortable. Godburgers, sexburgers, hamburgers. The node just plugged into a giant needery. You sit there and need – we do the rest! Green stamps given.[34]

173. **Peter Cook: Control and Choice, 1967.** A system which is responsive to moods which are in turn mostly responsive to technological capabilities.

174. **Archigram: 'Instant City',** made up from balloons, travelling cranes, robots and light/sound equipment, 1969. Week-end Pop festivals such as Woodstock showed the potential form and content of such 'instant cities'.

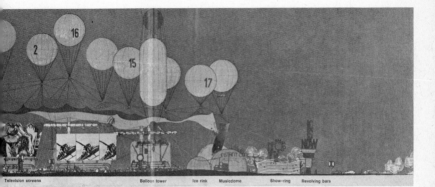

Television screens   Balloon tower   Ice rink   Musicdome   Show-ring   Revolving bars

One might ask, why be a nomad if it's all brought to you and it's all the same anyway? But the question merely brings up Archigram's intended lack of consistency: 'All sorts of inconsistencies appear (what is the meaning of consistency)...' Or as Banham put it: 'To show you have a mind, you have to change it.'

It is this intention to respond quickly and actively, no matter what the implications, which is at the base of the British *avant-garde*. Archigram make this clear when they summarize their philosophy: 'An active architecture – and this is really what we are about – attempts to sharpen to the maximum its power of response and ability to re-

spond to as many reasonable potentials as possible' [175]. They see pluralism and the quickness of reaction as of more importance than the actual content of reaction. Imagination is prior to politics. Yet naturally underlying their work is a very consistent nexus of ideas and hence political position. As for the philosophy, it moves very consistently from such ideas as flow, movement, expendability to metamorphoses, change, plug-in to consumer choice, freedom and individual emancipation.

Thus a paradox is that, in spite of all the claims, there is very little change – at least change of initial assumptions. However, there is a coherent development of these fixed assumptions and forms which comes from the constant critical feedback: from the first *Archigram* based on the flow of people through hardware to the latest scheme being built in Monte Carlo – the movement of software around people. The great contribution of the British *avant-garde* has been to open up and develop new attitudes towards living in an advanced industrial civilization where only stereotyped rejection had existed before, to dramatizing consumer choice and communicating the pleasure inherent in manipulating sophisticated technology. If these strategies will not solve the deeper social and political urban problems, at least they open up new alternative routes for thinking about consumer society and urbanism.

175. Archigram: Monte Carlo Entertainments Building, 1969– . A concrete dome under the park holds a grid of services on a six-metre module. Seating banks, stairways and service robots are all movable depending on location for the type of event involved.

8. THE INTERNATIONAL SCENE - LARGER THAN ARCHITECTURE

... I suggest the name 'Oedipus effect' for the influence of the prediction upon the predicted event ... whether this influence tends to bring about the predicted event, or whether it tends to prevent it. (KARL POPPER)

While architects have always been concerned with city planning in the past, it is really only quite recently that this concern has grown into a primary preoccupation. This is true of architects in Holland, Japan, Germany, South America, etc. - not only the countries we have already surveyed - so that we can actually speak of a growing international consciousness about urban problems. Part of this new interest comes from the realization that architectural solutions alone, however brilliant, cannot overcome the limitations of the urban fabric in which they are placed, while the other part comes from the general 'crisis' in urban affairs itself.

Most obviously the reason for this crisis is the massive migration of the people into the cities combined with what is variously described as the population 'balloon' or 'mushroom', or more melodramatically still, 'explosion'. It is a commonplace that more buildings will be built in the next forty years than in the total past history of man - and these will be built mostly in vast conurbations. But the causes for this crisis are really manifold and cannot be found in any one place or under any one traditional area of specialization - a situation which no doubt adds to the pervasive feelings of anxiety. Indeed one of the interesting facts which emerges from a study of urban problems is the circular way in which the thoughts and pronouncements on 'crisis' tend to exacerbate the deteriorating situation which they are meant to cure.

One can see this circularity or what Popper calls the 'Oedipus effect' in, for instance, the urban planning metaphors of 'cancer, decaying blight, slum and death'. First put in circulation by Patrick Geddes in the 1890s ('slum, semi-slum, super-slum to this has come the evolution of our cities') the metaphors of cancerous growth reached cancerous proportions by mid century. There was the summation of the work of CIAM in 1944 in the book and question *Can Our Cities Survive?* which was answered unequivocally 'no' by 1961 in Jane Jacobs's *The Death and Life of Great American Cities* or more simply by Doxiadis as just *The Death of Our Cities*. In any number of books and pamphlets the growth and haphazard operation of cities was discussed in eschatological and hysterical terms.[1]

Thus it was not surprising, given the general tenor of planning metaphors, that they had their metaphorical revenge and directed planners to design salubrious and sterile solutions which had overtones of the hospital and operating theatre. For this the solutions were themselves condemned in a similar language and tone to the original cancerous growth. The New Town and *Ville Radieuse* were seen to be as dead as the city they were meant to replace. Thus in effect what appeared more and more obvious in the early sixties was that an overriding part of the 'crisis' was caused simply by the fact that those people who were talking about it and supposedly trying to cure it were so committed to hygienic metaphors and professional values that their cure was equal in virulence to the very disease. Jane Jacobs's attack on the mentality of professional planners was representative of this new mood:

Who would prefer this vapid suburbanization to timeless wonders? . . . An all too familiar kind of mind is obviously at work here : a mind seeing only disorder where a most intricate and unique order exists ; the same kind of mind that sees only disorder in the life of city streets, and itches to erase it, standardize it, suburbanize it.[2]

From one attack to a counter-attack, from one self-fulfilling metaphor to another self-denying prophecy, the history of urbanism has lurched back and forth more like a wandering drunk than a clearly developing science and cumulative tradition. Perhaps it would be more accurate to say that there are many discontinuous traditions running side by side and often opposed which do in fact show internal, cumulative development. In any case, it would be premature and quite impossible to synthesize them towards one overriding direction. All that they have in common is an agitated, sometimes apocalyptic, pursuit of new solutions, new relations between form and content and new methods. These last vary, in their discontinuity, from such things as the attempt to re-establish urban identity to the sophisticated model building of systems engineers. No grand integration of these traditions will be attempted here, but for reasons of conceptual clarity they will be treated under common themes which do emerge – the defence and attack on the concept of 'place' and the development of the idea of an 'open society'.

PLACE - NON PLACE

FROM PLACE TO SPACE

During the 1950s the sociology of urbanism managed to achieve what amounted to a consensus about the effects of living in large metropolitan areas. This consensus was based on a convenient fiction, like 'economic man', which was necessary to discuss broad trends in terms of ideal types. Naturally, no real man ever behaved exactly as the ideal type which the economist formulated, but this did not diminish the power of the fiction because it allowed the economist to treat large statistic samples as if they were one, motivated thing. In the same way, sociologists formulated the image and personality of the urban man, and he was termed by at least one writer the 'Orgman',[3] short for 'the organization man'.

By the end of the fifties, sociologists had fixed the out-lines of Orgman. He was, as one might guess, basically nondescript, but in so far as he had a character it was 'other directed' rather than 'inner directed'; that is made up of socially conditioned drives rather than personally created goals. To fill out this composite portrait, he was characterized as a technician rather than a workman, a specialist rather than a 'Universal Man', a member of a committee rather than an entrepreneur, and a man in a 'Grey Flannel Suit'. As the book titles of the time portrayed the stereotype, urban man was likely to be a member of 'The Lonely Crowd' in which roles of efficiency were substituted for pre-urban relations of personal friendship; he was subject to and conditioned by 'The Hidden Persuaders' which lay behind every advertisement and were dreamed up by 'The Managerial Class' of 'The Affluent Society' which was otherwise controlled by 'The Power Elite' of the military/industrial 'Establishment'. How far this collective portrait actually applied I will consider later; at this point I only wish to accentuate the fact that an ideal type of urban man, Orgman, was a commonplace of cultural criticism and that for sociology, at least, he represented a well documented and interviewed standard. The researcher could point with pride to the overwhelmingly consistent evidence for his existence. A sceptic, such as Harold Rosenberg, might object that the myth of Orgman was really partially just the result of the sociologist talking about himself, talking in 'orgprose' about his own alienation and lack of roots – 'The Orgman is, with necessary additions and disguise, none else than the new intellectual talking about himself'[4] – but this did not necessarily refute the large amount of evidence. It all pointed to two inescapable conclusions: the life of urban man was becoming more anonymous and mobile; or in architectural terms there was an inexorable movement from symbolically rich systems to impoverished ones, from cultural roles to functional ones, or just simply from place to space [176]. It was as impossible to resist this movement as, in Le Corbusier's words, an 'overwhelming flood'.

BACK TO PLACE

Yet resistance was exactly what the mainstream of architectural activists tried. The history of CIAM to Team Ten, from 1953 to 1963, is basically the history of an attempt to re-establish the basis for urban identity: 'The feeling that you are somebody living somewhere', as

176. Ray Affleck and Partners; Place Bonaventure, Montreal, 1962-6. A huge urban scheme typical of the sixties, with a programme including, from top down: a hotel, offices and International Trade Center, Merchandise Mart, gigantic exhibition hall, shopping centre and various transport links including rail. None of these functions find appropriate or striking articulation, the lumpish mass being merely an echo of Rudolphian corduroy concrete [117]. Hence the characteristic transition from urban 'place' to semantically reductive 'space', surrounded by parking lots.

Peter Smithson phrased it. In fact to counter the usual Orgman feeling that he is 'No one living nowhere' the Smithsons put forward two strategies: the first called significantly 'Urban Re-identification' (1952) was meant to re-establish identity through a clarifying order based on 'a significant road hierarchy'. The second means for clarifying identity was completely different: through *inducing* the emerging order of 'human associations'. To see exactly what this meant, one has to recreate the thinking behind urbanism in the second quarter of this century.

Basically due to Government planning agencies and such unofficial forums as the CIAM, there existed a very strong consensus on how to cut up the city into conceptual chunks. Most planners then, as now, think in terms of land-use chunks and separate zoning. This is a perfectly natural thing to do since almost all cities can be divided up into similar functional parts, each with a certain statistical make-up. For instance, land-use statistics for the New Town of Reston, USA, cut the urban cake into the following typical slices: Residential 56·1 per cent, Commercial and Industrial 14·6 per cent, Public Rights-of-Way 9.8 per cent, Institutional 5 per cent, Open Space 14·5 per cent. In short, almost the same 'four functions' which CIAM laid down in the early thirties. If one starts with a finite area of space, one's first act is to differentiate it in terms of different mental sets or categories. Quite naturally there is a continual attempt to make these categories closer to the facts, usually called 'induction', but what is interesting from an historical point of view is really how inflexible or unchanging they turn out to be. For instance planners still make use of categories current in the thirties: the neighbourhood idea, the Radburn idea, the superblock, the separation of pedestrian and vehicle, the separation of the four functions (later, happily, augmented to five). A perfect illustration of the way these abstract ideas could generate a physical plan is Chandigarh, or even better, Brasilia [177]. From the air one can easily pick off the purified five functions: the public core to the south; the circulation cross which determines the overall

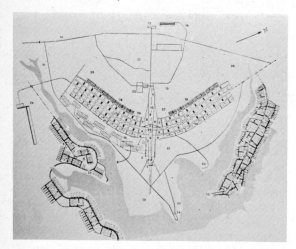

177a, b. Lucio Costa: Plan of Brasilia, 1956, and Oscar Niemeyer: Government Buildings, Brasilia, 1956–60. The architecture of functional zoning and Platonic purism. Here the two congress halls, in quarter spheres, are set opposite their secretariat and the State Chancellery in the background.

shape; the dwelling superblocks located on the cross-bar; the open, recreation space surrounding the city; and the work areas located along the spines.

It was so transparently obvious to architects in the early fifties that this kind of abstract Platonic thinking was inadequate that the major shift from CIAM to Team Ten occurred over this point:

It became clear [1954] that what goes to the making of life falls through the mesh of the four functions – lies, in fact, *beyond the scope of analytical thinking.* The meeting [of CIAM X] therefore attempted to formulate a *new way of thinking* about urbanism that would consider each problem as a unique example of Human Association at a particular time and in a particular place.[5]

In fact this 'new way of thinking' was really the old way of thinking dressed up in terms of new categories of human association – not surprisingly four in number: 'the city, town, village and homestead'. The Smithsons, who were largely responsible for taking over these categories from Patrick Geddes, were very conscious of the problem they implied. No less then three times in this Draft Framework it is insisted that these categories are merely a symbolic beginning from which to start planning for identity. In other words, as is also stated throughout, the architect must *induce* the emerging pattern of association: 'the appreciated unit'. Thus what is meant by

'induce' is probably two things: the architect must induce a new city growth as a magnet can induce a new flow of electricity in a wire, and the architect must induce his general laws about cities from the study of those facts 'at a particular time and in a particular place'. That the latter point was the main difference between CIAM and Team Ten was made clear in the argument over 'morality' between Walter Gropius and Jacob Bakema:

> To oversimplify, the idea of 'social responsibility' (Gropius) was directive, an imposition. Whilst the idea of 'Moral Function' (Bakema) is libertarian in that the onus placed on the architect is to seek out the existing structure of the community and to allow this structure to develop in positive directions. Induction instead of deduction.[6]

Thus this summary of a participant John Voelcker also lets loose one of the oldest philosophical hares, but before we start chasing it (in this section and under Parametric design, p. 351), it is important to see what it led to in

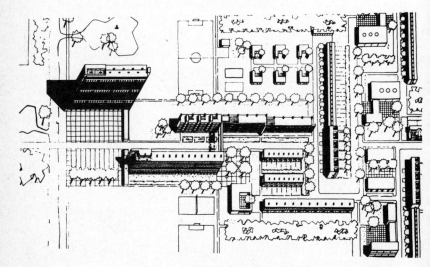

architectural terms. A characteristic project of Team Ten during the fifties was that of Van den Broek and Bakema [178]. In their Kennemerland Scheme they try to give identity to an urban area by mixing up low, medium and high building on a transitional scale. The highest buildings are placed closest to the main road, whereas the lowest ones are, conversely, in scale with the pedestrians, while the six-storey flats provide an intermediate link. Thus in effect the architects have tried to provide a greater variety of accommodation which can take into account more com-

178. Van den Broek and Bakema: Project for Kennemerland, 1959. Mixture of land-use and density to accommodate future growth.

plex social structures than the previous CIAM categories. Furthermore they have provided for an 'open-ended' growth in size which will not disturb the overall structure.

This idea of giving a comprehensible form to urban variety spread very fast throughout the world and was in fact brought to fruition by Van den Broek and Bakema themselves [**179**]. Their Marl Town Hall shows both the same complex articulation and room for expansion which characterized their earlier projects. Apart from these methods, the idea of a 'cluster city' made up of many centres of intensity instead of just one centre became another prevalent means of giving identity to an otherwise amorphous growth. In fact the idea of cluster planning was first put forward by Kevin Lynch in 1954; it

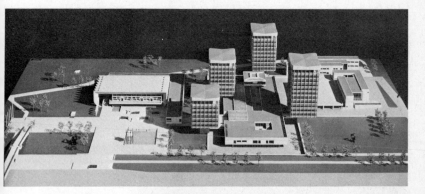

179a, b. Van den Broek and Bakema: Marl Town Hall, Marl, Germany, 1964–9. Variety of volume for different functions. The main civic functions are within the giant folded plate structure to the left, while administrative work goes on in the office towers (which are hung on tension cables and can expand vertically!).

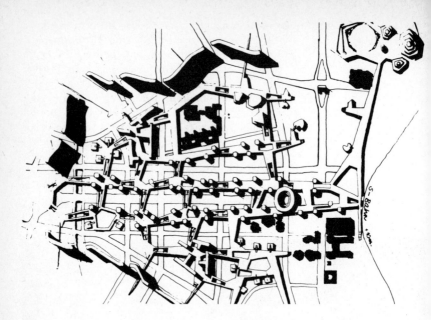

was next taken up and developed by Denys Lasdun in his Bethnal Green Cluster Block (1956) and finally generalized by the Smithsons to the level of a whole city, in their Berlin scheme of 1958 [**180**]. In this last scheme one may trace the rather hybrid thinking which still underlay urbanism. On the one hand, there was still the emphasis on functional separation and green fingers, but on the other there was an introduction of new concepts and 'keywords' such as growth and change, mobility and the inverted profile. This last concept provided for a 'Chinese Wall' of thirty-storey office buildings which were to surround the centre and give it a very strong identifying 'image'. In short, this project carried out the Team Ten manifesto laid down in 1954, because it provided a significant image' of the 'emerging patterns of human association' which would give 'identity' to a 'changing' area.

From an academic point of view, this cluster of ideas went back to its source and culminated in a carefully argued book of Kevin Lynch called *The Image of the City* (1960), which, curiously enough, did not mention the Smithsons or the European work at all. Perhaps the reason for this was that Lynch was trying to be even more em-

180. Alison and Peter Smithson: Berlin-Hauptstadt Scheme, 1958. Three new means of giving identity (the wall of buildings, the pedestrian net, and cluster blocks) which were later developed by Shadrach Woods [**202**], [**204**].

pirical and inductive than Team Ten; he tried to base his categories just on social surveys, questionnaires and field work. What he appeared to induce from these studies was

181. Affonso Eduardo Reidy: Pedregulho Estate, Rio de Janeiro, 1947–53. The curvilinear housing block which defines the 'edge' of a city has been a preoccupation of architects since Le Corbusier's schemes of the thirties. Here, however, the linear form does not have the further justification for use as a super-highway and serves mostly to 'make legible' the contour of the hill.

that there were five main categories which, if accentuated, could make a city 'comprehensible' to its inhabitants: 'paths, edges, districts, nodes and landmarks' [181]. Of course he admitted a conceptual bias at the start, which was that the 'legibility' of a city is absolutely necessary and crucial, but then no one would really quarrel with this assumption. After all, people have to navigate from one point to another, so that some means of order are necessary. However, what could be disputed were the particular categories and the idea that these, rather than others, should be accentuated. For how was one to know that the chosen concepts were right for the problem? They might not spring from an 'objective' analysis of the particular situation as Christopher Alexander pointed out[7] and would be just one more example of imposing deductive categories. Besides, the imposition of any such concepts is ultimately a political act which would be immediately felt by a particular culture. For instance, it would be gratuitous to apply them to an African village or a black ghetto in Harlem.

The idea that 'legibility', or the *form* of a city, was an end in itself, while never admitted into the morality of the idealist tradition, made its covert entrance through the projects of the Townscapers, the Smithsons and the Metabolist Fumiko Maki, all of whom made elaborate suggestions for making a city comprehensible. For instance Maki,[8] opposed to the categories of the former two, put forward such clarifying devices as 'compositional form, megaform and group-form' [182]. All this was acceptable. However, when the issue of the autonomy of form became more blatant than this and was tinged with historical overtones, it brought forth an outburst of moral opprobrium with the charge that the architect had retreated from 'modern architecture'.[9] In the sense that the idealist tradition stood for a comprehensible relation between form and content, inside and outside, the argument now had to be conducted on the level of plausibility and information theory, because most design situations,

182. Maki and Ohtaka: Shinjuku project illustrating three types of clarifying order: group form upper left, compositional form lower right, both on top of a large frame or Megaform.

like television sets and motor cars, had become both too complex and too simple: the interior had to work and the exterior had to sell. However, there were some architects who nevertheless tried very tenaciously to keep a resolution between the exterior and interior, task and symbol, and thus provide the multi-meaning in form which was the primary reality of 'place' in pre-urban societies.

Prime among these architects, and hence a strong influence on the idealist tradition in the sixties, was Aldo Van Eyck. He stated the proposition to Team Ten very clearly in 1959:

Whatever space and time mean, place and occasion mean more. For space in the image of man is place, and time in the image of man is occasion . . . Provide that place, articulate the inbetween . . . make a welcome of each door and a countenance of each window . . . Get closer to the shifting centre of human reality and build its counterform – for each man and all men, *since they no longer do it themselves.*[10] (My italics)

To substantiate the last point, Van Eyck said of Holland what could be said of most urban areas:

Instead of the inconvenience of filth and confusion, we have now got the boredom of hygiene. The material slum has gone – in Holland for example it has – but what has replaced it? Just mile upon mile of organized nowhere, and nobody feeling he is 'somebody living somewhere'.

But if all this were true, if the sociologists of Orgman were right, then there was an unforeseen problem for the inductivists of Team Ten. Because, as Van Eyck said, 'If society has no form – how can the architect build the counterform?' This could be rephrased to 'If society has no clear conception of itself, or even unconscious identity, then how can the architect induce the counterform?' Or put differently still, the problem was to generalize from particulars which turned out not to exist. A difficult, not to say impossible task. Strictly speaking of course, Van Eyck and the sociologists were wrong: society did have a form, a very complex one made up of many stratified layers each with its own identity, including the very recognizable identity of Orgman. But nevertheless, the problem of induction versus deduction remained.

One way this problem could be resolved was shown by Van Eyck himself in his paradigmatic Children's Home (1960). In the design of this he showed a continual oscillation from general to particular and back until the factual requirements had modified the original concepts and vice-versa. The building represented a near-perfect example of cybernetic design and the way out of the philosophic conundrum. In fact, Van Eyck was quite conscious of this when he insisted, in presenting the building, that 'to establish the "inbetween" is to reconcile conflicting polarities. Provide the place where they can interchange and you re-establish the original dual phenomenon.' What he called the dual phenomenon or 'twinphenomenon' of every object was its ability to function both as an autonomous whole *and* as a subordinate part of the next larger twinphenomenon. In short he argued that there is a continual relation between all the parts (or isolated 'functions' in the CIAM sense) and that these relations are just as important as the parts. By stressing these relations in his buildings and by continually relating the functions to form (and vice-versa in a lengthy cybernetic design process), Van Eyck achieved a multi-

183a, b (*opposite*). **Aldo van Eyck: Children's Home, Amsterdam, 1958-60.** Entrance and the semi-public space half-way in the Home.

184. **Aldo van Eyck: Children's Home.** Pavilions at the most private points providing sleeping above and play below for each age group.

valence of meaning which could establish the sense and reality of 'place'.

For instance, the entrance [183a] is made to serve many different but precise meanings in an unobtrusive way. There is a slight change of pavement pattern and the

313

slightest rise in step: two door-steps and two strange out-door lamps articulate the place between the outside world and the home. This subtle transition is a crucial event because it is between a somewhat alien world (the children are orphans) and their adopted home, both of which should presumably interpenetrate so that the transition both ways is mediated. This is further reinforced by providing a semi-public area beyond the main entrance [183b] which both invites the outside world inside and controls it by a series of subtle articulations – the administration bridge and bicycle ramp. A further sequence of transitional areas, or locks, continue until the completely private sleeping areas are reached [184] furthest

185a, b. Aldo van Eyck: **Children's Home.** Roof-scape and plan. A series of locks, organized on the diagonal, lead from public to private, from older children to younger. The repetitive geometry is varied in amount or broken in kind for functional and semantic reasons.

from the public and noise. In fact these areas are made even more private and personal by being raised off the ground and broken in their overall symmetry. That is, the general, repetitive geometry is made more particularized by being changed where a bedroom differs in size.

If one questions the use of elements, one finds the same dual phenomenon. There is a limitation to six main ele-

ments – dome, cylinder, clerestory, window-wall, brick
and doorstep – which repeat throughout and impose an
overall geometry. Yet this deductive order is broken from
below and changed to suit the particular context, either
by being distorted – the bedrooms cited above – or by
being varied in amount [185]. The same duality exists also
between the orthogonal unit and the diagonal organization, or the centralized domes and their off-centre sub-
division. While some of this variation is on the formal
level, it also has its counterpart in content, since Van
Eyck has provided for all sorts of possible activities, such
as wading and admiring one's reflection in surprise
mirrors, located in unlikely places.

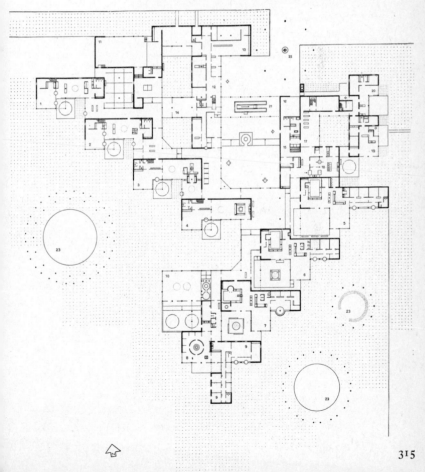

The reasons for analysing this building in some detail are that it is intrinsically a multivalent work and also one which has had the greatest effect on 'place-making' in the sixties. In two further projects,[11] Van Eyck augmented his methods for crystallizing place. One, a project for a Protestant Church, showed again that place was dependent on 'multi-meaning', or what he also called 'labyrinthian clarity'. By this Van Eyck meant (among other things) the complex clarity that results whenever similar forms are overlaid (in this case circles) to produce a dual order: both centralized and decentralized, etc. Another project, actually built, the Arnheim Pavilion, developed further the idea that place depended on the slow unfolding of an ordered experience. For instance, his description of the partially veiled, partially revealed approach [186]:

> Central to my idea was that the structure should not reveal what happens inside until one gets quite close, approaching it from ends.
> Bump! – sorry. What's this? Oh hello!

This idea that place is dependent on occasion, on multi-meaning and on the significant image was taken up explicitly all over the world,[12] but nowhere so strongly as in Van Eyck's native Holland.

In fact one could almost speak of a Dutch School springing from Van Eyck and related to the twenties

Dutch movement of *De Stijl*. The coincidence of forms is more than just fortuitous, as is the constellation of similar ideas. For instance the buildings of Piet Blom and Herman Hertzberger share with Van Eyck and *De Stijl* the quality of being made from many, small, autonomous units added together in complex relationships. The inten-

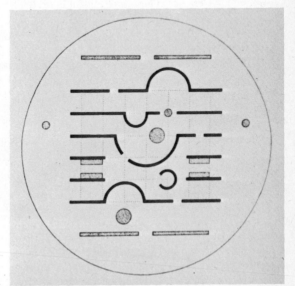

186a, b, c. Aldo van Eyck: Arnheim Pavilion, 1966. Place conveyed through the occasion of controlled suspense.

tion is to make 'A Village of Children, A Village like a Home' (Blom) or 'A house is a tiny city, a city a large house' (Van Eyck) or 'Every corner and every space must be programmed for multiple roles' (Hertzberger). I have deliberately cross-quoted here to bring out the undeniably similar thought patterns which continually revolve around the idea of multivalence. This is also evident in the built-

form – the factory extension by Hertzberger [**187**] which is built over the roof of an early twentieth-century factory. Hertzberger says that each unit of the whole 'must be open to the maximum number of interpretations', must be 'autonomous' and when added into a sequence always 'complete in itself'.[13]

Thus in effect these units are those 'twinphenomena' of Van Eyck which have a certain degree of autonomy and a great degree of multivalence. It is this last quality which is contrary to the general trend towards univalence of form, and abstract, neutral space. But it was not the only attempt to re-establish the reality of place through the multiple-functioning object. There were at least two other directions which reversed the large-scale trend towards impersonalization: regionalism and historicism.

187a, b. **Herman Hertzberger: Factory Extension, Amsterdam, 1964.** Autonomous parts which can be clipped on without disturbing the whole. Compare with the open-ended growth of [**201**].

THE CONTRIBUTION OF LOCALE

If multivalent architecture is one way of establishing place and giving a strong identity to form, then another obvious

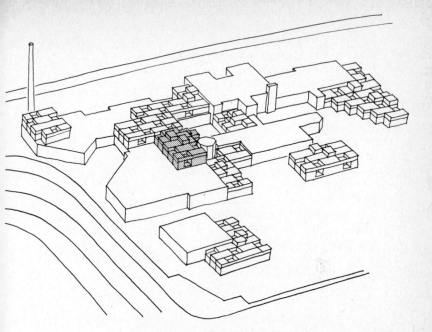

way of place-making is simply by taking into account the
locale and its traditions. This was perhaps the greatest
single departure of the idealist tradition in the late fifties,
from its previous claims to universality and it thus inevitably brought forth a flurry of attacks and calls to
order. Before considering these it makes more sense to
consider the departure in its most favourable and defen-
sible light since it would be unfair to treat it only in its
worst aspects. As for the most closely argued justification,
it occurred in Christian Norberg-Schulz's *Intentions in
Architecture*, 1964. Although he was not explicitly defending regionalism or localism, he was clearly making an
argument which had these implications. Basically it consisted of the overwhelming evidence gathered from
psychology that all form, including urban form, is perceived culturally: i.e. through schemata learned from a
culture. His conclusion was that meaning in architecture
is transactional between cultural intentions and the object
of perception: the one modified and the other in an endless
cybernetic process of hypothesis and correction. Thus
urban form was not and could not be entirely value-free

from all meanings, even if they were the single meanings which characterized the modern metropolis. The implications of this argument for urban design were not unlike those developed by Team Ten: to wit, the architect must set his new creation into a particular time and place so that it provided an intermediary link between the past and future meanings, between the 'urban villagers' and 'Orgman' (to instance the two extreme ideal-types).

Hence the theory underscored the relativism which was so repugnant to those who wished to establish architecture on an absolute base, and hence it justified the more responsible kind of regionalism which had been going on for ten years. The question became: what should the relation be between such universal requirements as the four functions and those determinants of the local situation? The answer, when implied, turned out not surprisingly to be a matter of degree: those solutions which were too overtly historicist or provincial were condemned, whereas those works which answered a specific need were praised.[14]

Of the latter one could say that the architecture was traditional almost in spite of itself. That is, the Scandinavian work of the Sirens was unmistakably Nordic in feeling, just as that of Max Bill and Eiremann was unmistakably Germanic in its tough efficiency. To underline the point about national identity, one only has to list the architects under their typical, national characteristics. Thus Scandinavian modern was generally nature-oriented and socially responsible, German was tough and ordered, Swiss was bourgeois and clean, Italian was vigorously modelled, sophisticated and slick to the point of decadence, Indian was strong and impoverished, Israeli was hexagonal and full of six-pointed stars, Japanese was constructivist, black on white, full of slight curves and so on [188].[15]

Of course all this national identity was continually eschewed or, where found, explained away and condemned. But this embarrassment did not make it any less of a fact. The point was that an architect would as inevitably use a traditional set of forms as he would speak a local language with national inflexions and certain built-in assumptions. Besides, the justification might continue, to avoid a solution just because it was traditional was as

188a, b. Kiyonori
Kikutake: Miyakonojo
Civic Centre, Japan,
1965-6. Accordion-like
auditorium over concrete
base. Although these forms
were justified in Metabolist
terms for showing different
rates of change, they clearly
show a Japanese flavour in
their bracket articulation.

silly as accepting it just because it was traditional. The same traditional form, the wheel, works equally well in a prehistoric cart as in a posthistoric turbine. To change it to a rectangle would amount to the sentimentality of the futurist.

In fact this was the kind of argument which Kenzo Tange used to justify his new use of old traditional Japanese forms. When asked by the Italian architect Rogers at a Team Ten meeting whether these forms were Japanese he responded hotly with the assertion that:

So-called regionalism is always nothing more than the decorative use of traditional elements. This kind of regionalism is always looking backwards . . . The same should be said of tradition. In my thinking tradition can be developed through challenging its own shortcomings and pursuing the meaning of continuum within it.[16]

What this meant Tange made clear in his other discussions of tradition as a catalyst: it sparks off new ideas and, as in the case of the wheel, can still be usable. For instance in his Kurashiki City Hall [189], Tange has used the traditional slight curve of the Torii Gate on the entrance canopy where it is both appropriately welcoming

189. **Kenzo Tange: Kurashiki City Hall, Japan, 1958-60.** The Metabolist distinction between different rhythms of change (long-term structure, short-term infill) is made clear. Compare illustrations **200** and **201**.

and useful. Furthermore he has used the interlocking beam method and post and lintel construction of Japanese architecture, because they happen to work with this particular organization. However, this cannot be said of the projecting beam ends and the interior which is a pastiche of Le Corbusier's work. In these cases, Tange has lapsed into the very regionalism he has just condemned ('the decorative use of traditional elements') simply because he has applied past forms without (as he insists) 'challenging' them. Nearly all of the Japanese Metabolist work, of which this is a part, has this curious mixture of being both radically new and radically old at the same time. For instance, Isozaki has proposed an urban system called a 'cluster in the air' [190] which is made up of many short-term elements bracketed on to long-term supports. The idea is explicitly based on traditional pagoda construction where brackets cantilever out from a central post to give (metaphorical) support to the roof. One could say in this case that the traditional distinction between load-bearing and decorative elements has been successfully transposed to make the Metabolist distinction between cycles of change. The forms, as opposed to being historicist, do not recall their previous use until *after* they are seen to work in their present context.

One could trace this permissible route to the past in much of the best work of the early sixties. While it

190. **Arata Isozaki: Clusters in the Air, 1962.** Traditional bracket forms act as a catalyst for totally new urban uses and also act as a semantic distinction between different cycles of change.

depended on function as a necessary justification, this was not sufficient; the other justification for place-making was based on the function of memory and memory-traces. A form which is from the past has a deeper set of relations and hence a wider spectrum of associations on which to call than an entirely new form. While this may be a positive disadvantage in most cases (because the spectrum is fixed in the mind and hence dead), in a few allusive cases when the past meanings are not quite known or sufficiently recollected they serve a kind of halo effect. That is, like a visual illusion, they continually suggest things not themselves. A good example of this kind of ambiguity is the Rinascente Department Store in Rome [191], which while entirely modern and functional is still disturbingly old and traditional. On the former level, one is at first taken in by the undulating, blank, exterior walls entirely appropriate

191. Franco Albini and Franca Helg: Rinascente Department Store, Rome, 1957-62. Is it a blank *cella* inside a surrounding colonnade or a Baroque palazzo with a heavy cornice? The corrugated walls contain service ducts while the exposed steel skeleton is extended from the wall for fire protection.

to a department store. The undulations contain the mechanical service ducts and the black steel cage is separated from the wall for reasons of fire protection. The six-storey elevation serves to unify the existing urban fabric. But suddenly one is conscious of strange overtones: an obvious attempt to fit into the masonry background of the Roman street produces an odd allusion. The same horizontal divisions, the similar projecting bays, the cornice with its heavy shadow line. Are these coincidental or the fruit of a painfully subtle attempt to show that the classical virtues of architecture are still attainable with modern means? This ambiguity has the effect of answering Team Ten's call for a 'memorable image', because it reverberates with overtones of historical place without ever quite admitting them. One could call it place-making through historical titillation which manages never to become erotic. Does she or doesn't she? The architect would never tell.

'THE RETREAT(S) FROM MODERN ARCHITECTURE'

But there were many critics who were determined to find out. The question really was if 'modern architecture' was becoming truly historicist – because then it was a retreat from the progressive ideal which very few would deny: that the architect must be relevant to certain qualities of contemporary existence. What exactly these were was a little difficult to establish, because of the great variability of contemporary existence.

Still there were fairly clear cases of historicist regression, such as the Arab villages of Frank Lloyd Wright and Walter Gropius,[17] the Neo-Gothic work of Yamasaki [120] and Rudolph and the Neo-Liberty of Gabetti and Figini. Some of this occurred in the middle fifties as did the more borderline cases of Brasilia [177] and the MIT work of Eero Saarinen – which were diagrammatic examples in a modern idiom of essentially classical buildings. Some of the first critical rumblings were sounded by Bruno Zevi, who identified 'the moral crisis' in Saarinen's 'Neo-Classical ideal' that 'geometry prevails over psychology, abstraction over reality, symbols over men'.[18] Soon after this, Le Corbusier's Ronchamp stirred up the 'crisis of rationalism', followed quickly by Utzon's Sidney Opera House which confirmed the 'crisis', since it was defended by Siegfried Giedion just at the same time as he was out on the field attacking the 'Playboy Architecture' for its irrelevancies [33].

The moral crisis of the idealist tradition reached its highest pitch by the end of the fifties when all consensus seemed to be breaking down about the permissible next moves. In his attack on Neo-Liberty (subtitled 'The Italian Retreat from Modern Architecture'), Reyner Banham tried to establish the plausibility of any moves made after the 'watershed' of the machine aesthetic, and condemn any historicism that referred to styles before this (i.e. the Liberty style was pre-machine aesthetic and *therefore* Neo-Liberty was irrelevant).[19] This caused a strong counter-attack by the Italian architect Ernesto Rogers (the questioner of Tange above) who pointed out the arbitrariness in reviving certain styles and ideas and not others. Banham wanted the revivals (if necessary) limited to periods which were culturally 'analogous' to the present, which was a reasonable enough idea. But, again, how was one to determine these? If one took the inductivist approach, then clearly, present society was pluralist enough to find just about any analogy with the past; which was clearly too much.

There was thus no easy way to determine the morality and hence the idealist tradition continued to define it in current examples which were close to hand. The prime one of these turned out to be none other than a work of Ernesto Rogers himself – the Torre Velasca [**192**] designed with his firm BBPR and presented up to the Team Ten forum for its judgement. The verdict was surprisingly harsh: Van Eyck, Tange, the Smithsons, and Bakema turned thumbs down unanimously, finding it guilty of 'eclecticism, regionalism and modernism' (Van Eyck's words).[20] Its crime? An ambiguous resemblance to certain historical forms such as medieval Milanese towers. This in spite of Rogers's protestations about functional determinants. Perhaps the reason why his claims did not carry any weight was that he had suppressed such contemporary realities as the parking garage and mechanical equipment behind semi-traditional forms and had thus failed to evolve the 'open aesthetic for the open society' (which

192. BBPR: Torre Velasca, Milan, 1957. Dwellings cantilevered out above offices for *rational* reasons; the form however happened to be similar to a medieval tower, for which coincidence it was heavily condemned.

was the ostensible charge against him). Even though the accusations against Rogers were somewhat true, they were out of proportion to their object which was being made to stand 'trial'[21] for the real culprits: Ed Stone, Yamasaki and others, who, not surprisingly, were missing from the forum.

Finally, these attacks culminated in the discovery that there was a veritable epidemic of heresies and deviations from the 'modern movement' around every corner and behind every façade:

327

The earliest retreat was what one may call neo-Accommodatory. Then there is neo-Liberty, the most talked about of these revivals. There is neo-Art Nouveau, which includes neo-Liberty and also includes neo-Gaudi. There is neo-*De Stijl*, there is neo-school of Amsterdam, there is neo-German Expressionism, and finally, to a certain extent neo-Perret.[22]

All these perverse departures were found by Nikolaus Pevsner in 1961, in a vein similar to those he had also found before in Michelangelo, Le Corbusier and Gaudi. No doubt such a zealous job of flushing out heresy was to be welcomed in those uncertain times of the early sixties, but one was left wondering at the appearance of so many fine shades of neo-this and neo-that, whether the judge was not taking altogether too much pleasure in the detailed inspection of every sin. Besides, could so much previously undiscovered historicism really exist, or was it more in the eye of the beholder? In any case, as a result of all these endeavours, the consensus of the modern movement was again established in relative terms. It was a question of how far too far one could go before place-making became 'infantile regression'.

FORWARD TO NON-PLACE

The whole question of the relevance of place took another turn, where it had originated, outside architecture in the fields of city planning, sociology and history. This time, with an impetuosity to be admired, it was decided that since the whole movement towards non-place was inexorable, one might just as well learn to accept it and, if possible, learn to love it. Effectively, one was told to stop complaining about Orgman and his ubiquitous Levittown, not just because all the complaints had no effect on him, but more because he was really a benefactor in disguise, with his many admirable gifts such as efficiency, pluralism, maturity and abundance.

This last argument was put forward in its most popular and influential form by Harvey Cox in his *The Secular City*, 1965. Basically, his argument consisted in summarizing the findings of urban sociology and concluding that the movement from tribe to village to city to technopolis is a liberating movement towards full maturity, because one is continuously cutting away superstition and the cosmologies of closed societies. Thus the qualities of uprootedness and pragmatism which characterize the Secular City were celebrated by Cox and this celebration caused a much greater storm of controversy than the usual condemnation would have, because it was (1) against the conventional wisdom of the time, and (2) took a position contrary to that of the Church from within the Church (in favour of secularization). The process of secularization, with its attendant 'death of God' philosophies, accentuated the possibility of widespread choice and self-determination. For Cox the ubiquitous question 'will it work?' replaced the metaphysical question 'what is it?' The positive use of anonymity and mobility replaced the agonizing over their existence. In short the whole attempt was to defatalize the environment of its gods, cut away the defeatist attitudes towards megalopolis and find out how to make the large bureaucracies work more effectively:

> The sore point is *not* that these massive bureaucratic empires exist: the problem is that we have not yet learned how to control them for the common welfare.[23]

If the attitude expressed here is not particularly exceptional, at least the book set off a controversy which clarified the social and cosmological issues in urbanism. For in *The Secular City Debate* (1966), the point became clear that the Secular City was like its father the Orgman, an ideal-type that never really quite existed in fact but whose presence was always just imminent.[24] That is, this debate pointed out how even in the most advanced technopolis there still exist a majority of systems which are pre-urban and personalized, either because they have continued from the past or because they have a tendency to crystallize in the present (in fact Levittown being one). Instead of a totally functional and rational form of behaviour replacing the former type, it was merely overlaid on it.

In effect then, the conclusion was that although there is a general evolution of culture from tribal to urban, from mythical to rational and thus also from place-oriented to space-oriented, still one mythology would overlay but not altogether annihilate the previous one, just as one city system would overlay but not entirely destroy the previous one. Thus any city, or culture, was shown to be a palimpsest of many separate sub-cultures each with its own mythology and spectrum of identity, extending from extreme tribalism and personalization to extreme anonymity and mobility. This conclusion was perfectly consonant with that of the urban sociologists Herbert Gans ('the urban villagers') and Melvin Webber ('the urban realms').

What Webber showed, and what he contributed to the concept of urban place, was that the physical place had less and less relevance in the modern world because the size and flexibility of communications were changing. Communities depended primarily, as their root-word shows, on communication, and that was increasingly independent of any particular place, then so too would be the community:

> The spatial patterns of American urban settlement are going to be considerably more dispersed, varied and space-consuming than they ever were in the past – whatever metropolitan planners or anyone else may try to do about it.[25]

The two ideas that Webber put forward to replace the place-community were the 'interest-community' and the 'urban realms'. The former, the interest community, was similar in concept to the functional organization, the bureaucracy, except that it also extended all the way up and down the urban realms from businesses to friendships. What these and other organizations had in common was their foundation in communication and common interest. One chose a job or friend more because of his interest and accessibility than because of his physical place. At least this was increasingly the case:

> Spatial distribution is not the crucial determinant of membership in these professional societies, but interaction is . . . we thus find no Euclidean territorial divisions – only continuous variation, spatial discontinuity, persisting disparity, complex pluralism, and dynamic ambiguity.

It was all an attempt to explain why Webber felt his much maligned Los Angeles was, after all, a most urbane place in spite of its sprawl: because its excellent communications allowed the same density of relationships that an old city did. As for the concept of urban realm, it bore out the inherent layered complexity of any city with the additional idea that this complexity extended to the individual himself. He was inevitably a traveller in space and time across the many subcultures that made up the city, or rather world-city. Almost all urbanites but the very poor spent their day in contact with many different groups and in the guise of many different roles, so that, even literally speaking, it often became necessary to have many different changes of clothes. The point was that it made less and less sense to speak of a man living where his house happened to be located, if in fact he lived throughout the world in a number of interest-communities. The difficulty was to find the new forms which corresponded to these new realms. Or, to take a different tack, one could say that as communication technology increased in efficiency and quality, then form was increasingly independent of content and hence place from space.

Thus to conclude the discussion of place, the last argument of Webber implied an answer that was surprising both to those who had attacked the idea of place (as regressive) and to those who defended it (as necessary). Since form was shown to be increasingly independent of content, then the architect could increasingly provide, or avoid, any strong images of identity he wished because they would have, in any case, less and less influence on the community. One could envisage a situation where physical planning was completely independent of social planning. In fact, urban sociologists such as Webber and Broady[26] questioned the pretension of architects to solve social problems with physical plans, calling it 'architectural determinism'. One would have to imagine from now on a situation where social and physical issues were worked out in parallel and then rather arbitrarily connected, just as this arbitrary connection is made between content and form in all sign systems.

It would appear then that the sanctions for place-making had lost their technical necessity and had become mostly psychological. One could provide place through the many means outlined above – the significant image, occasion, historical overtones, multi-meaning, etc. – or simply avoid it and provide 'no-place'. In fact, by a happy linguistic accident, it turns out that 'no-place' is actually the original meaning for the word Utopia, all of which would underline the non-physical aspect of the problem.

If the planner wanted to create that 'no-place' of the perfectly interacting community all he might do is increase the communications facilities and let the rest take care of itself. Or he might also decide that since all communication has to take place in some place, then he might give them all a memorable image. Either way, whatever he did its arbitrary nature was bound to appear and also the fact that it reflected a particular ideology or philosophy. The whole question of place–non-place was thus in a sense rendered obsolete by the growing awareness that all urban problems were based on certain shared values – a conclusion which brings us to a discussion of certain philosophies and their effect on urbanism.

CLOSED - OPEN

THE CLOSED AND OPEN SOCIETY

As already mentioned in the attack on Ernesto Rogers (p. 326), there was a very strong ideology underlying the forum of Team Ten, albeit an ideology whose main idea was to end all ideology (or at least hold it open to criticism). One can find this idea expressed by many different architects in many different ways. For instance the Polish member of Team Ten, Oscar Hansen, meant by an 'open architecture' one which could accept change without becoming obsolete and wasteful of resources, whereas Christopher Alexander meant one that could accept the multiple and expanded friendships characteristic of our age (rather than the closed, hierarchical *groups* of friends characteristic of a closed society).[27] These two meanings were similar to those which the Smithsons were putting forward to Team Ten in their idea of the 'open aesthetic': a formal system which was never finished, never imposing a limit to the possibility of functional change and never reminiscent of a past social order. That these meanings of the open society were in the air, especially among the English-speaking architects, was a testimony of the great, although indirect, influence of Karl Popper's book *The Open Society and Its Enemies.*

First published right after the War in 1945, the book was really an attack on all forms of the closed society from tribalism to the archetypal Platonic society of the West to Hitler's Germany. This last case was especially important because it was an immediate and relevant illustration of the way the uprooted and anonymous city dweller could be effectively re-tribalized – for among other reasons because he was such an easy and willing victim to all forms of progressivist myths and historical determinisms. Nazi Germany was thus in a sense the paradigm of all urban problems working in the worst possible mix. A tribal, closed mythology grafted on to the most advanced technological state. The way this strange marriage could come about was shown in Popper's closely reasoned and sometimes bitter book. Basically at the root of the closed, tribal society was 'the magical attitude towards social custom . . . Its main element is the lack of distinction between the customary or conventional regularities of social life and the regularities found in "nature"; and this often goes together with the belief that both are enforced by a supernatural will.'[28] In other words, what has been called here a belief in the natural and unalterable connection between form and content.

With such a naturalistic ethic and aesthetic, the next step is to find the underlying laws of natural change – whether economic, social or technical – and then predict the future state which must come about with inexorable necessity. This kind of 'historicism' (different both from architectural revivalism and the relativism of historians) Popper found underlying the most modern states from Marxist Russia to Hitler's Germany. In fact he himself had to flee this type of historicism and he dedicated the book called *The Poverty of Historicism* to those: 'Who fell victim to fascist and communist belief in Inexorable Laws of Historical Destiny'.

In opposition to these beliefs, Popper put forward a mixture of present social tendencies – the substitution of impersonal, rational functions for personal contacts – and the ideology of critical rationalism, both of which he combined together to give a picture of the Open Society. Now this ideal-type community with its basis in constant criticism and 'piecemeal, social engineering' was opposite to all forms of holistic, Utopian planning, and thus parallel to the general tendencies of post-war urbanism. The idea again was that one could only make measurable progress by changing a few things at a time, rather than all at once, because only this way were decisions controllable and values measurable. The attempt was to lessen error, get rid of mistakes and pursue positive goals (which could be rationally argued) one at a time. Popper outlined the long revolution, started by the Greeks and yet only still beginning, towards this perfect state of openness.

FROM UNICENTRE TO POLYCENTRE

For architecture the most obvious formal difference between an open and closed society became apparent in the question of centrality. The question which architects tried to answer in the late fifties was how to give identity to a polycentred sprawl [193]. As described already, cluster city and the inverted profile were two means which the Smithsons evolved [180]. A third and fourth were the ideas con-

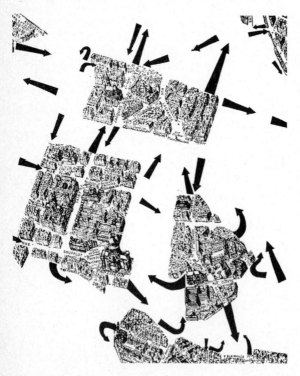

193. Guy Debord: Situationist Map of Paris, 1961. The modern city works and is experienced as a series of semi-autonomous 'chunks', each with their own identity and functioning. One navigates through a city by dividing it into meaningful chunks just as one cuts up the continual flow of speech into meaningful sub-sets. A problem arises in city planning when the functional and visual sub-sets become too discontinuous or even opposed.

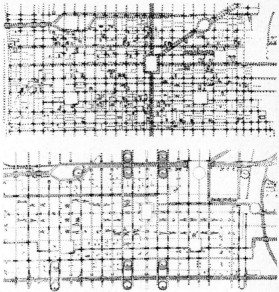

194 (*above*). **Alison and Peter Smithson: Soho Route Building and Road Net, 1959.** 'Flow is best served by a net', because at any junction point the driver only has to make one decision and the rotary space is the least possible. Compare [**207**]. The route buildings (dark) have internal movement systems such as travelators.

195 (*right*). **Louis Kahn: Existing and Proposed Philadelphia Movement Patterns, 1952.** Movement systems reduced to the same abstract language and treated as a continuous whole of 'traffic architecture'; a reduction which was necessary before city traffic problems could be solved in terms of time and quality of movement.

nected with road forms: the route building and the net [**194**]. The triangulated net, as the Smithsons and others have pointed out, is the best form for highway building in a city because it consumes the least amount of urban land at juncture points and is most open to flexibility and change. Yet their real reason for proposing this and their route buildings (buildings with internal moving sidewalks) was to provide 'the structure for a scattered city' which was on a gigantic enough scale (like the moats and fortifications of past cities) to give urban identity. This idea itself comes from a concept of 'movement patterns' which Louis Kahn devised as early as 1952 [195] and ultimately goes back to the Futurists who were the first to consider flow as a frozen, abstract thing-in-itself. But it wasn't until the Smithsons and others worked out the interaction of movement systems into the idea of the 'interchange' [196] that frozen movement patterns really came into their own. Because all too often one would think of a fast system by itself (air travel) whose benefits would largely be nullified by its relation to the environment (traffic jams around air-

196. Richards and Chalk: Interchange, 1966. Four movement systems together form a fifth which has to be worked out separately to make speed and transition an enjoyable affair.

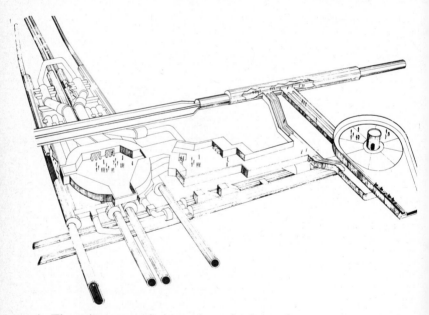

ports). The point was to devise an interrelated set of differing movement systems so that they and all their interchange points could be as agreeable and fast as possible. Although no integrated system has yet been built, much of the theoretical study has been made including the very necessary 'comparative anatomy' of systems [**197**]. These comparative studies themselves showed a shift in thinking away from the Utopian and *a priori* approach. Instead of laying down a master plan dependent on a few fixed variables, architects now began proposing flexible strategies. Their method would be to take an existing part of a city and add for instance a travelator, a mini-rail, a monorail and the interchange between them and then see how this would integrate with route buildings and the environment. All this led to new ways of evaluating movement. For instance the Buchanan Report (1963) showed that if the quality of 'environmental areas' were considered primary, then this would allow only a certain amount and kind of traffic. While the idea is obvious to anyone giving the subject a moment of thought, apparently no one had, so that, at least on the popular level, the

197. Brian Richards: The comparative anatomy of movement systems, 1966.

COMPARATIVE PLANS OF TRANSPORT SYSTEMS (drawn to the same scale) scale in feet 10 0 50 100 150 200	COMPARATIVE SECTIONS FOR 2 DIRECTIONS scale in feet 10 5 0 10 20 30 40	ECONOMIC DISTANCE BETWEEN STOPS OR STATIONS	PASSENGER OR VEHICLE CAPACITY PER HOUR ONE WAY	AVERAGE SPEED	ECONOMIC RUNNING COST PER CAR OR PASSENGER MILE
PRIVATE CAR ON SURFACE STREET IN CITY		as required	700–900 v.p.h. 1,500–2,000 v.p.h.	up to 30 m.p.h.	2·3–3·0d per vehicle mile 2·9 cents
PRIVATE CAR ON AUTOMATED MOTORWAY (AUTOLINE) SYSTEM	40' radius	interchange points 2 mile intervals (minimum)	7,200–9,000 v.p.h.	40–70 m.p.h.	as above plus possible toll
MINI CAR ON SURFACE STREET IN CITY (no other traffic) MINI CAR ON ELEVATED AUTOMATED ROAD (STARRCARR) SYSTEM	6' radius	as required interchange points ·25–·5 mile intervals	2,000 v.p.h. One 8' wide lane 3,000–5,000 v.p.h.	30 m.p.h. 15 m.p.h. (city use)	·5d ·5d
EXPRESS BUS ON GRADE SEPARATED ROAD (one lane)	66' radius	1 mile	1,450 v.p.h. 60,000 people	35 m.p.h.	4d 30 cents per car mile
DOUBLE DECK BUS ON SURFACE STREET IN CITY	70' radius	·2 mile	120 v.p.h. 7,200 people	8–15 m.p.h.	4·4–6d per car mile 2·5d per pass. mile
TELECANAPE (non-stop system)	47' radius	·2 mile	8,300	8 m.p.h.	·25d per pass. mile
CARVEYOR 4 SEAT (non-stop system)	12' radius	·2 mile	5,000 seated 10,000 seated and standing	15 m.p.h.	
MINIRAIL	50' radius	·2 mile	5,000 seated	8–15 m.p.h.	·25d
NEVER-STOP RAILWAY	15' radius	·2 mile	12,600 seated 18,000 seated and standing	15 m.p.h.	·25d

idea caused quite a stir. Perhaps less obvious and more shocking were the conclusions of Christopher Alexander who took time rather than distance as the point of departure. He came to the unlikely conclusion that the ideal-type street pattern should be in parallel rows of right-turning, one-way streets [**198**]. Although the distance travelled in most journeys would be longer, the time and psychic disturbance would be much less because there are no cross-streets and the speeds can be as high as possible. Finally the motor car would be used in a way which took advantage of its difference from the horse and foot (it can go faster and does not get tired) and the morality of animal energy would not be misapplied to the machine.

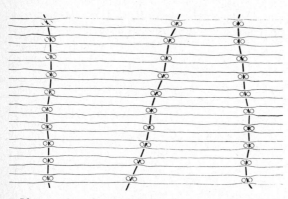

198. Christopher Alexander: Ideal type street pattern based on nine parameters. The logic of the machine has changed the statement 'I live X miles from downtown' to 'I live Y minutes from downtown'.

If one took an open-minded attitude towards what the machines (or media) were doing to the form of the city, then one reached the conclusion of Webber mentioned before. The car, the telephone, the TV and radio were all tending to disperse the form and give an even, suburban density throughout – which could be partially justified for its many advantages. For instance in the thirties, Frank Lloyd Wright had shown in his Broadacre City how the motor car really meant the possibility of more private, autonomous working conditions (hence independence), because it allowed people and their goods to be decentralized [**199**]. Herbert Gans showed in his book *The Levittowners* (1967) that contrary to the myth of Orgman the suburbanite often led a richer, more diverse and active community life than he did as a city dweller and than he

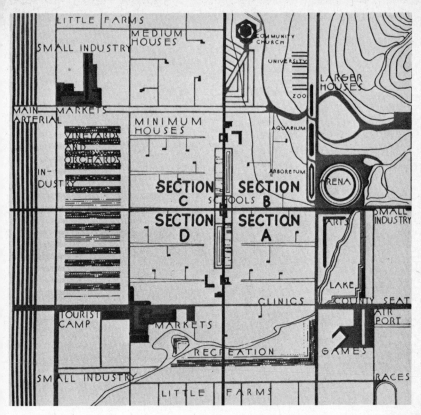

199. Frank Lloyd Wright: Broadacre City, 1934. Two advantages to the dispersed city: increased independence and the efficiency of home production in moving goods rather than people.

was supposed to (according to all informed opinion). The advantages of suburbia were its flexibility, malleability and freedom to change. Given these advantages and the inescapable fact of polycentred sprawl, a really important question became how to structure it.

'THE IDEAL INFRASTRUCTURE'

For a high-density area the idea of the megastructure became very popular in the early sixties and could be found on every student's drawing board, perhaps because of its irresistible imagery. The designer could manipulate such attractive things as pipes and ducts at a scale where they had an appealing virility and differentiation. For

instance the Metabolist Kisho Kurokawa put forward his theory of metabolic cycles which differentiated objects into six, separate *regenerative* rates. This sliding scale of change was then further used to differentiate the visual and functional elements into autonomous elements with 'intermediate' spaces between. Thus one could replace any particular element without altogether disrupting another on a different level, because of their loose connection [200a]. Or one could add or clip on an element without disturbing the whole [200b]. Or one could slowly transform a radial-concentric city into a linear chain without massive disruption [201]. These then were the three basic types of change (regeneration, growth, transformation) which the Metabolists sought to accommodate in

200a. Kenzo Tange and the Metabolist Team: Tokyo Bay Plan, 1960, model of office area. Different rates of change divide the city up into different levels of circulation and function. The road pattern, connecting sectors, works on a principle similar to Alexander's [198].

their megastructure. Whether in fact this megastructure was really 'the open form for the open and changing society', as they claimed, was another question altogether which Peter Smithson raised in his critique of the Tokyo Bay Plan.

200b. Kenzo Tange: Yamanashi Press Centre, Konju, Japan, 1967. Like the office area opposite, the architecture is made up from service pylons plus office bridges between, with empty places left for expansion.

201. Kenzo Tange: Tokyo Bay Plan. Different growth rates divide the plan into cycles and sub-cycles which can be easily added in five-year increments without internal disruption.

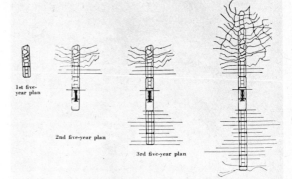

1st five-year plan

2nd five-year plan

3rd five-year plan

4th five-year plan

202a, b (*opposite*).
Candilis, Josic and
Woods: STEM idea at
Toulouse-le-Mirail,
France, 1961–. Open-
ended pedestrian streets
composed of all activities
and services and separate
from high-speed traffic
below. On the semantic level
there is a curious inversion:
the 'servant' spines
predominate over the
'served' activities in this
scheme and the Berlin
University.

203. John Andrews:
Scarborough College,
Toronto, 1964–6. A linear
pedestrian spine extending
from a central 'meeting
place' – left to the science
laboratories, right to the
humanities wing. Although
a linear 'stem', this scheme
would have great difficulty
in expanding because the
ends are too far from the
fixed, symbolic centre.

The difficulty was that the Metabolists had accepted the
projections of sociologists without seeing the political
problems they raised. Although they were perhaps right
to accept a megalopolis of ten million people comprised
largely (60 per cent) of those in 'tertiary industries' (communication), still they did not take into account the massive political and economic integration such a megalopolis
implied. In effect their massive concentration provided
an effective megastructure to plug into, but none to plug
out of:

One should be free to opt out, or to work in ways that might
in the long run redirect the economy. That would be a real open
society. The centralized nation-city seems to be the opposite of
this.[29]

Smithson then goes on to find the same inflexibility
built into the office bridges [200a] because they are all
supported on similar cores in each direction and because
they compromise the space below. Furthermore, he says,
the pyramid housing also compromises the internal functions by being on too large a scale.

Even if this critique were overstated, it did point to the
underlying *dual* aspect of urbanism, its physical and social
side, and the necessity for a smaller device than a megastructure – what Shadrach Woods called 'a minimum
structuring device'. In fact Woods proposed a series of
such devices which grew out of the previous Team Ten
thinking. For the Smithsons' idea of deck housing on a
linear route, he substituted the idea of 'stem' [202 and
203]; and for their idea of a two-dimensional net, he sub-

343

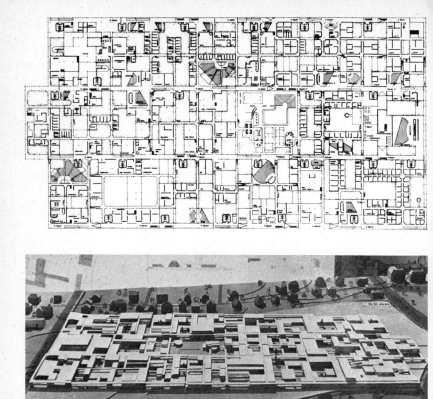

stituted the idea of 'web' [**204**]. These substitutions were of course new creations, but they nevertheless did reflect the overall climate of opinion as can be seen by Woods's ideological summary of closed and open patterns: 'A point is static, fixed. A line is a measure of liberty. A non-centric web is a fuller measure.' Thus again we have the idea of the open form being polycentred and extendable in one or two directions, qualities which signify the open society. But there is another idea of openness which is different from those before:

No one of the stems has been given greater importance than the others . . . so that it may become polycentred through use. The arbitrary decision of the architect as to the nature and location of 'centres' is replaced by the real choice of the people

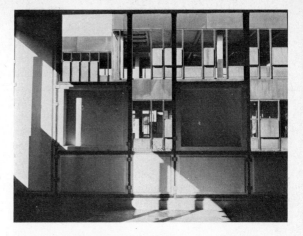

204a, b, c. Candilis, Josic and Woods: web idea at the Free University of Berlin, 1963- . The web is basically the stem idea in two directions, with a major and minor axis. The small scale, only three storeys, was more in keeping with economic realities than the megastructure. **(c)**, interior, under construction.

who use the system. It is assumed that the need for symbolic or representative geometry has disappeared – if it ever existed.[30]

In other words open form means here that the people have the right to choose and mould it without having the architect impose 'symbols, monuments or crutches of authority'. In adopting this *laissez-faire* attitude, Woods does not account for the fact that perhaps the people will choose symbols and monuments, because he believes that this need has disappeared with the coming of the 'universal society'. Of course this belief or wish on his part is questionable, as the survival of pre-urban patterns shows. But still what is of interest in Woods's work is the curious paradox to which this kind of belief leads: the fact that, as in Louis Kahn's distinction which Woods has borrowed, the 'servant spaces' (the stems) predominate over the 'served spaces' (the activities). This is the strange inversion of means and ends which has its counterpart on a semantic level: the paradox is that the infrastructure does not symbolize nothing, as Woods intended, but rather in a very emphatic way merely systems of movement.

Not surprisingly, Woods shares this semantic inversion with the Futurists, Kahn and most of the other urbanists because they often end up by reifying the means – the infrastructure; but that does not necessarily detract from their ideological contribution. For they all clarified the form of the open society as polycentred, open ended and

345

changeable. Again, it might be objected that on a literal level the radial-concentric city was in fact more open, flexible and expandable than a web. Indeed there were many comparative studies which just sought to determine the literal parameters of each form-type.[31] But most of these tended to confirm the prevailing ideology.

For instance, Colin Buchanan's *South Hampshire Study* (1966) again compared the centripetal structure with the linear and grid and like so many others also concluded that the most flexible was 'the directional grid' [205]. The coincidence of this form with Woods's web seems more than just fortuitous until one remembers that almost every American city has been planned on a grid-iron with major and minor routes of traffic. Indeed the Directional Grid appears everywhere in modern urbanism from Doxiadis's *Dynapolis* to the year 2000 plans for Washington DC. With such an overwhelming consensus one is left with the impression that the time is ripe for the definitive comparison of all city forms according to the same parameters. No doubt this will soon be made when someone can afford the research and computer time. For the present, however, one is confined to comparative studies made on limited and often exclusive parameters.

Some of these have questioned the superiority of the orthogonal system and have put in its place hexagonal and hybrid systems. Indeed nearly every real system in the world is a hybrid of some kind and most of them, for historical reasons of growth, also happen to be concentric. Yet under the pressure of further growth even the radial, concentric systems seem to distort on a smaller scale along a series of orthogonal axes, so that they soon come to resemble Dynapolis, or the stellar plan with many rays shooting out along communication lines. The hexagonal star is a 'natural' type of growth and settlement pattern as shown long ago by Christaller because it is the most efficient occupation of space. That is, only the hexagon can be packed tightly with itself and still have its centre close to all points on the circumference. A circle cannot be closely-packed and a square has the corners far from the centre. So, given certain parameters, the most economical city form is the hexagon and it has been so favoured by many theorists. One of them, Lionel March, has combined it with the proposition that it makes much

205. Colin Buchanan: Directional Grid, 1966. Similar to Woods' WEB idea, this form along with the hexagon [206], trihex [207] and star-shape became the form-type for the open society.

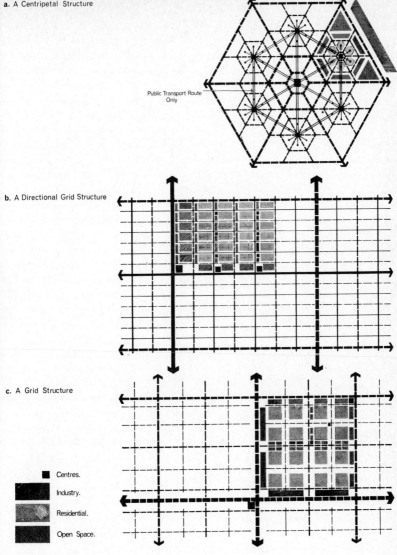

a. A Centripetal Structure

Public Transport Route Only

b. A Directional Grid Structure

c. A Grid Structure

■ Centres.

▨ Industry.

▨ Residential.

■ Open Space.

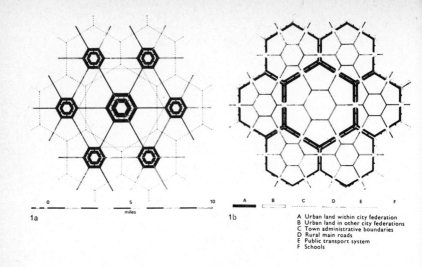

1a

1b

A Urban land within city federation
B Urban land in other city federations
C Town administrative boundaries
D Rural main roads
E Public transport system
F Schools

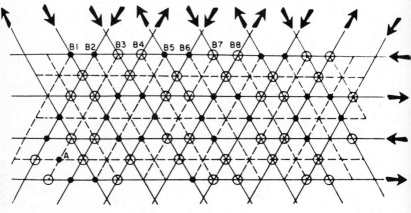

ONE-LEVEL INTERSECTION ●   PEDESTRIAN PATH — — —
TWO-LEVEL INTERSECTION ○

TRIHEX

	Length of path Car : Pedestrian	:	Intersections Total : 2-level
AB1:	4 : 5	:	3 : 2
AB2:	6 : 5	:	2 : 2
AB3:	5 : 5	:	4 : 2

ORTHOGONAL

Length :	Intersections Total : 2-level
6.53 :	6 : 3
2.47 :	2 : 2
4.53 :	4 : 2

more environmental sense to turn the present-day 'blob-like cities' inside out into 'line-like cities' and organize these on a hexagon (or grid) of transport lines [206]. The advantages with this linear pattern are that growth is not self-congesting and that one has all the amenities right at one's doorstep (with urbanity at the front door and country at the back). Furthermore, contrary to expectation, one can still achieve higher densities and a higher volume of traffic by building in lower buildings along lines of a ribbon strip than in tall point blocks. This can be shown empirically in such new urban forms as Route One City, Florida, or Los Angeles's Wilshire Boulevard – all downtown shopping centres flattened into a line by the car. Further thinking along hexagonal lines has answered one of its major short-comings which is the unusual geometry and constant turnings. A new pattern for occupying urban space called 'the trihex' [207] combines both the distributional advantages of the hexagon with the straight-line advantages of connected triangles.[32] The two geometries mesh to satisfy certain measurable parameters.

But all these models – the web, the directional grid, the trihex – were in a sense rendered obsolete by the appearance on the scene of 'the ideal infrastructure' itself, or at least a project of that name by Yona Friedman.[33] The significant thing about Friedman's infrastructure was not the particular ideals, which were rather prosaic, but the fact that he went about devising and presenting them in a way which allowed public comparison and choice. Here was an example of Parametric Architecture (discussed next) that gave a hint of what was possible on the level of an open, consumer democracy. One could imagine a situation where the measurable factors in an architecture were clearly specified and the public could choose between alternative designs in a very sensitive way (not even now possible with consumer products).

What Friedman did was to formulate all possible spatial organizations into a series of explicit axioms and then to devise a system (the Spatial City [208] and [209]) which could change from any one type to another with the minimum of friction and loss of energy. Actually, as one can see, he has just put the directional grid or web up on elevated shafts and turned it into a three-dimensional

206. Lionel March: Parameters of Form, 1967. Cities organized along lines of a hexagon give certain advantages: better access to amenities, easier growth, greater space saving and open space.

207. Le Ricolais: Trihex, 1968, combines the close-packing and distribution of the hexagon with the straight-line travel and single decision of the triangle.

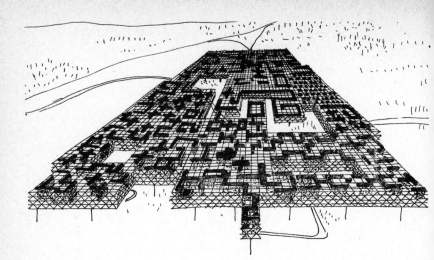

growth form. But the axiomatic basis for doing this is the important thing. Friedman starts off with the exaggerated claim that '. . . this system of axioms covers completely any human activity', which it does not. But he does specify those activities that it covers, and shows their spectrum of organization in terms of extremes:

Space can be organized in (A) a continuous way, or (B) in a discontinuous way. Groups can be formed on (A) a biological base (family), or (B) on a social determinant base (same age, interest, religion, etc). Distribution can be (A) centralized (you have to go to a defined place for a commodity, for example theatre), or (B) homogenized (you can get the commodity at any place you are, for example, television).

Now, one of the two techniques applied for every field of these axioms give us eight combinations. These eight combinations present all possible organization patterns (i.e. town patterns) . . . this allows us to comprehend intuitively any possible towntype as *predominantly* fitting into one of these patterns. (The eight extremes are then listed.)

(a) Existing occidental towns belong to type B A A, characterized by discontinuity in space organization, family groups and centralized distribution (you have to go to the department store, to your working place, to the central town), etc.

Now the objections that one could make to this study are that the axioms are too general to be of much interest and that they are quite arbitrarily chosen and not ex-

208. **Yona Friedman: The Spatial City, 1961.** This three-dimensional web can undergo all possible transformations with the least amount of friction. The 'ideal infrastructure' carries all the services and functions on a space frame supported at 200-feet intervals and would ideally disappear when fully clothed by a living culture (as opposed to other infrastructures) (see [202]).

209. Wimmenauer, Szabo, Kasper and Meyer: City Superstructure above Düsseldorf, model, 1969. A spatial city to be built over the old one without, as in Friedman's schemes, ultimately replacing it. Structurally, cities could bear such *ad hoc* additions and the only things prohibiting them are building codes and land values.

haustive as Friedman claims. While these objections are fair and relevant, they do not nullify the model unless we expect it to be perfect. But we may only demand that it work adequately well and reduce certain forms of error. For instance, Friedman explicitly claims for his ideal infrastructure that it can just change from any one of the eight possible forms to another with 'maximum efficiency'. So we clearly know his utilitarian criteria and his eight parameters and we can thus adopt his package or reject it consciously and selectively. Another criterion he makes clear is that his mechanism would disappear when used: '. . . these objective elements (the infrastructure) don't determine the character of the town. The character of a town should arise intuitively, formed by the inhabitants themselves (as in the historical past) or by their trustees.' In other words the ideal infrastructure withers away like Marx's ideal state, as opposed to becoming the final goal of the design as in so many megastructures. The servants do not take over from the served.

PARAMETRIC DESIGN

The general trend towards rational design and making criteria explicit reached its apogee in the logical tradition with the systematic design methods of the middle sixties.

351

Prime among these methods were those outlined by Christopher Alexander in five key works. The first of these, *Community and Privacy*,[34] took thirty-three parameters for an urban house and showed how (by breaking them up into interacting sets) they could be resolved together to produce the most satisfactory balance of conflicting forces. Each force, or each parameter, was carefully scrutinized to see if it was important and was not biased by semantic weighting. Then they were divided up into tightly interacting bundles, or sets, so that their conflicts could be worked out on a low level (where it is much easier to resolve differences). Finally they were synthesized into a whole which satisfied all the various needs between community and privacy.

The immediate objection to this method, as before, was over the arbitrary choice of criteria. For instance the Smithsons in their 'Criteria for Mass Housing' and Buckminster Fuller in his 'Universal Requirements of a Dwelling Advantage' had listed completely different kinds of criteria for the house and, as the titles suggest, with completely different semantic weighting. How was one to get the right list or best list or complete list? Secondly, how was one to choose the right theoretical model to synthesize the list? Alexander admitted in his next book, *Notes on the Synthesis of Form*, that the choice of both parameters and logical model was essentially arbitrary and not fully justifiable.[35] But this did not mean that the method was pointless (as many critics contended): rather, not infallible or perfect. It was just a method which could reduce certain kinds of error such as incompatibility and omission of criteria.

Besides, in any design problem, there are always *certain* needs which can be specified within maximum and minimum limits, and furthermore, as Alexander pointed out,[36] the choice of a logical model could be varied with the type and complexity of the problem to be solved. For instance, to give an example of parametric design which became rather prestigious in the sixties, there was the problem of moving a man to the moon and back without losing his goodwill and life. This could be conceptually divided into the sub-problems of designing a sufficient environment for him, inventing the necessary rockets and selling the idea to the tax-payer. Obviously three different kinds of design model would be used in each case, but common to all three would be the conceptual similarity of the parameter. Certain parameters, with their maximum and minimum limits, had to be invented and then satisfied.

The method which Alexander outlined in his *Notes* consisted of first listing all the possible criteria one could think of which might be *relevant* to the problem. (There is obviously no indisputable criterion of relevance itself.) Next, one was to break these criteria down into as small physical entities as possible and cleanse them of their inevitable semantic and cultural weighting. The idea of this step was to avoid those preconceptual categories which, as we have seen, have circumscribed all designers from the CIAM deductivists to the Team Ten inductivists. In other words, the idea was to be more empiricist than Team Ten by basing one's design on thousands of atomic needs and minute data rather than such arbitrary, verbal sets as 'street, village or infrastructure', which might not apply at all. In effect, Alexander wanted to find out what 'the problem wants to be' in itself, rather than what the designer wanted the problem to be.

[All designers'] Concepts and categories, besides being arbitrary and unsuitable, are self-perpetuating. Under the influence of concepts, he not only does things from a biased point of view, but sees them biasedly as well. The concepts control his perception of fit and misfit – until in the end he sees nothing but deviations from his conceptual dogmas, and loses not only the urge but even the mental opportunity to frame his problems more appropriately.[37]

Although obviously Alexander was overcompensating for the negative power of preconceptions he was nevertheless stating the extremist form of inductivism in a clear manner. One could just as well take the opposite position and insist that the designer should proceed from pre-existing categories, just as Mother Nature works with old, hackneyed hypotheses, but whether or not one agreed with the basic assumption, at least the extreme inductivist position of the logical tradition was now out in the open.

To return to the method, after brainwashing the criteria of all their built-in values, one was to synthesize them into interrelated sub-sets and provide each one of these with a form-diagram [**210**]. Finally one could take these form-diagrams and put them together as an hierarchical 'tree'. The result was fantastic. Not only did the final form reflect all the criteria (141 in the case of the Indian Village), but the criteria were even unusual and interesting (such as No. 10, 'Need for elaborate weddings'), and the form was pure, forceful, honest and strictly relevant. It had all the passionate intensity and rigour of the soap bubble – which in fact was also a pure response to specifiable parameters:

In this case, the formal descriptions and the functional descriptions are just different ways of saying the same thing; we can say, if we like, that we have a unified description of a soap bubble. This unified description is the abstract equivalent of a constructive diagram. It is the aim of science to give such a unified description for every object and phenomenon we know.[38]

And it was the aim of Alexander to give a unified description of how one should design every object we know from the teacup to the city, so it was not suprising that he next found a major fault in his own previous method and the fact that this fault also happened to underlie the mistakes of all past urban designers. Thus, contrary to his former hierarchic sub-sets, as he said in the title of a most influential essay, 'A City Is Not a Tree', nor should design

210. Christopher Alexander: Form Diagram for an Indian Village, 1962. Not only does the form reflect a great number of parameters, they are even interesting ones.

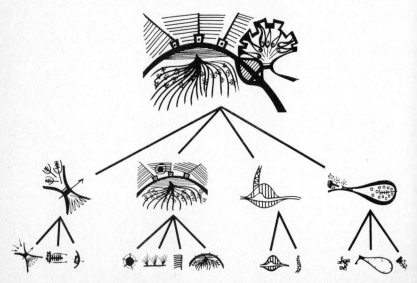

be either. To see what revolutionary implications this harmless sounding phrase carried, one has to reconstruct the conceptual perplexity into which it was introduced.

As mentioned before, part of the conventional wisdom underlying urbanism in the sixties was that the city was not *just* a physical or 'artistic problem' as Jane Jacobs put it. Nor, as she also put it, was it *just* a statistical problem in 'disorganized complexity' as the CIAM and others, who divided it into functions, had claimed. Rather it was both these things and in addition a problem of 'organized complexity', a problem akin to biological and life processes which could only be understood with new conceptual tools. These were the conclusions of Jane Jacobs's seminal book on urbanism. She wanted the planners to look for 'unaverage clues' such as the safety of streets and opportunity for jobs which gave a hint to the underlying, 'real' processes of a city. Now all of these processes not only 'fell through the four functions', but they also fell through the other conceptual categories of 'Cluster, Change, Metabolism' which were meant to replace them. No matter what new biological concepts and lively key-words an architect might propose, they seemed inadequate fixes and allowed too many criteria to 'fall through'. The same was true of New Towns designed for variety, complexity and richness [211]. In fact, even the solution that

211. Hugh Wilson and others: Cumbernauld New Town, Centre, Scotland, 1956– . Like Hook, another New Town project, Cumbernauld is an attempt to achieve the urban diversity, variety and life of old cities by mixing functions in a compact, 'downtown' centre. While the intentions were positive, the results were less than perfect because of the oversimple methods used: for instance, the Centre is not closely connected to the neighbourhoods and the children's life is carefully removed from it.

Jacobs herself proposed, of designing for processes, was inadequate because all it would lead to was the formalization of frozen processes (as in a Metabolist City).

Into this conceptual distress, 'A City Is Not a Tree' fell like a bountiful nut. It was picked up immediately by many magazines and re-published around the world, gaining particular influence in Italy, France, England and Japan. It was given the Kaufmann Award for being one of the most effective statements in the field of design published in the last five years. Why? Because it changed the previous tree-like simplicity of form into a lattice-like complexity and it showed how the latter was the only adequate way of dealing with those complex processes that Jacobs had pointed out.

Basically, the argument was similar to Alexander's previous one with the emphasis again on the way the designer's categories predetermine constricting forms, except now he found exactly this fault with his own previous sub-sets. In fact, he claimed, any historic or 'natural' city is rich in 'overlap' of sub-sets which accounts for their diversity, or multivalence, or in Jacobs's terms 'organized complexity', or in layman's terms 'life'. Thus the answer was to find a richer set of connections across the sub-sets, or what he called a semi-lattice:

> We may see just how much more complex a semi-lattice can be than a tree in the following fact: a tree based on 20 elements can contain at most 19 further sub-sets of the 20, while a semi-lettice based on the same 20 elements can contain more than one million different sub-sets [212].

> This enormously greater variety is an index of the great structural complexity a semi-lattice can have when compared with the structural simplicity of a tree. It is this lack of structural complexity characteristic of trees, which is crippling our conceptions of the city.[39]

Given this new way of thinking and method of design, it was now at least theoretically possible to solve urban problems in their rich complexity. An extension or refinement of these ideas took place in Alexander's next two books, called *Houses Generated by Patterns* and *A Pattern Language Which Generates Multi-Service Centres*. As can be seen by the titles of these books, there was a shift back towards deductivism (the 'patterns') and the *a priori* (the process of 'generation'). In fact, the attempt

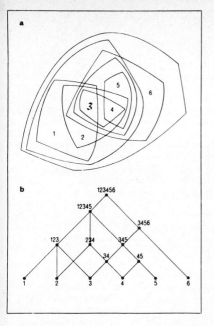

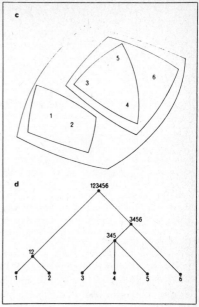

212. Christopher Alexander: Semi-Lattice (*left*). compared with Tree (*right*). The former corresponds to organic cities which have grown in linkage and diversity over time, while the latter represents the modern city which lacks this diversity and overlap.

was to establish an *a priori* basis for city design which had parallels with Noam Chomsky's *generative grammar*. Alexander explained the basis for the sixty-seven 'patterns' he evolved:

A pattern defines an arrangement of parts in the environment, which is needed to solve a recurrent social, psychological or technical problem.

And he went on to apply these patterns to one specific design problem – the *barriada* or squatter settlements of Peru [**213**]. The results were unique and radical: Alexander and his team designed a new, cheap construction system out of bamboo and urethane foam and they incorporated such traditional requirements as the *mirador* and *sala* without being historicist or condescending. Furthermore, the squatters could continue to build their own houses as well as choose their type and location. It was the incorporation of many such parameters into their design which distinguished it from those of the other architects who entered the government-sponsored competition. Nevertheless, there remained some unresolved problems with

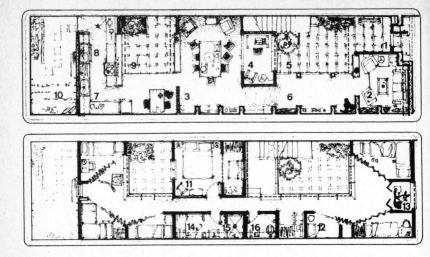

the parametric method of design,[40] the prime among which was the fact that it was only a method and not a mode of action for getting things done on a practical, city scale. For this, other approaches were more relevant.

CONSUMER PLURALISM AND ADVOCACY PLANNING

Two general tendencies of urbanism which have so far been mentioned are the trend of certain architects towards more rational methods of design which specify their parameters and the trend of cities towards larger impersonal organizations. These two trends have opposite implications for society. The former means that quite likely a true 'parametric architecture' will grow that reflects some of the qualities which its founder (in name anyway), Luigi Moretti, demanded. It will be clear and crystalline at the points where parameters can be specified with exactitude (like those of a soap-bubble or bridge) and everyone will be able to read off those determinants with little trouble, or slight training. In short, it will be a public architecture which makes manifest those qualities which it must 'satisfice' (to use a word of parametric designers). The point in using this ugly word is to underline the permissiveness or 'slack' inherent in any parameter. One could

213. Christopher Alexander and Centre for Environmental Structure: Generic plans for a barriada house, Peru, 1969. The ground floor (above) is divided by patios into a public formal part and a family area. The first floor (below) is divided into sleeping alcoves on each side of the parents' bedroom. A 'mirador' looks over the street life below.

say that as long as a product gets between certain, vague maximum and minimum requirements, then it 'satisfices' the user's or consumer's demand. That this 'satisficing' is partially malleable by such things as advertisement is a fact well known to large corporations – which brings us to the other side of the question.

If it had long been an assumption of capitalism that supply followed demand, then by the sixties it had become equally clear that demand follows supply, when this supply is dependent on advanced technology. John Kenneth Galbraith outlined and popularized the qualities which attend any advanced industrial state.[41] First of all, as he pointed out, there is a tendency for wealth and power to accumulate in the hands of a few large corporations: the five hundred largest in the United States produce almost half of all the goods and services of the entire society. Secondly, to ensure their own survival and security, there is a necessity for them to keep pace with a changing technology which is all the time becoming more complex and sophisticated. In order to do this, they must call in expert opinion, which in turn effectively means that the knowledge of any one group or individual is not enough for a decision to be made upon. This decentralizes decisions. For instance, to use an example which Galbraith cites, to launch the 'Mustang', Ford Motor Company took three and a half years and spent nine million dollars on engineering and 'styling' and fifty million just on tooling up for special production. The tools alone were so specialized that Ford had to call into play the 'organized knowledge' of many experts in order just to solve such sub-set problems as the chassis or brake. Who designed the Mustang? Not the Board of Directors, nor the 'Director of Styling', nor the consumers through their representative the market researcher, but rather the vast and deep 'technostructure' – a term Galbraith coins to signify the anonymous sets of experts and specialists who worked out satisfactory answers to specifiable parameters. With so much at stake in terms of time, money and experts, the Mustang had to work, the public had to be conditioned to accept it, or simply, it had to sell. This it did in fact beyond all expectations.

In spite of its unusual success, the Mustang is still a paradigm for the products of large industrial corporations.

The counter example, the 'Edsel' which did not sell in spite of the same process, is only an exception to the general rule that where sophisticated products are concerned demand follows supply with an amazing dexterity:

The general rule with fewer exceptions than we would like to think, is that if they make it we will buy it.[42]

Thus we have an inversion of both the capitalist ethic and the morality which underlies almost all designers and architects. For the Open Society or consumer pluralism which they purport to serve in fact turns out to be a partially Closed Society which limits the amount and sensitivity of choice. One kind of freedom is being exchanged for another; the freedom to buy an article tailor-made to one's needs is being exchanged for the freedom to select from a limited number of technically sophisticated and conformist products [214]. Or put in the terms of urbanism, the right of interest-communities to determine their specific needs and livelihood is being limited by the affluent majority.

214. Consumer Democracy possible through vast, new electric technologies. Potentially, if all the parameters of a product were cross-referenced, then the individual consumer could specify his needs which would then result in a range of alternative products. Such technologies and the 'Consumer Movement' pose at least two means of making the supply more responsive to individual demands.

It is this kind of the formulation of the problem which the concept of 'Advocacy Planning' was meant to solve. First outlined by the planner Paul Davidoff in 1965, the concept of advocacy was taken over direct from legal practice and applied to urbanism.[43] It was meant to supplant the idea that a planner would design for the community from his disinterested point of view, with the idea that he would represent a special-interest group as a lawyer would in court. The confrontation of many such advocates all pleading the minority interests which they represent would more easily lead to the interests being satisfied than presently occurs under the majority system. For in the present system planners avoid a strong defence of the good life as seen by a minority group, and they certainly avoid defending assumptions which might threaten the *status quo* and their own position within it. The result is that there is no effective advocate for either the larger public-interest or the smaller minority-interest. Or, to revert to the example of motor vehicles, there is no legalized effective spokesman who objects when the cities become polluted or who insists that a low-priced electric car be developed – two extremes of the demand spectrum. What happens in the majority of cases, in the United States at any rate, is that the ideology and interests of the vast middle class are served while everything else suffers. One thus has the paradox of private wealth and public squalor, or generalized growth and increasing inequality, or rising productivity and rising slums.

Advocacy Planning has grown since its inception into a fairly large movement with Advocate groups now helping some poorer communities in Boston, Harlem, San Francisco, Syracuse and many other American cities. Basically, these groups have aided blacks in the ghetto and poor urban whites in preparing renewal plans and taking advantage of complex, bureaucratic aids. Yet, as Robert Goodman argues in *After the Planners*, their positive results in the way of new housing and community services have been non-existent.[44] They can stop most socially disruptive activity such as highway building through a community, but, Goodman contends, without 'mini-socialism' or a 'decentralized, democratic socialism', their constructive efforts are doomed to failure. Thus many of the Advocate Planners, like Goodman, see positive urban action only possible within a radical, political movement, and they have tried to create various links with the activists on the Left – anarchists, Yippies, socialists and Marxists. The political nature of planning and architecture, on a ideological as well as practical level, was finally being acknowledged. Any city planning for the future would have to take into account the pluralistic goals and social forces whose nature was irreducibly political.

As Karl Popper showed in many works discussing the Open Society, the future is theoretically unknowable, because (among other reasons) if one knew it with certitude then one could take steps to avoid it and it would no longer come about. Or another reason why it is impossible to know the future is that whatever it will be, it will be largely shaped by inventions which are presently unknown and in theory unpredictable. We cannot know when the next transport vehicle will be invented which solves many of the specified urban problems, yet we do know that when it occurs it will have a great effect on the environment (which is one reason that urbanists try to predict and hasten its existence).

In spite of such obvious difficulties, many prophets have offered their predictions as if they were certain and based on scientific laws of historical inevitability, or a rigid determinism. Such prophecies are termed by Bertrand de Jouvenel futurology because like so many other 'ologies' they claim to be scientific, or at least knowable in principle. Although this claim is of course false, still the suffix 'ology' can remain to indicate its relation to other bogus scientific pursuits such as astrology, and scientology. For the more modest and reasonable study of coming events the term 'futuribles' was coined by Bertrand de Jouvenel to signify that the future is partially open and that we can choose from a 'fan of possibles' if they are clearly and explicitly set forward.

The actual working of futuribles in everyday life can be seen for instance in the architect designing for a set of possible urban futures, or the businessman making certain selections among a group of speculative stocks. The future implicates the present and the past so inextricably in a changing society that everyone is forced into the game of futuribles almost by necessity. Any large corporation devotes some of its money to 'Research and Development' and any urban planner maps out at least three predictions of certain parameters: a maxima, minima and likely state. While the field of futuribles is still in its infancy, there are already several corporations and forums which are continuously involved in forecasting and they have already evolved fairly sophisticated methods for doing so.[45]

These methods can be roughly divided into three main types: the normative forecasting, or predicting the future one wants; the projective or likely future assuming no major shifts in ideology and power; and the invented future or the inventions which certain experts think likely to occur. To start with the last one first, there is for instance the Delphi technique which amounts to a Gallup Poll of experts and when they think certain inventions are likely to occur [**215**]. As one can see from the kind of invention

215. Delphi Technique, 1967. Experts predict when an invention is most likely to occur, given a certain latitude on either side of the white dot.

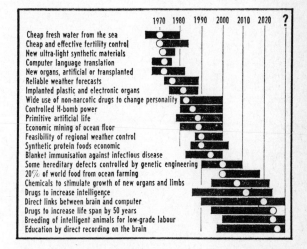

they predict, their hopes follow their interests and projects. The new creations are almost always technical rather than social, although obviously they have social implications. Still it is very significant that no group of sociologists or politicians has been as active and daring as the scientists. Perhaps this conservatism can be traced to the fact that society looks to all social forecasting as shades of *1984*, or the kind of determinism associated with futurology. Nevertheless, as de Jouvenel insists, the quality of life is for most people much more affected by social factors than technical ones; and so one would expect prediction to concentrate on the former:

Take this very simple example – the life of the German family since 1913. Would we say what has principally affected it are changes resulting from technological progress? Surely it was far more affected by World War I, the ensuing inflation, the Great Depression, the advent of Hitler, World War II, the division of the country, and a protracted crisis of conscience.[46]

Nevertheless in a field such as urbanism, one wants to know the likely technical inventions since these have such an influence on form and location (if not content). The following scenario will contrast what an 'expert', Gabriel Bouladon, thinks might happen in the field of urban transport with what a 'committee', headed by Buchanan, thinks likely to happen (the projective method).

Bouladon predicts that by 1982 the central urban areas will be so glutted with movement and pollution that all cars will be banished except silent, fumeless, miniaturized, electric ones that are small enough to be stored on 'linear,

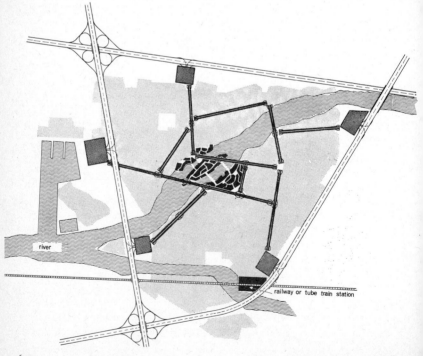

river

railway or tube train station

mobile parks'.[47] In even tighter urban centres, such as the historic core, the car will be altogether replaced by such conveyors as moving sidewalks (which can move up to ten miles per hour). But surrounding these two inner rings will be many transfer points and large car parks which connect up to faster means of travel – like gas turbine cars and the turbotrain (capable of speeds up to 200 mph) [216]. In addition to this there will be supplementary systems, the most exotic and desirable of which is the 'Pneumatic Logic Tube Train'. This will be a completely transparent train riding on a cushion of air, driven by air pressure and capable of up to 500 miles per hour. Indeed the speeds of all types of movement will increase fantastically just by electronic devices which will keep a high, steady, average flow.

This set of predictions, or 'scenario', is now almost feasible from a technical viewpoint. What makes it unlikely from a realistic point of view are the conservative factors in society combined with the cost. So one wants a cost/benefit form of prediction and a projective method which first projects all the present trends and allows for minimum social effort. For instance, Buchanan predicts that in Britain the amount of motor vehicles will increase three or four times by the year 2000. He also assumes (falsely to my mind) that even with the technical developments the future vehicle will 'present most of the problems' it does today.

Therefore *certain minimum strategies naturally follow* if environmental standards are to remain at least on the level of today: through traffic will have to be channelled away from 'environmental areas'; a hierarchy of distributors will have to surround each area, and a series of local tactics will have to be used such as closing off streets, increasing parking costs, public transport and so on. As one can see by these proposals, their monetary cost to society indicates a *shift* in relation to the past whereas their nature indicates just a *drift* from past planning ideas. It seems likely that society will not meet the financial shift, but will try to drift through its urban problems which are quite low on its priority scale. Thus one could make the conservative prediction that given the advantages and appeal of the automobile it will never disappear, but rather evolve itself into something which includes all its advantages and

216. Gabriel Bouladon: Transfer System Network for the Future, 1967. Discontinuous transfer systems lead from the parking lots and railway stations towards the centre of the city. Compare with the dual-mode system which is continuous [218].

transfer systems

parking

historic city

c

new city

0   500   1000   1500   2000
                          metres

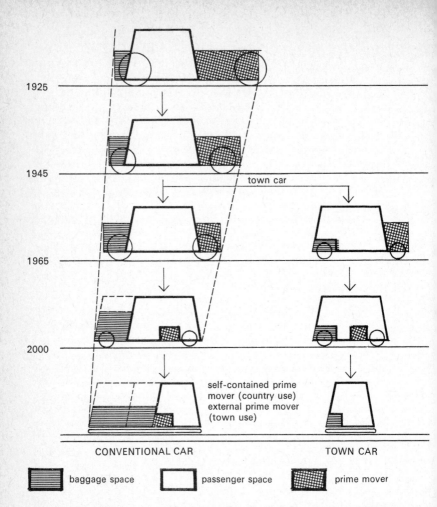

1925

1945

town car

1965

2000

self-contained prime
mover (country use)
external prime mover
(town use)

CONVENTIONAL CAR

TOWN CAR

baggage space   passenger space   prime mover

excludes all its disadvantages (fumes, smell and noise). In short, a mini-electric or steam car [217]. In biological terms, the species 'car' will assimilate those genes which will make it evolve slowly rather than be killed off suddenly by other species (as Bouladon suggests) and thus contrary to Buchanan it will not present 'most of the problems it does today' except congestion. Yet congestion and slow urban speeds are still not aggravating enough ills to warrant the shift in money and invention which Buchanan demands. At least from the most conservative view.

217. Gabriel Bouladon: Car of the Future having evolved so that all the present negative parameters are absent.

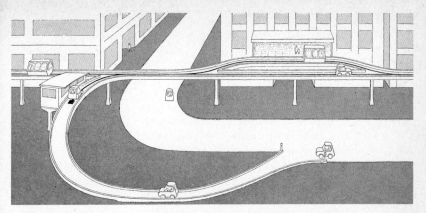

218. Systems analysis applied to urban transport comes up with the unexpected conclusion that the most economic and 'beneficial' system for American cities is a modified form of personal transit shown here. The suggested personal transit system combines the advantages of a private car with the speed of a rail system called the 'guideway'. Average speeds of 60 miles per hour are predicted by the model. The two advantages of systems analysis are that: (1) it is much easier to build a *model* of a city and test that and not the city itself, and (2) the parameters from many different systems may be dissected out and recombined positively. See Hamilton and Nance, 'Systems Analysis of Urban Transportation', *Scientific American*, July 1969, p.21.

Whether or not these conservative priorities are right or wrong is another question completely, which brings us to the normative type of forecasting and back to the political realm. Here the ideal would be to set before society the alternatives open to it, with the cost and benefit of each one weighed on a comparative scale. The difficulties of this, in spite of such sophisticated methods as 'systems analysis' [218] are staggering simply because of the difficulty of deciding and measuring what is valued. And yet any attempt to avoid this measurement will lead, by default, to the present condition where certain unstated values are just *given* their respective priority. This lack of formulated choice becomes a particularly ridiculous affair expecially in such affluent countries as the United States where freedom is lost without ever acknowledging its existence. Society does not formulate intelligible alternatives; no one sees *the possible routes on a comparable scale*. Decisions are thus precluded because they are not thought about. In this sense, it becomes 'irresponsible' not to speculate, critically, about the future.[48]

Modern architects were, of course, aware of this fact, as can be seen by the large number of their normative forecasts (compared to other fields). The *Ville Radieuse* of Le Corbusier, the *Citta Nuova* of Sant'Elia, or Fuller's Dymaxion World were all attempts to predict and direct the future according to explicit norms. In a sense they were all too successful in their attempts and we are now coming to see that their variety of norms was too limited. This perhaps explains the major shift in normative forecasting which is now more flexible in its approach. It proposes developing plans and alternative strategies rather than one final goal. On a bureaucratic scale, there are the 'development plans' for each city in Britain, or the 'model cities' programme in the United States; or on a theoretical scale the time-dependent plans of Doxiadis, or the phased sequences of Archigram [219]. What distinguishes these predictions from those of the past is that they actively seek multiple alternatives rather than single ones, and, at best, provide a constant feedback mechanism with their clients so that, as the slogan went in the sixties, it can be 'planning with rather than planning for'.

There are very few examples of this type of forecasting. In fact the Goodmans' *Communitas* (revised 1960) is virtually the only example of an urban 'futurible' which clearly shows the economic, social and physical parameters in a way that allows comparison and choice. Yet no matter how rudimentary the Goodmans' models are, they are more developed than other schemes simply because the social and physical values are explicit:

219. **Archigram.** Future Possibilities over time rather than a single goal of one time. Shown is the metamorphosis of a house in phases to 1985.

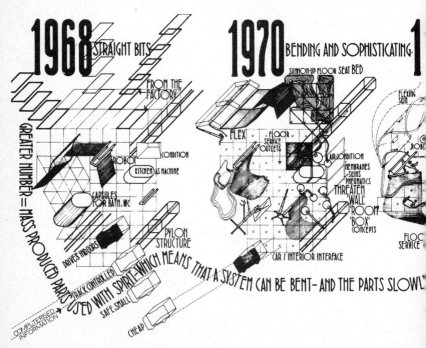

We have chosen to present our thoughts in the form of three community models of our own. Given the complex and *incommensurable* factors of the subject, this seems to us the simplest as well as liveliest method of presentation: to give typical important *value-choices as if they were alternative programs and plans.*[49]

The second model, or paradigm, which the Goodmans actually favour over the other two [**220**], is crystallized around one basic value: that work can be a positive way of life. Thus they propose on the physical side such efficient mechanisms as a partial home economics (it is often cheaper to move things than people) and on the social side such ideas as diversified education (so that the worker can understand all parts of his labour, from the initial invention to production and consumption). Yet around this major value of liberated work, they show what other values are necessary to sustain it. So that one *can clearly see and choose* which overall set of values is desired while cutting away the rest. Effectively then one has on a large scale what other Utopian architects have given collectively on a small scale: a set of possible futures. One can imagine,

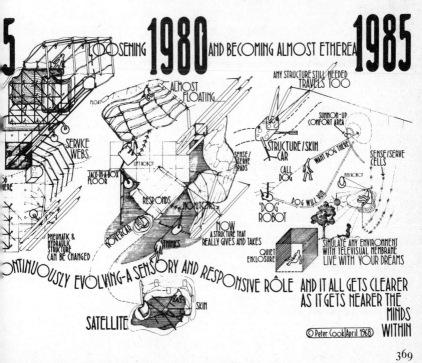

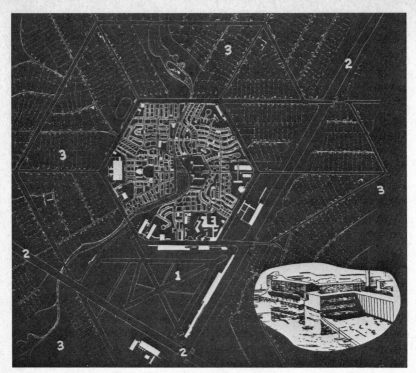

as the result of such efforts and other disciplines such as comparative anthropology and urban sociology, that in the future urbanists will project bundles of related values and forms which people can select and discard with the full knowledge of what they are getting.

It is obvious that we are still very far from having the kind of open philosophy and self-determination advocated by Popper, de Jouvenel, the Advocacy Planners, and the Goodmans, but at least we can see what is desirable. That is a political arena, and effective 'surmising forum' as de Jouvenel puts it, where power is decentralized and in the hands of those who need it; and a philosophy of purposeful change which supports men in pursuit of a future goal. Whether this power and philosophy would make any difference in the actual course of future events is of course an open question, but at least it is clear that most of the other competing questions which regard the future as determined are closed.

220. Paul and Percival Goodman: 'A new Community; The Elimination of the Difference between Production and Consumption', 1947-60. The first Utopia to give the idea of multiple land uses and diversity. Each square has enough diverse tissue to regenerate a whole city.

POSTSCRIPT

ARCHITECTURE AND REVOLUTION

... divide the counties into wards ...

(THOMAS JEFFERSON)

One of the conclusions to be drawn from a study of recent architecture is the problematic nature of architecture itself. Not only is it thrown into doubt by those who would replace it with a 'social service', or engineering, but it is questioned even by successfully practising architects. The reason is not hard to find. It concerns the consumer societies for which architecture is built and the undeniable banality of their building tasks and commissions. At present the most talented architects are designing beautiful candle shops and boutiques for the sophisticated [23], office buildings for soap and whiskey monopolies [17, 53], playthings for the rich of Monte Carlo [175] and technical gadgetry for the Worlds Fairs [34]. Such designs are in every formal and technical way provocative and carried through with great integrity, but they can never transcend the limited social and political goals for which they were created. When the content is so trivial, the brilliant form just drives the point in with further gusto. Hence we have reached the ironic position of having what may well be the most inventive and excitingly formal architecture ever produced, with surely the most ridiculous content.

If architecture is to regain a credibility among both architects and the public, then two different things will have happened. From within the profession the question of giving certain tasks monumental and symbolic expression will have been faced straightforwardly and answered without the present evasion or embarrassment. Since

architecture is a conscious, often selfconscious, crystalli-
zation of certain cultural values, architects will have to
acknowledge explicitly their responsibility in presenting
and dramatizing them. The present custom of proffering
such substitutes as functionalism, or vernacular architecture, or servicing, bears eloquent testimony to the
architect's lack of faith in his social role and the current
public realms. But these substitutes only evade the question
of his responsibility towards rhetoric, they don't answer it.
Architecture, 'the art or science of constructing edifices
for human use' (OED), has always been, as this French
definition of 1563 suggests, concerned with 'edifying' and
educating the public through a conscious symbolic
medium – the façade. Obviously such limited definitions
of edification are out of date, but they still suggest that
area for which the architect is pre-eminently responsible:
the symbolic, the meaningful, the perceived. Architecture
crystallizes specific cultural values, and not others, and the
architect, as opposed to, say, the sociologist or engineer,
has been delegated to this role by society.

But of course this is only half the question, and if a
viable architecture is to emerge, then society will have
changed in important ways as well. Consider those
explicitly cultural commissions which society has given
its major architects: the Guggenheim Museum [81] and
Lincoln Center in New York [115], the Opera House in
Sydney [33], and the Royal Festival Hall in London
[148]. Each one of these projects is formally interesting,
but each one is being asked to fulfil a role in city life
which was previously filled either by the church or state.
As Matthew Arnold and so many aesthetes of the nineteenth century predicted, culture, literature and the arts
are becoming the religion and politics for a new, secular
society. But, as so many others have also pointed out,
culture is a poor substitute for both. Hence, in architectural terms, what one often finds in these buildings is
either a Camp presentation of failed seriousness or an overblown gesture of exaggerated importance. The fault
probably lies if anywhere more with the lack of serious
commissions than with the architects. But what about
those buildings which do have an intrinsic seriousness of
programme – The Imatra Church of Aalto [109], the
Boston City Hall [139], the government buildings in

Dacca by Louis Kahn [146] and Chandigarh by Le Corbusier [93]? These religious and public buildings have all the qualities, including architectural excellence, that one could ask for – except a credible religion and politics. Here the actual content, the activity within the physical shell, proves the problematic issue. It has become increasingly clear, especially to the architects involved, that the politics consist mostly in representative, élite government rather than direct, participatory democracy, and that the religion is mostly ossified, anachronistic ritual. The effect of this begins to tell on the architects: they remain unchallenged and unexcited.

It is this general loss of credibility in politics and religion which, in a strange way, has even been the cause of 'modern architecture'. For the fantastic celebration of engineering structures, the Eiffel Tower and railroad shelters which occurred in the nineteenth century and their counterpart in the twentieth, the moon shot, the Space Program, the Vehicle Assembly Building [132] are brilliant substitutes for more serious cultural tasks. When architects found in the nineteenth century that conventional social tasks were no longer challenging, they quite naturally looked to emergent areas of expression: the new technologies and materials. It was only in such marginally social areas as housing [45] and sports stadia [38], that they kept a general commitment. But then another problem immediately arose, for like Le Corbusier, they tried to elevate the house to the palace, the private to the public and the utilitarian to the cultural. By contrast, it was only in post-revolutionary Russia and only for a short time that architects achieved a renewed faith in significant social functions – the Palace of Labour is an example [44] – and they achieved this by re-inventing these functions along with society. As a result, they produced an architecture which was both formally brilliant [221] and explicitly tied to social goals that were progressive, idealist and believable (at the time).

If the affluent consumer societies offer no better building tasks than an occasional Worlds Fair or *ersatz* public realm mistakenly termed 'democratic', then architects with a sense of purpose are rather restricted in their alternatives. Some, like Robert Venturi, have tried to make architecture out of the negative forces by either contradict-

ЛЕНИНГРАДСКАЯ **ПРАВДА**

15 ⁱ⁰ ЧАС

ПАРИЖ

БЕРЛИН

ЛЕНИНГРАДСКАЯ ПРАВДА

ПРОЕКТ

221. Vesnin Brothers:
Project for the Pravda
Building, 1923. A pure,
elegant geometry carries
such utilitarian elements as
a loudspeaker, searchlight,
and projection of the daily
news.

ing or expressing them ironically [134] and one has to
admit that this critical approach is far superior to the
usual suppressions because it acknowledges the true
nature of these forces. Other architects have proposed
subversive critiques and idealist alternatives to the present
system without having much hope of seeing them built.
The situation is intractable, complex and unlikely to
change. Yet even admitting these difficulties, at least one
can begin to see hints of an answer.

For brief moments in man's history there have emerged
forms of political organization that reveal an enormous
ability for realizing certain human potential. These forms
have sometimes been concretized in the laws, institutions
and the architecture of a society: the Greek agora, the
Roman forum, the medieval communes and American
townships were all variants of an institution which
allowed particular human qualities to emerge and furthermore protected their continual ability to do so. What were
these qualities? First of all the public realm promoted free
and open discussion on issues which affected the community as a whole. The benefits of this public realm were
not just the obvious ones of self-government – control
over decisions affecting oneself – but extended beyond
this to areas of enjoyment which sound almost quaint to
our ears: 'public happiness', the delight in appearing in
public to disclose one's personal identity,[1] the enjoyment of debate, sharing one's opinions with others even
including an opposition, the pleasure taken in public
speaking, rhetoric, the art of persuasion where artifice
becomes a satisfying substitute for physical coercion.
These are the attributes of acting, the world of the
theatre, and it was the genius of the public realm to create
a space where almost anyone could act out a significant
role if he wished. The enormous satisfaction which this
stage function could generate becomes apparent today
only at odd moments such as a crisis which catalyses a
group of people, a sporting event or pop festival, where
the nature of a spontaneous talented gesture is immediately shared in a collective, but credible, way.

Other benefits of the public realm which democratic
theorists such as Rousseau have stressed concern its educational aspect. By taking part in a democratic process,
the individual is forced to widen his special interests to

the point where he can see how they intersect with general, public interests: for Rousseau the democratic situation naturally 'forced' the individual to develop into a responsible citizen because he was given a degree of control over collective decisions and this control naturally brought with it the development of accountability, foresight, tolerance and intelligence. However, the more general justifications of a public realm conceived in democracy concern its functional rather than psychological aspects, and in a proposal for dividing the city of New York up into a metropolis of fifty communities, the 'Citizens for Local Democracy' go back to the traditional claims that this system alone provides justice and self-rule [222].

As a mass of men with local democratic institutions we find ourselves hovering on the brink of catastrophe. The public interest is unrecognized or subverted. Special interests flourish and irresponsible bureaucracies are free to serve themselves. This is the direct result of the absence of local democracy in New York City . . . Local democracy is the essence of democracy in this republic. Citizens who do not live in self-governing communities can scarcely be termed citizens, for they lack that which makes a person a citizen, namely a voice in their own government

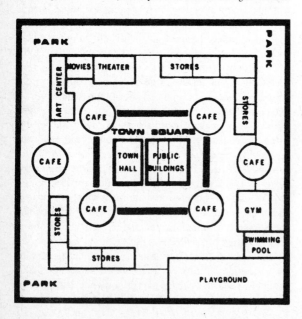

222a, b. Citizens for Local Democracy: 'What a Democratic New York Would Look Like', 1970. Each community, with its town centre, would control its schools, sanitation, housing, hospital, etc., whereas the municipal government would be a federation of such bodies with larger duties such as public transportation and central parks.

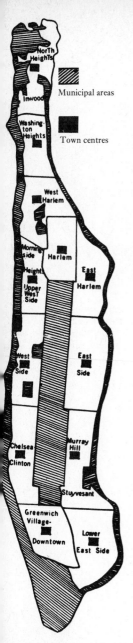

Municipal areas

Town centres

and a share in public power. In quite a literal sense such people are not even part of our republican government, for the basic 'unit of the republic' is the self-governing township.[2]

Theoretically acute as such statements are, they still suffer from a lack of historical probability. The 'Citizens for Local Democracy' propose their Jeffersonian ward system as a liberal piece of legislature as if participatory democracy could be brought into existence within the prevailing system by a stroke of the pen. Unfortunately, however, no representational democracy with its party system has ever been seriously interested in legislating itself out of existence and the only time in recent history when the federation of wards has ever had a practical chance of existence is within *popular*, urban revolutions.

Quite spontaneously, and without the aid of professional revolutionists or their theory, the same kind of self-governing group has emerged in every popular revolution since the English one of 1640.[3] The American townships of 1776, the French popular societies of 1793 (there were over 5,000), the popular clubs of 1848, the Paris Commune of 1871, the Soviets of 1905 and 1917, the *Räte* which emerged in Germany for a brief period in 1918, the Syndicates in Spain, 1936, the Workers' Councils in Hungary, 1956, the *barrio* groups of Santo Domingo, 1965, the Action Committees of Paris, 1968 [**223**], and so on. In every uprising which was more than a *coup-d'état* or palace revolution or guerrilla based takeover, this form of participatory democracy has sprung up out of the 'events' themselves. Perhaps this organization from direct action – as opposed to organization on class or ideological lines – explains the interesting similarities which these groups share even across different cultures.

They all become political forums rooted in public debate where the several 'freedoms' become the prime issues. They all eliminate the bureaucratic form of solving problems by substituting immediate and direct action at a local level. In this way they are quicker, more delicate and actually more efficient than prevailing modes of government. For a small élite of representative interpreters, they substitute a federation of groups familiar with the specific problems at hand. Thus they contain a local expertise foreign to bureaucracy and their fraternity

377

grows out of particular functions. Leon Trotsky wrote of the 1905 Soviet in Russia:

223. Action Committee, Sorbonne, Paris, May 1968. The public realm as it emerges in revolution.

> The Council of Workmen's Delegates introduces a free press. It organizes street patrols to secure the safety of the citizens. It takes over, to a greater or less extent, the post office, the telegraph, and the railroads. It makes an effort to introduce the eight-hour workday. Paralysing the autocratic government by a strike, it brings its own democratic order into the life of the working city population.[4]

Hannah Arendt has described how the Hungarian Councils of 1956 were also organized along lines of common endeavour and expertise:

> Thus neighborhood councils emerged from sheer living together and grew into country and other territorial councils; revolutionary councils grew out of fighting together; councils of writers and artists, one is tempted to think, were born in the *cafés*, students' and youths' councils at the university, military councils in the army, councils of civil servants in the ministries, workers' councils in the factories and so on. The formation of a council in each disparate group turned a merely haphazard togetherness into a political institution.[5]

A final pattern which occurs in all popular revolutions is that the council system comes into being through a *dis-*

appearance of power, and hence, contrary to say Marxist theory, is not founded in violence, bloodshed and terror. In fact it makes sense to say that popular revolutions are peaceful whereas it is counter-revolutionary seizures of power which are violent and have given revolution its unfortunate image. On this score it is interesting to note that such 'professional' revolutionists as Robespierre, Trotsky and Lenin, who proclaimed the importance of self-organizing groups at first, later brought about their downfall in the terror and counter-revolution. In the French and Russian Revolutions, it was a case of centralist theory taking over from a decentralist practice even when the theorists initially came to power through decentralized groups. Indeed these groups have more often been suppressed by sympathizers who believe that they are incapable of continued existence than by reactionaries from the outside. In any case, crushed they have been, not from any intrinsic faults, but by the combined forces of all centralist élitists: liberals, Bolsheviks, parliamentarians, socialists and conservatives alike.

Happily this situation has an opportunity of changing in the future since, for the first time, revolutionary theory is beginning to catch up with two hundred years of practice. Such disparate theorists as the linguist Noam Chomsky, the philosopher Hannah Arendt and the major protagonist of the May Events Daniel Cohn-Bendit have reached much the same conclusion about the significance of these groups from very different starting points.[6] A consensus of decentralist theory might easily crystallize, in which case during the next upheaval the reimposition of a centralized bureaucracy will become that much more difficult and the council system might survive.

Meanwhile in architectural terms what can be done? At the very least, the architect can continue to offer ideal alternatives such as Bruno Taut's Community Centre [29] or Tony Garnier's Industrial City (1904), with its clearly defined public realm and basis in Utopian socialism – alternatives which serve the purpose of keeping alive a critical opposition to the present system and articulating a positive course of action should a revolution occur. One can see that unless a live architectural tradition exists at the time of upheaval, the cultural alternatives are radically limited. While the same spontaneous creativity emerges in all popular revolutions – the street art, slogans, graffiti, etc. of Russia 1917, Paris 1968 – it is only those which combine with an already live tradition which can blossom fully into flower, such as Constructivism in 1921. It is true that the popular revolt acts as a major catalyst for creative expression. In post-revolutionary France all the rituals and conventions of a Christian society were transformed into new modes of behaviour based on reason and nature. The Cult of Reason was worshipped, in the form of an outstanding actress, on the high altar at Notre Dame. In Russia, mass demonstrations, *agit-prop* and street painting were transformed into a new kind of theatre based on circus and vaudeville conventions – culminating in annual re-enactments of the storming of the Winter Palace. An industrialized symphony conducted between different factories, played on sirens and steam whistles, was carried out from time to time. But these inevitable, popular manifestations only reached a greater significance because they were aided by a tradition which was already prepared for their emergence – the *Philosophes* in France, the Cubo-Futurists in Russia. Perhaps one factor which kept these traditions creative under the previous systems was their active dissent. Even when working for the old system, they managed to express counter-themes, alternatives, ironic tensions, contradictions to the prevailing ideology. A viable architecture in the present situation will do the same. If architecture concretizes the public realm and if that realm has lost its credibility because it is founded on a false idea of what allows men to govern themselves, then its whole expressive nature, and therefore its essence, is thrown into doubt. In that situation all the architect can do is clarify the situation theoretically, design dissenting buildings for the system, provide alternative models and wait for the propitious moment. Le Corbusier ended his polemic with the alternative 'Architecture or Revolution. Revolution can be avoided'. But today if we are to have a credible architecture, it must be supported by a popular revolution that *ends* in a credible public realm, the council system. Architecture *and* revolution.

NOTES

Introduction: The Plurality of Approaches

1. Nikolaus Pevsner, *Pioneers of Modern Design*, Penguin Books, Harmondsworth, 1960, first published as *Pioneers of the Modern Movement* in 1936 by Faber & Faber. Pevsner ended this first edition justifying the modern style as 'genuine' and 'totalitarian'.

2. Nikolaus Pevsner, 'Architecture in Our Time, the Anti-Pioneers', *Listener*, 29 December 1966, p. 953.

3. Michael Lane, *Structuralism, A Reader*, Jonathan Cape, London, 1970. As de Saussure pointed out in 1916, the relation between the sound and sense in language is for the most part initially arbitrary or unmotivated; the same holds true for the relation between form and content in architecture; see also the next note for references.

4. Charles Jencks, 'History as Myth', in George Baird and Charles Jencks, *Meaning in Architecture*, Barrie & Jenkins, London, 1970. This essay analyses the patterns of historical interpretation over the last fifty years.

5. See E. H. Gombrich, *Norm and Form*, Phaidon Press, London, 1966, pp. 81-3.

6. The idea of imaginative fusion has a long history in literary criticism, culminating in S. T. Coleridge. See I. A. Richards, *Coleridge on Imagination*, Routledge & Kegan Paul, London, 1934.

7. See Peter Serenyi, 'Le Corbusier, Fourier and the Monastery of Ema', in the *Art Bulletin*, December 1967. In 'The Marseilles Block', Le Corbusier writes: 'Look back. Think of Charles Fourier, and his "wild ideas" of houses supplied with communal services . . . "water itself will be conducted through iron pipes into every house". That was 1830 and Fourier was dismissed as a madman. So don't let's be afraid of ideas' (p. 22).

8. Le Corbusier, *Oeuvre Complète*, Volume V, 1946-52, Zurich, 1953, p. 195.

9. This argument, which is terribly complex, is put by I. A. Richards in *Principles of Literary Criticism*, Routledge & Kegan Paul, 1924, pp. 43, 140, 46. Some criticisms of it can be found in W. H. N. Hotopf, *Language, Thought and Comprehension, A*

Case Study in the Writings of I. A. Richards, Routledge & Kegan Paul, London, 1965, pp. 230–35.

10. Only a small number of the recent, relevant architects could be discussed in a book of this size and nature, and if it were more of a survey of the period since 1945, it would have included buildings of the following: *in Finland*, Ervi, Korhonen, Siren and Pietila; *in Denmark*, Arne Jacobsen and Bo & Wohlert; *in Sweden*, Erskine, Nyren, Lewerentz and Markelius; *in Norway*, Grung and Fehn, Norberg-Schulz, Lund & Slatto; *in Germany*, Ungers, Eiremann, Bohm, Schultze-Fielitz, Schwarz, Platz; *in France*, Prouvé, Wogensky, Bodianski, Egger, Boudon, Schein; *in Holland*, Blom, Van Stigt, Verhoeven; *in Austria*, Haus-Rucker, Pichler, St Florian, Feuerstein, Rainer; *in Israel*, Neumann, Glickson, Gerstel; *in Canada*, Safdie and Andrews; *in South America*, Villenueva; *in Poland*, Soltan, Hansen; *in Australia*, Seidler; *in the USA*, Neutra, Breuer, TAC, Cambridge 7, Ant Farm, Stern, Giurgola, Barnes, Polshek, Netch, Esherick, Wachsmann, Kiesler; *in Japan*, Maekawa, Sakakura, Maki, Otani, Okada, Raymond; *in Spain*, Coderch & Valls, Martorell, Bohigas & McKay, Correa, Oiza, Paredes, Alba, Higueres; *in Switzerland*, Gisel, Atelier 5, Foderer, Otto, Zwipfer, Stucky; *in Africa*, Simounet, Studer; the Italians mentioned in Chapter 1, note 31 and Chapter 8, note 15 – and countless other individuals in Russia, Asia, Greece and the satellite countries.

1: The Six Traditions – Politics and Architecture

1. For a discussion of how this evolutionary tree was derived, see Charles Jencks, *Architecture 2000*, Studio Vista, London, 1971, pp. 35–48, and *Architectural Design*, 1970, p. 527.

2. See Bibliography, pp. 397–8.

3. From an uncompleted manuscript, 1931. The idea can be traced to the early twenties and is developed in Reyner Banham, *Theory and Design in the First Machine Age*, London, 1960, pp. 151, 152.

4. ibid., p. 151.

5. Théo van Doesburg, 'Vers un style Collectif', *Bulletin de l'effort moderne*, Vol. 1, No. 4, 1924, p. 16.

6. Le Corbusier, *Towards a New Architecture*, Architectural Press, London, 1927, pp. 229–31.

7. By the Swiss Alex von Senger. It was partially instrumental in Le Corbusier losing this competition.

8. Le Corbusier, op. cit., p. 250.

9. Le Corbusier, *The City of Tomorrow*, London, 1929, trans. Frederich Etchells, pp. 300–301.

10. Ulrich Conrads, *Programmes and Manifestoes on 20th Century Architecture*, Lund Humphries, London, 1970, p. 111.

11. ibid., p. 112.

12. Letter to author, in Donald Drew Egbert, *Social Radicalism and the Arts*, Alfred Knopf, New York, 1970, p. 661-2.

13. U. Conrads, op. cit., p. 169-70.

14. See also for instance the quote of Kallmann, p. 228 below.

15. See p. 369 below for a discussion of the Goodmans' work.

16. Paul Schultze-Naumburg, *Kunst und Rasse*, Munich, 1928, p. 127, quoted from Barbara Miller Lane, *Architecture and Politics in Germany, 1918-45*, Harvard University Press, Cambridge, Mass., 1968, p. 139. See also Paul Schultze-Naumburg, *The Face of the German House*, Munich, 1929, p. 90.

17. Barbara Miller Lane, op. cit., p. 258, note 57.

18. Sibyl Moholy-Nagy, *Journal of the Society for Architectural Historians*, March 1965, p. 84.

19. Barbara Miller Lane, op. cit., p. 181, also quoted more fully below, page 119.

20. See for instance, Stanislaus von Moos, *Le Corbusier, Elemente einer Synthese*, Verlag Huber, Stuttgart, 1968, pp. 220, 236, 265-71.

21. William Shirer, *Berlin Diary*, Alfred Knopf, New York, 1941, p. 213.

22. See Giulia Veronesi, *Difficolta politiche dell'architettura in Italia*, Milano, 1953.

23. Nikolaus Pevsner, *An Outline of European Architecture*, Penguin Books, 7th edition, reprinted 1964, p. 411. See also above, page 11 footnote 1.

24. Gio Ponti, *Domus Magazine*, June 1961, p. 3.

25. Cleveland Amory, 'Philip Johnson', *Vogue*, May 1964, p. 205.

26. I have tried to explore this nexus of factors in 'La Trahison perpetuelle des Clercs', in *Architecture 2000, Predictions and Methods*, Studio Vista, London, 1971, pp. 20-29.

27. I owe this parallel to Sibyl Moholy-Nagy; see her answer to the letter in the *Journal of the Society for Architectural Historians*, October 1965.

28. Hans Hollein, in *Arts and Architecture*, California, 1963, p. 14.

29. Conrads, op. cit., p. 181.

30. Quotes are taken from various unpublished papers of Superstudio, 1968.

31. A representative list would include Luigi Moretti, Gio Ponti and Alberto Rosselli, Carlo Scarpa, Joe Colombo, Gae Aulenti, Hans Hollein, Ettore Sottsass, Archizoom, Superstudio,

Maurizio Sacripanti, Haus Rucker Co., Walter Pichler and, with some qualifications, Ricardo Bofill and Kiyonari Kikutake.

32. Ricardo Bofill, 'The Present Situation of Architecture in Spain', *Zodiac 15*, 1966, p. 196.

33. ibid., p. 197.

34. Walter Gropius, 'Programme of the Staatliches Bauhaus in Weimar', quoted from Ulrich Conrads, op. cit., pp. 49–53.

35. Walter Gropius, *Ja! Stiemmen des Arbeitsrates für Kunst in Berlin*, Charlottenburg, 1919, pp. 32–3.

36. Bruno Taut, 'Architektur-Programm', Berlin, 1918, quoted from Ulrich Conrads, op. cit., p. 43.

37. Le Corbusier, *The Radiant City*, Orion Press, New York, 1967 (1933), pp. 192–3.

38. Conrads, op. cit., p. 157.

39. ibid.

40. Ulrich Conrads and Hans Sperlich, *Fantastic Architecture*, Architectural Press, London, 1963, p. 142–3.

41. U. Conrads, *Programmes and Manifestoes on 20th Century Architecture*, pp. 172–3.

42. Kenzo Tange, 'On Vitalism', in *CIAM 59 in Otterlo*, ed. Oscar Newman, Alex Tiranti, London, 1961, pp. 171–2.

43. Buckminster Fuller, '2000+', *Architectural Design*, February 1967, p. 63.

44. ibid., p. 63.

45. Pier Luigi Nervi, 'Is Architecture Moving Towards Unchanging Forms?', in *Structure in Art and Science*, ed. Gyorgy Kepes, George Braziller, New York, 1965, p. 101.

46. See Anthony Jackson, *The Politics of Architecture, A History of Modern Architecture in Britain*, Architectural Press, London, 1970, p. 172.

47. Evgeny Ruzhnikov, 'Housing Construction in Moscow', Novosti Press Agency, 30 May 1965.

48. U. Conrads, *Programmes and Manifestoes on 20th Century Architecture*, p. 159.

49. Friedrich Engels, *Zur Wohnungsfrage*, Leipzig, 1887. Quoted from Anatole Kopp, *Town and Revolution, Soviet Architecture and City Planning 1917–35*, Thames & Hudson, London, 1970, p. 33.

50. Camilla Gray, *The Great Experiment: Russian Art 1863–1922*, Thames & Hudson, London, 1962, p. 216.

51. ibid.

52. Leon Trotsky, *Literature and Revolution*, 1923.

53. Klara Zetkin, *Reminiscences of Lenin*, New York, 1934, quoted from D. D. Egbert, *Social Radicalism and the Arts*, p. 57.

54. C. Gray, op. cit., p. 286.

55. Anatole Kopp, op. cit., p. 94.

56. See Claude Schnaidt, *Hannes Meyer, Buildings, Projects and Writings*, Alex Tiranti, London, 1965, p. 95.

57. ibid., p. 123.

58. ibid., pp. 31 and 57.

59. William Mangin, 'Squatter Settlements', *Scientific American*, October 1967, and John Turner, 'The Squatter Settlement', *Architectural Design*, August 1968.

60. Gabriel and Daniel Cohn-Bendit, *Obsolete Communism, the Left-Wing Alternative*, Penguin Books, Harmondsworth, 1969, p. 79.

2: The Problem of Mies

1. See Lewis Mumford, *The Highway and the City*, Secker & Warburg, London, 1964, p. 156.

2. See Sigfried Giedion, *Space, Time and Architecture*, Harvard, Cambridge, Mass., 1967, 5th edition, p. 617. One must distinguish here the 'integrity of form' from the 'integrity of consistency'; obviously Mies has the latter as he never deviates from exploring to their fullest certain *a priori* principles. However, these principles are themselves too limited to result in the 'integrity of form' because they eschew function and a changing technology.

3. For William Jordy's defence see *Zodiac 8*, Milan, 1960.

4. See Alison and Peter Smithson, *Architectural Design*, 7, 1969, p. 363. Other two quotes are pp. 363, 365.

5. ibid., p. 366.

6. See William Jordy, 'Seagram Assessed', *Architectural Review*, December 1958.

7. See Thomas Creighton, 'Seagram House Re-assessed', *Progressive Architecture*, June 1959.

8. See Werner Blaser, *Mies van der Rohe*, Thames & Hudson, London, 1965, p. 11.

9. Quoted from Giedion, op. cit., p. 616.

10. See above, pp. 40–51, and for a discussion of Popper and the Open Society, below, pp. 332–4, 362.

11. Quoted more fully below in the discussion of Camp architecture, where the consequences are explored further, pp. 189–93.

3: Gropius, Wright and the Collapse into Formalism

1. Conrads and Sperlich, *Fantastic Architecture*, London, 1963, p. 137.

2. It is interesting to see what 'Modern Architecture' looked like to a German observer in England at the time; the series of articles in *Architectural Review* written from 1922–3 discusses Gropius, Mendelsohn, B. Taut, Poelzig and the Dutch Expressionists.

3. This plausible idea was suggested to me by Reyner Banham;

whatever the causes were, however, the extraordinary thing is that no participant or historian has tried to explain them and that the revolution took place without a whisper. The positive reasons for the change are dealt with later in the text.

4. See Walter Gropius, *Ulm Magazine*, 10/11, 1964.

5. See Walter Gropius, *The Scope of Total Architecture*, Collier Books, New York, 1962, p. 39.

6. ibid., p. 13.

7. Reyner Banham, Kenneth Frampton and Camilla Gray have done a lot to revalue the influence of the Constructivists and Van Doesburg, but no one has yet explored the Dadaist contribution to the Machine aesthetic and anti-art (in an architectural context that is). Hans Richter's *Dada, Art and Anti-Art*, Thames & Hudson, London, 1965, supplies much of the missing material on Picabia and the Berlin Dadaists, etc.

8. See H. L. C. Jaffe, *De Stijl*, Amsterdam, 1956, p. 20.

9. Source unknown.

10. See Bruno Zevi, *Poetica dell'Architettura Neo-Plastica*, Tamburini, Milan, 1953.

11. Not only had Le Corbusier's and Ozenfant's writings circulated through the Bauhaus by 1922, but they had also been continuously commented on in *De Stijl* since February 1921. Gropius's two buildings of 1911 and 1914 are often cited as proof that he had come to all the same conclusions eleven years earlier, but we are interested here in *direct causes of the Expressionist shift*, not antecedents. The earliest datable sign of a switch in Gropius I can find is February 1922. See *50 Years Bauhaus*, catalogue, London, 1968, p. 145, but obviously the switch had not occured until June as the Schlemmer letter makes clear.

12. *50 Years Bauhaus*, op. cit., p. 20. The last phrase is reminiscent of Lissitzky's *Proun* (objectivity objects) concept, published in *De Stijl*, May 1922.

13. ibid, p. 36.

14. Gropius's stated reasons for leaving the Bauhaus in 1928 were to go back into private practice and take the Nazi pressure which was directed at him off the Bauhaus; the latter reason does not seem plausible, given the fact that he appointed the quasi-Communist H. Meyer as his successor.

15. See Barbara Miller Lane, *Architecture and Politics in Germany 1918–1945*, Harvard, Cambridge, Mass., 1968, p. 181.

16. See *The Scope of Total Architecture*, p. 21.

17. The Pan Am controversy was well aired in the architectural magazines. See especially *Progressive Architecture*, April 1963, *Architects' Yearbook 10* and, for the exchange between Bruno Zevi and Gropius, *L'Architettura*, April 1964. The controversy was touched off mainly by the fact that 25,000 workers plus many times that number of visitors would congest even more one of the most congested areas of the world. This didn't in fact occur

and Gropius seemed right in his defence that a vertical business centre was a necessary and good thing. But the controversy was then aggravated by the fact that some critics thought that the building somehow cut down the view down Park Avenue, whereas Gropius thought it unified the multifarious building heights. The critics then suggested that the lobby space was a crude amalgamation of too many shiny materials, and Gropius pointed out how he had integrated objects of art into his building. The critics then asked why such a little turn was made in the octagon plan, since this really didn't diminish the bulk, and Gropius answered that his main reason was not so mundane. 'The greater width of the tower in its middle part results logically from . . . ' the elevator core; and the blocking of the Park Avenue vista results logically from the air conditioning loads (orientation). The window wall which Gropius had designed to give scale and plasticity to the large volume was also criticized as meaningless because it was imperceptible from far off – where one would see it.

18. See *Architectural Record*, June 1964, p. 140.

19. See *The Scope of Total Architecture*, p. 85.

20. Formalism as a restricted genre like farce is discussed in the chapter on Mies; formalism as failed seriousness is discussed below under 'Camp-Non Camp', Chapter 6.

21. See *50 Years Bauhaus*, op. cit., p. 9.

22. See Norris Kelly Smith, *Frank Lloyd Wright, A Study in Architectural Content*, Prentice Hall, New Jersey, 1966, p. 30 ff.

23. Some of these were 'the Ready-Cut Houses' of 1913, 'All-Steel Houses' of 1937, 'House for a Family of $5000-6000', 1938, 'Suntop Houses', 1939 and 'Cooperative Homesteads', 1942.

24. See *Architectural Forum*, January 1951.

25. The inherent relation of certain geometries to certain functions is discussed in the chapter on Urbanism, pp. 339–50.

26. See Iovanna Lloyd Wright, *Architecture, Man in Possession of his Earth*, New York, 1962, p. 40.

27. A verbal acknowledgement showing that he kept a certain scepticism even then, quoted by Walter Segal in *The Architects' Journal*, 11 June 1969, p. 1548: 'And I was caught red-handed by my own sentimentality. It was forever claiming me and every time it did I would not only lose face but my patience: and [find] someone or something to blame.' Or, 'Naturally (I well remember) I became less and less tolerant and, I suppose, intolerable. Arrogant, I imagine, was the proper word.'

4: Charles Jeanneret – Le Corbusier

1. See Maurice Besset, *Who Was Le Corbusier?*, Editions d'Art Albert Skira, Geneva, 1968, pp. 8 and 196. Unable to offer an interpretation, Besset quite rightly abjures a judgement.

2. Quoted from *Aujourd'hui, Art et Architecture*, No. 51, November 1965.

3. Treated more fully below in the discussion of Alvar Aalto, pp. 176–9.

4. Quoted from *Modern Artists on Art*, ed. Robert L. Herbert, Prentice Hall, New Jersey, 1964, pp. 61–2. *Le Purisme* actually appeared in the fourth issue of the magazine, January (?) 1921.

5. This point is discussed for its relevance to Pop art in Chapter 7, pp. 273–5.

6. Karl Popper has argued that monistic and pluralist systems of philosophy have been unable to stand up to the attack from a dualist position because of its inherent strength; he then goes on to argue for a trivalent system as better than all three alternatives; see *Encounter*, February 1969, p. 63, for a report of this argument.

7. The difficult and probably impossible question to answer is 'who wrote how much and what of *Vers*?' It seems that Jeanneret and Ozenfant were about equal collaborators on *Le Purisme* and their pseudonyms Le Corbusier-Saugnier appear *in all* the articles which were later to make up *Vers*. In retrospect, Ozenfant felt rather bitter about being excluded from co-authorship of *Vers*, which he still claimed to have partially written (*Foundations of Modern Art*, Dover Publications, New York, 1952, p. 328). Judging by his other writings one imagines that he was instrumental in convincing Le Corbusier of both the Purist 'constants' and 'the Engineer's Aesthetic', which is to say the major sub-arguments of *Vers*. But then why should he alone have reviewed *Vers* in *L'Esprit Nouveau 19* and not mentioned his own pseudonym Saugnier? On the other hand, why should Van Doesburg have thought that Le Corbusier-Saugnier was Ozenfant alone? (*De Stijl*, September 1921). A major job of revising history seems to await the person who can get to the bottom of this.

8. In 1929 with *Défense de L'Architecture*, reprinted in *L'Architecture D'Aujourd'hui*, 1933, and *Précisions*. Quotes are from the former article, my translation, pp. 61, 44.

9. A course advocated by Reyner Banham at the end of *Theory and Design* (op. cit). Contrary to what Banham claims here (p. 329), the theorists of the First Machine Age were pre-eminently concerned with opposing all sorts of human values to the process of technological development. They were not just 'norms and types' however, but included such things as the Constructivists' social Utopianism and *De Stijl*'s abstract forms. I don't think there was one movement of this period which was *solely* committed to following technological process, although all of them may have given this impression from time to time.

10. The main criticism of 'The Contemporary City' or equally the Ville Radieuse has been that its imagery and function are banal – a static monument to the status quo, a rigid class-

distinction which favours industrialists and an inhuman scale which allows no choice, place to meet nor live open spaces. Jane Jacobs also criticizes it for its economic naivety and functional separation (see below, pp. 355-6). All these criticisms, however, overlook the positive values which Le Corbusier was offering.

11. See *My Work*, Architectural Press, London, 1960, p. 147.

12. Quotes are taken from *My Work* and *Œuvre Complète*.

13. There are many casual references to 'superficial modernism', the betrayers of his generation, etc. He also supported Team Ten against CIAM.

14. *Le Corbusier 1910-65*, Edition Girsberger, Zurich, 1967, p. 176.

5: Aalto and the Means of Architectural Communication

1. See *Alvar Aalto*, Editions Girsberger, Zurich, 1963, p. 73.

2. For a general discussion of this point see E. H. Gombrich, 'Visual Discovery through Art', in *Psychology and the Visual Arts*, ed. James Hogg, Penguin Books, 1969, p. 232.

3. Quoted from E. H. Gombrich's 'Expression and Communication' in *Meditations on a Hobby-Horse*, Phaidon Press, London, 1963, p. 61. An essay which gives the best explanation of the relative merits of information and expressionist theory that I have found.

4. See E. H. Gombrich, op. cit., pp. 58-62.

5. See Reyner Banham, *Guide to Modern Architecture*, Architectural Press, London, 1963, p. 126.

6. See Alvar Aalto, *Zodiac 3*, p. 78.

7. See *Alvar Aalto*, op. cit., p. 7.

8. See *RIBA Journal*, February 1957, p. 128.

6: Recent American Architecture: Camp - Non Camp

1. See Philip Johnson, *Hound and Horn*, No. 7, 1934, p. 137.

2. Burchard and Bush-Brown, *The Architecture of America*, 1967, p. 420.

3. See above, p. 40.

4. Susan Sontag, 'Notes on Camp', in *Against Interpretation*, Eyre & Spottiswoode, London, 1967.

5. See *Progressive Architecture*, March 1961; the word is Philip Johnson's.

6. *Journal of the Society of Architectural Historians*, March 1965, p. 46.

7. See *Perspecta 7*, New Haven, 1961, p. 51.

8. Both quotes from Cranston Jones, *Architecture Today and Tomorrow*, McGraw-Hill, New York, 1961, p. 175.

9. *Time Magazine*, 15 November 1963.

10. C. Jones, *Architecture Today and Tomorrow*, op. cit., p. 108.

11. The first five epithets are of English coinage and, for the most part, abusive.

12. See John Johansen, *Architectural Forum*, January 1966.

13. *Architectural Review*, September 1950, pp. 152–9.

14. Quoted from an interview, part of which was shown on BBC TV, November 1965.

15. The adjectives and attitude are, of course, traditional and common.

16. See Paul and Percival Goodman, *Communitas*, Vintage Books, New York, 1960, p. 80, who discuss the social implications of Fuller's Dymaxion World: equality through equal isolation and dispersal. The goals are greater productivity and no conflict or social and political intercourse.

17. See below, page 285, for a discussion of 'une architecture autre' and pp. 351–8 for a discussion of 'parametric architecture'.

18. See Robert Venturi, *Perspecta 9/10*, p. 33.

19. Robert Venturi, *Complexity and Contradiction in Architecture*, New York, 1966, quotes from pp. 22–3. Venturi's idea of an inclusive architecture is similar to the idea of multivalence developed here, but as I pointed out in a review of his book (*Arena*, June 1967, pp. 4–5) he does not go into the deeper theoretical reasons for his whole position. Thus his arguments, however sound, tend to seem as if they were nothing more than his personal taste.

20. Explicitly he has attacked the Smithsons over this point; see *RIBA Journal*, August 1969.

21. See David Gebhardt, *Architectural Forum*, March 1969, p. 79.

22. See below, pages 301–32 for a discussion of 'place'. The quote is from Robert Stern, *New Directions in American Architecture*, George Braziller, New York, 1969, p. 70.

23. See G. Kallmann, *Architectural Forum*, October 1959, pp. 132–7.

24. See Louis Kahn, *Perspecta 10/11*, New Haven, 1967, p. 305.

25. ibid., p. 310.

26. See Vincent Scully, *Louis Kahn*, Braziller, New York, 1962, pp. 114–21.

27. See *Architectural Review*, February 1961 and March 1962. Kahn is criticized for being 'ideal' where he should be 'practical' and vice versa.

28. See Louis Kahn, *Perspecta 7*, New Haven, 1961, pp. 14–17.

29. The problem with fundamentalism is, obviously, that it refuses to deal with complex realities that transcend its initial

beliefs, but against this one should remember that the only group to stand up consistently to Hitler, and now to the Soviet Union under dictatorship, was the Jehovah's Witnesses.

7: Recent British Architecture – Pop – Non Pop

1. For this argument and for the quote see 'The Politics of Architecture. English Architecture 1929-1951', by Anthony Jackson, *Journal of the Society of Architectural Historians*, March 1965.

2. See G. E. Kidder-Smith, *The New Architecture of Europe*, New York, 1961, p. 36.

3. Particularly by the New Brutalists and New Palladians. See for instance Joseph Rykwert, 'Review of a Review', *Zodiac* 4, 1959.

4. See *Architectural Review*, June 1947, December 1949, January 1950, April 1954, for these main ideas.

5. *Architectural Review*, May 1953.

6. See *Arena*, February 1966, p. 184.

7. *Architectural Design*, April 1957.

8. Quoted from Reyner Banham 'The Last Formgiver', *Architectural Review*, August 1966; see also discussion of Corbusier's influence, above, p. 153.

9. *Architectural Design*, September 1965.

10. *RIBA Journal*, May 1965.

11. ibid.

12. Osgood and Sebeok, *Psycholinguistics*, Indiana, 1965, p. 177 ff. In one sense we spend our life doing nothing else but building up codes (linguistic and otherwise) to formulate or match a set of real events.

13. See *The New Brutalism*, op. cit., p. 63, and *Pop Art*, op. cit., p. 32.

14. L. Lippard, *Pop Art*, London, 1966, p. 32.

15. Reyner Banham, 'Who Is This Pop?', *Motif No. 10*, Lodon, 1963.

16. Karl Popper's *The Open Society*, Chapters 3 and 4.

17. *ICA PUBLICATIONS, II*, 1958.

18. *Architectural Design*, March 1958.

19. According to Hamilton who showed me his unanswered letter with its long list of 'Pop' elements. The elements were originally intended for another exhibition, but when the Smithsons did not answer the letter, Hamilton incorporated them in this painting.

20. For the first two ideas see *Architectural Design*, October 1966, p. 493; for the third idea see the *Fun Palace*, 1961/3; for the fourth idea see *Archigram II*, 1962; the last idea was at least implied in a lecture to the AA on the Anti-University, 1968.

21. See particularly *The New Brutalism*, Chapter 5.2 where the idea is discussed. The camp fire and the drive-in-cinema come closest to realizing a non-architecture of pure content. Of course one cannot escape from form altogether, just as one cannot have a language free from form (i.e. sound), unless the content just remains in the mind alone. All sign systems are inevitably doubly articulated as semiologists have shown.

22. *New Society*, 2 June 1966.

23. See George Baird, 'La Dimension Amoureuse', *Arena*, June 1967, p. 30. It is really rather difficult to ascertain how much behavioural 'conditioning' the Thinkbelt implies; presumably it would have such mechanisms as teaching machines which are in themselves passive instruments of conditioning. But knowing Price's persistent interest in creativity and dissent and having found out in conversation that he intended his service as 'air conditioning', I suppose it would contain a sufficient amount of 'foul air' or slack to keep its inhabitants from using it altogether as an efficient tool for conditioning people to acceptance of their 'process'. The great problem, however, remains of education as a value-free service; think of all those wonderful services which US universities have provided in Vietnam. Here education has been rather well integrated with manufacturing: death. The great advantage of 'classical education', which Price somewhat rejects, is that it teaches dissent, criticism, scepticism, debate, etc. or the very built-in 'foul air' which a service avoids. Again however, Price has pointed out to me in conversation that classical education is rather weak on criticizing its own assumptions; something which he is not. Thus we find here the reason for his paradoxical positions.

24. Banham mentions the problem as it arose in the fifties. See his 'Atavism of the Short-Distance Mini-cyclist', *Living Arts*, 3, London 1964, p. 92. That the same problem has remained in the sixties was apparent at the Folkestone Conference (1966) where the political implications of consumer architecture were an issue of debate. For a neo-Marxist critique of Archigram, see *L'Architecture d'Aujourd'hui*, September 1968, p. 90.

25. *Design Quarterly*, 1965, p. 30.

26. Now partially reprinted in the latest edition of *Space, Time and Architecture*, Harvard, 1967, p. 586.

27. See C. Doxiadis, *Encyclopaedia Britannica, Book of the Year* 1968, p. 21. For another condemnation see Peter Hall, 'Monumental Folly', *New Society*, 24 October 1968. While it is no doubt true that the Walking City resembles a war machine, it is manifestly untrue that Archigram's intentions are anything like totalitarian. Critics continually fail to make this distinction.

28. See Reyner Banham, 'Atavism . . .', op. cit., p. 96.

29. For these main ideas, see the Smithsons' essays in *Archi-*

tectural Design, July 1965, July 1966, November 1966, January 1967.

30. *The Architects' Journal*, 1960, p. 415.

31. *Art in America*, April 1965.

32. ibid.

33. *Industrial Design*, September 1965.

34. *Archigram 8*, 1968.

8: The International Scene – Larger than Architecture

1. The work of Le Corbusier, Lewis Mumford, and Constantinos Doxiadis is particularly rich in eschatological metaphors. For a current list including cancer, suicide, rats and the sudden death of a mother wheeling her baby carriage, see *Community and Privacy*, by Chermayeff and Alexander, Penguin Books, 1963, pp. 26, 70, 40 and 82.

2. See Jane Jacobs, *The Death and Life of Great American Cities*, Penguin Books, London, p. 460.

3. See Harold Rosenberg, *The Tradition of the New*, McGraw-Hill paperback, 1965, chapter called 'The Orgamerican Phantasy'.

4. ibid., p. 284.

5. See *Draft Framework 5*, of *CIAM X*, prepared by the later members of Team Ten; *Arena*, June 1965, p. 13 (my italics).

6. John Voelcker, ibid., p. 13.

7. See below under discussion of parametric design, page 351.

8. See Fumiko Maki and Masato Ohtaka, 'Some Thoughts on Collective Form', in G. Kepes, *Structure in Art and Science*, Braziller, New York, 1965.

9. See 'The Retreats from Modern Architecture', below, page 325.

10. See the *Team Ten Primer*, ed. Alison Smithson, London 1965, p. 43. The additional quotes are pp. 15, 7.

11. See *World Architecture III*, and *IV*, ed. John Donat, Studio Vista, London, 1966, 1967.

12. It is interesting to note that the concept of 'place' diffused so quickly that it spread all over the globe without any acknowledgement of the sources. For instance, it underlies Moore and Lyndon's Condominium in California, 1964, the work of Denys Lasdun on universities, Karmi's work in Israel, Decarlo's Urbino work, Utzon's Kingo houses and finally even gets written into the policy for British New Towns such as Washington. See *World Architecture IV*, called *Place and Environment*.

13. *World Architecture III*, op. cit., p. 141.

14. The fact that this sentence turns out to be a tautology is significant because there is no way that one can define historicism, or going too far except *post factum*; it is always 'too far' for certain

critics' and societies' thresholds which are in fact relative, moving things.

15. Of course these archetypal terms are inadequate even to classify the different nations; however, some national classification obviously does exist and that is all I wish to contend. I am thinking of such architects as Valle, Vigano, Albini, DeCarlo, Michelucci, Morandi, Gardella, BBPR, Ponti, Roselli, Portoghesi, Colombo, Castiglioni, Nervi and Moretti in Italy. Just taking this group, it is at once intuitively obvious that they are all very 'Italian', but a careful study would have to establish their common attributes.

16. See *CIAM '59 in Otterlo*, ed. Jürgen Joedicke, Alex Tiranti, London, 1961, p.182.

17. See Chapter 3.

18. See 'Three Critics Discuss MIT's New Buildings', *Architectural Forum*, March 1956, pp. 156-8.

19. See R. Banham, 'Neo-Liberty, etc.', *Architectural Review*, April 1959.

20. See *CIAM '59 in Otterlo*, op. cit., pp. 27, 96, 182, 220.

21. Another indication of the mood at this time is the series of articles by Reyner Banham called 'On Trial', published by the *Architectural Review* during 1962.

22. See *RIBA Journal*, 3rd Series, LXVIII, 1961.

23. Harvey Cox, *The Secular City*, MacMillan & Co., New York, 1965, p. 174.

24. *The Secular City Debate*, ed. Daniel Callahan, MacMillan & Co., New York, 1966. See especially pp. 101-26.

25. See Melvin Webber, 'Order in Diversity: Community without Propinquity', 1963, p. 23, or 'The Urban Place and Non-Place Urban Realm', in *Explorations into Urban Structure*, Pennsylvania, 1964.

26. See Webber, *JTPI*, January 1968, 'The New Urban Planning in America', or for quote M. Broady, 'Social Theory in Architectural Design', *Arena*, January 1966.

27. See *CIAM '59 in Otterlo*, op. cit., p. 190, and Christopher Alexander, 'A City Is Not a Tree', *Design*, February 1966, p. 51.

28. Karl Popper, *The Open Society and its Enemies*, Routledge & Kegan Paul, London, 1966, p. 172.

29. *Architectural Design*, October 1964, p. 479.

30. See *World Architecture II*, op. cit., 1965, p. 117.

31. For instance see Kevin Lynch, 'The Pattern of the Metropolis', in *The Future Metropolis*, Daedalus, Winter 1961. Five ideal-types are compared here.

32. See Le Ricolais, 'The Trihex', *Progressive Architecture*, February 1968, p. 118.

33. See for instance Yona Friedman, 'Towards a Coherent System of Planning', *Architectural Design*, August 1964, p. 371.

34. *Community and Privacy*, Serge Chermayeff and Christopher

Alexander, Doubleday, 1963. The other four key works were *Notes on the Synthesis of Form*, Harvard, 1964, 'From a Set of Forces to a Form' in *The Man Made Object*, ed. G. Kepes, Braziller, 1966, 'A City Is Not a Tree', in *Design*, February 1966, *Houses Generated by Patterns* (with Hirshen and Ishikawa), California, 1969.

35. See p. 194, note 12, loc. cit.

36. Three different models are discussed in 'From a Set of Forces, etc.', op. cit.

37. See *Notes*, op. cit., p. 70.

38. ibid., p. 90.

39. See 'A City Is Not a Tree', op. cit., p. 49.

40. The main difficulties aside from those already mentioned are two: (1) In fact design and nature are radically traditional. They both modify pre-existing traditions (or sub-sets). The designer of the Mach III Stratocruiser does not proceed from scratch any more than nature does. (2) A rational, conscious method of design tends to discourage all the unconscious, delightful and spontaneous parts of creation that give any work its life. Although there may not be any necessary reason why this should be so, it incontestably is so. Where systematic designers try to be witty and frivolous they inevitably become trite and cute – which may have more to do with psychological types than methods. Still the problem exists.

41. See J. K. Galbraith, *The New Industrial State*, Houghton Mifflin, Boston, 1967, particularly Chapters 2 and 18, for the arguments used here.

42. See Andrew Hacker, 'A Country Called Corporate America', in *New York Times Magazine*, 3 July 1966.

43. See Paul Davidoff, 'Advocacy and Pluralism in Planning', *JAIP*, November 1965.

44. Robert Goodman, *After the Planners; Politics and Architecture for Liberation*, Penguin Books, Harmondsworth, 1972, Ch. 7.

45. Besides Bertrand de Jouvenel's group SEIDS there is the 'Commission on the Year 2000', such corporations as Rand, Group 1985, Mankind 2000, Hudson Institute, etc. For a partial bibliography see Stanford Anderson, *Planning for Diversity and Choice*, MIT, 1968, John McHale, *The Future of the Future*, Braziller, 1969, and Charles Jencks, *Architecture 2000, Predictions and Methods*, Studio Vista, London, 1971.

46. See Bertrand de Jouvenel, *The Art of Conjecture*, Basic Books, 1967, p. 284.

47. See Gabriel Bouladon, 'Transport', *Science Journal*, October 1967.

48. For this argument see Dennis Gabor, *Inventing the Future*, London, 1963, and I. C. Jarvie, 'Utopian Thinking and the Architects', in Anderson, op. cit.

49. Paul and Percival Goodman, *Communitas*, Vintage paperbacks, New York, 1960, p. 119 (my italics).

Postscript: Architecture and Revolution

1. For these arguments see Hannah Arendt, *The Human Condition*, Doubleday Anchor Book, New York, 1959, pp. 158 ff.

2. Citizens for Local Democracy, 'What a Democratic New York Would Look Like – a Plan without a Master', *New York Review of Books*, 22 October 1970, p. 27.

3. For a complete development of this idea see Hannah Arendt, *On Revolution*, Viking Press, New York, 1963, the last chapter; for the views of 'professional revolutionists' see Krishan Kumar, *Revolution, The Theory and Practice of a European Idea*, Weidenfeld & Nicolson, London, 1971, pp. 19-24, 121-55.

4. Leon Trotsky, *Our Revolution*, New York, 1918, p. 152.

5. Hannah Arendt, *The Origins of Totalitarianism*, 2nd edition, New York, 1958, p. 500.

6. See Noam Chomsky, 'Notes on Anarchism', *New York Review of Books*, 21 May 1970, pp. 31-5; Daniel and Gabriel Cohn-Bendit, *Obsolete Communism, The Left-Wing Alternative*, Penguin Books, London, 1969; for Hannah Arendt see notes 3 and 5 above.

BIBLIOGRAPHY

For the more particular studies of single architects and national contributions, see the notes to each chapter.

Without question, the three most serious, general histories are: Sigfried Giedion, *Space, Time and Architecture*, Cambridge, Mass., and London, 1941, 5th edition revised and enlarged, 1967; Leonardo Benevolo, *Storia dell'architettura moderna*, 2 vols, Bari, 1960; and Reyner Banham, *Theory and Design in the First Machine Age*, London, 1960. The first and last mentioned are written from relatively opposed viewpoints, disagreeing over the roles of aesthetics and technology, whereas the middle one is more balanced and comprehensive, but less interesting. To fill them out with the views of practising architects, one should read Ulrich Conrads, ed., *Programmes and Manifestoes on 20th-Century Architecture*, Berlin, 1964, London and Cambridge, Mass., 1970, and the soon-to-appear Kenneth Frampton, *A Concise History of Modern Architecture*, London, 1973.

On the descriptive and encyclopedic level, the best sources are: for specific issues, Gerd Hatje, *Encyclopaedia of Modern Architecture*, London, 1963; for photographs, references and bibliography, Jürgen Joedicke, *A History of Modern Architecture*, London, 1959, and his *Architecture Since 1945*, London, 1969; for formal tendencies and fashions see Henry-Russell Hitchcock, *Architecture: Nineteenth and Twentieth Centuries*, London and Baltimore, 1958, and John Jacobus, *Twentieth Century Architecture 1940-65*, London and New York, 1966; for theoretical currents see Bruno Zevi, *Storia dell'architettura moderna*, Turin, 1950, and Peter Collins, *Changing Ideals in Modern Architecture 1750-1950*, London, 1965.

For accounts of specific architectural movements see Nikolaus Pevsner, *Pioneers of the Modern Movement from William Morris to Walter Gropius*, London, 1936, revised and rewritten as *Pioneers of Modern Design*, London, 1960; H. L. C. Jaffé, *De Stijl*, London and Amsterdam, 1956; Ulrich Conrads and Hans G. Sperlich, *Fantastic Architecture*, London, 1962; Oscar Newman, *CIAM 59 in Otterlo*, London and New York, 1961; Reyner Banham, *The New Brutalism; Ethic or Aesthetic?*,

London, 1966; Dennis Sharp, *Modern Architecture and Expressionism*, London, 1966. The all-important influence of Constructivism has finally been brought out in the following works: Camilla Gray, *The Great Experiment: Russian Art, 1863-1922*, London, 1963; Vittorio de Feo, *URSS-architettura 1917-1936*, Rome, 1963; Vieri Quilici, *L'architettura del Costruttivismo*, Bari, 1969 (very good for manifestoes); El Lissitzky, *Russia: An Architecture for World Revolution* (1929), reissued 1970, London and Cambridge, Mass.; Anatole Kopp, *Town and Revolution*, London and New York, 1970.

There are countless books and monographs on specific architects and the recent architecture in each country; for instance the series of George Braziller, New York, 1960, and Studio Vista, London, 1968. For an analysis of the ideological bias of recent histories, see Charles Jencks, 'History as Myth', in *Meaning in Architecture*, ed. Charles Jencks and George Baird, London and New York, 1970.

LIST OF ILLUSTRATIONS

1 Le Corbusier: Unité d'Habitation, Marseilles, France, 1947–52, explanatory section and elevation (Artemis Verlag, Zurich). 2 Unité d'Habitation, east façade (Charles Jencks). 3 Unité d'Habitation, section and plan (Artemis Verlag, Zurich). 4 Unité d'Habitation, roofscape (Charles Jencks). 5 Unité d'Habitation, window-seat-table (Artemis Verlag). 6 Frederick Gibberd: Liverpool Cathedral, 1960–67 (Elsam Mann & Cooper). 7 Liverpool Cathedral, cut-away perspective and ground plan (Tony Lofthouse). 8 Liverpool Cathedral, aluminium baldachin (Snoek). 9 Liverpool Cathedral, entrance and bell-porch (Snoek).

10 Le Corbusier: Unité d'Habitation, west façade (French Government Tourist Office). 11 Evolutionary Tree, 1920–70 (Charles Jencks, Studio Vista). 12 Theo Van Doesburg: L'Aubette Cafe, Strasbourg, 1927 (van den Bichelaer). 13 Le Corbusier: A Contemporary City of 3 Million, City Centre, 1922 (Artemis Verlag, Zurich). 14 Le Corbusier: Freehold Maisonettes, 1922 (Artemis Verlag, Zurich). 15 Ernst May: Bruchfeldstrasse low cost apartments, Frankfurt, 1926–8 (Langewiesche-Köster). 16 Mies van der Rohe: Monument to Karl Liebknecht and Rosa Luxemburg, Berlin, 1926 (Hedrich-Blessing). 17 Skidmore, Owings & Merrill: Lever Brothers Building, New York City, 1951/2 (Charles Jencks). 18 View down Park Avenue, New York City, 1970 (Charles Jencks). 19 James Stirling: St Andrews Residence, Scotland, 1964–9 (Richard Einzig).

20 Mies van der Rohe: Reichsbank Elevation, 1933. 21a Guerrini, Lapadula & Romano: Palace of Italian Civilization, EUR, Rome, 1942 (Italian State Tourist Office). 21b Gio Ponti: Pirelli Building, Milan, 1961. 21c Alberto Rosselli: Light-scraper Project, 1965. 22 Moscow, Palace of the Congresses, 1961 (Novosti Press Agency). 23 Hans Hollein: Projects, Vienna (Hans Hollein). 24 Archizoom: Dream Bed, 'Presage of Roses', Florence, 1968 (Archizoom). 25 Hans Hollein: Aircraft Carrier in the Austrian Wheatfields, 1964 (Hans Hollein), 26 Haus Rucker Co.: Pulsating Yellow Heart, Vienna, 1968 (Haus Rucker Inc). 27 Superstudio: The Continuous Monument, Arizona Desert,

1969 (Superstudio). **28** Ricardo Bolfill and Partners: Xanadu, Calpe, Spain, 1967 (Deidi von Schaewen). **29** Bruno Taut: Design for a Community Centre, 1918.

30 Frei Otto: German Pavilion, Expo 67, Montreal (German Embassy). **31** Felix Candela: Church of the Miraculous Virgin, Mexico City, 1954 (Handisyde). **32** Hans Scharoun: Philharmonic Hall, Berlin, 1956–63 (Reinhard Friedrich and JLSE Buhs). **33** Jorn Utzon: Sydney Opera House, Australia, 1957– (Australian News and Information Bureau). **34** Kenzo Tange: Theme Pavilion, Expo 70, Osaka (Masao Arai). **35a** Kiyonari Kikutake: Landmark Tower, Expo 70, Osaka (Taisuke Ogawa). **35b** Peter Cook: Montreal Tower Project, 1964. **36** Kisho Kurokawa: Takara Beautilion, Expo 70, Osaka (Tomio Ohashi). **37** Buckminster Fuller: Union Tank Car Company, Louisiana, 1958 (USIS). **38** Pier Luigi Nervi: Palazetto dello Sport, Rome, 1958–9 (Italian State Tourist Office). **39** Ezra Ehrenkrantz: SCSD, 1964 (SCSD).

40 Russian pre-fabricated dwellings, 1965 (Novosti Press Agency). **41** Matthew, Johnson-Marshall: University of York, 1965 (De Burgh Galway and Architectural Press). **42** Ezra Ehrenkrantz & BSD: Fibershell Kit-of-Parts, 1970 (SCSD). **43** Vladimir Tatlin: Monument to the Third International, 1919–20. **44** Alexander, Leonid and Victor Vesnin: Palace of Labour, 1923. **45** Moses Ginzburg and I. Milinis: Narkomfim Communal House, Moscow, 1928–9. **46** Drop City, Arizona, 1966 (Drop City). **47** Barriada, Peru (John Turner). **48** J. P. Jungman: Dyoden, 1968 (J. P. Jungman). **49** Mies van der Rohe: Lafayette Park, Detroit, 1955–63 (Artemis Verlag).

50 Mies van der Rohe: Seagram Building, New York City, 1958, external corner (Charles Jencks). **51** Mies van der Rohe: Lafayette Towers and Court Houses, Detroit, 1955–63 (Hedrich-Blessing). **52** Mies van der Rohe: Gallery of the Twentieth Century, Berlin, 1962–8 (Hedrich-Blessing). **53** Mies van der Rohe: Seagram Building, with Philip Johnson, New York City, 1958 (Charles Jencks). **54** Seagram Building, internal corner (Charles Jencks). **55** Mies van der Rohe: Farnsworth House, Fox River, Illinois, 1945–50 (S. Mintz). **56** Farnsworth House, entrance (Hedrich-Blessing). **57** Mies van der Rohe: Crown Hall, IIT, Chicago, 1962 (USIS). **58** Mies van der Rohe: Barcelona Pavilion, 1929, cruciform column (Hedrich-Blessing). **59** Walter Gropius, with TAC: Baghdad University, 1958, central area and auditorium (TAC).

60 Frank Lloyd Wright: Grady Gammage Memorial Auditorium, Tempe, Arizona, 1959–66 (Photographic Service, Arizona State University). **61** Walter Gropius: Monument to the March Dead, Weimar, Germany, 1921–2 (Bauhaus Archiv). **62** Walter Gropius with Adolf Meyer, 1922–3: Mass-production Housing (Bauhaus Archiv). **63** El Lissitzky: Lenin Tribune,

1920. **64** Walter Gropius with Marcel Breuer: Chamberlain House, Weyland, Massachusetts, 1939 (TAC). **65** Walter Gropius with TAC: Pan Am Building, New York, 1958 (Charles Jencks). **66** Walter Gropius with TAC: Temple of Oheb Shalom, Baltimore, Maryland, 1957 (Louis Reens). **67** Walter Gropius: Baghdad Mosque (TAC). **68** Frank Lloyd Wright: Grady Gammage Memorial Auditorium, Tempe, Arizona, 1959–66 (Photographic Service, Arizona State University). **69** Frank Lloyd Wright: Froebel Constructions, after Grant Manson (Grant Manson).

70 Frank Lloyd Wright: Unity Church, Oak Park, Illinois, 1906, lighting fixture and balcony (S. Myers). **71** Frank Lloyd Wright: Midway Gardens, Chicago, 1914–18 (F. R. Yerbury). **72** Frank Lloyd Wright: Hollyhock House, Los Angeles, 1916–20 (John Winter). **73,74** Frank Lloyd Wright: Price Tower, Bartlesville, Oklahoma, 1953–5 (Joe D. Price). **75** Price Tower, plan (Joe D. Price). **76** Price Tower, angular furniture (Joe D. Price). **77** Frank Lloyd Wright: typical Usonian house, Okemos, Michigan, 1939. **78** Frank Lloyd Wright: Johnson Wax Building, Racine, Wisconsin, 1938 (USIS). **79** Johnson Wax Building, pyrex glass tubing (John Winter).

80 Johnson Wax Building, Laboratory Tower, 1950 (John Winter). **81** Frank Lloyd Wright: Guggenheim Museum, New York City, 1943–59 (Guggenheim Museum). **82** Frank Lloyd Wright: Marin County Civic Center, San Rafael, California, 1959–64 (Thom Jestico). **83** Le Corbusier, sketch. **84** Le Corbusier: illustration of Purisme from *L'Esprit Nouveau*. **85** Le Corbusier: Ville Radieuse, 1930–38 (Artemis Verlag). **86** Le Corbusier: Plan Voisin, Paris, 1925 (Artemis Verlag). **87** Le Corbusier: Ronchamp, painting (Lucien Hervé). **88** Ronchamp, France, from the south-east (French Government Tourist Office). **89** Ronchamp, axonometric (Artemis Verlag).

90 Ronchamp, interior (French Government Tourist Office). **91** Le Corbusier: Chandigarh, India, Court of Justice, 1956 (Information Service of India). **92** Chandigarh, section of the two assemblies (Artemis Verlag). **93** Chandigarh, south-west façade (Information Service of India). **94** Chandigarh, interior of Assembly Building (Lucien Hervé). **95** Chandigarh, acropolis planning (Artemis Verlag). **96** Chandigarh, sign of the open hand (Artemis Verlag). **97** Le Corbusier: Venice Hospital, 1965 (Artemis Verlag). **98** Le Corbusier: Le Corbusier Centre, Zurich, 1965–8 (Charles Jencks). **99** Le Corbusier Centre, interior (Charles Jencks).

100 Henry Van de Velde: Werkebund Theatre, Cologne, 1914. **101** Alvar Aalto: Viipuri Library, Viipuri, Finland, 1927–35 (Museum of Finnish Architecture). **102** Alvar Aalto: Wolfsburg Cultural Centre, Wolfsburg, Germany, 1959–62, main entrance (Museum of Finnish Architecture). **103** Wolfsburg Cultural

Centre, plan (Museum of Finnish Architecture). **104** Wolfsburg
Cultural Centre, elevation (H. Heidersberger). **105** Wolfsburg
Cultural Centre, aerial view (Museum of Finnish Architecture).
106 Alvar Aalto: Säynätsalo Town Hall, Säynätsalo, Finland,
(Museum of Finnish Architecture). **107** Säynätsalo Town Hall,
doorway (Museum of Finnish Architecture). **108** Säynätsalo
Town Hall, struts (Museum of Finnish Architecture). **109** Alvar
Aalto, Imatra Church, Imatra, Finland, 1957-9 (Museum of
Finnish Architecture).

110 Imatra Church, view towards altar (Museum of Finnish
Architecture). **111** Imatra Church, acoustic model (Museum of
Finnish Architecture). **112** Alvar Aalto: Pensions Bank, Helsinki,
Finland, 1952-6 (Museum of Finnish Architecture). **113** Imatra
Church, exterior (Museum of Finnish Architecture). **114** Imatra
Church, juncture (Museum of Finnish Architecture). **115a**
Albert Speer: Zeppelinfeld, Nürnberg, Germany, 1934 (Library
of Congress). **115b** Lincoln Cultural Center, New York City
(Charles Jencks). **116** Numerical taxonomy (Charles Jencks).
117 Paul Rudolph: Arts and Architecture Building, New
Haven, 1963 (USIS). **118** Edward Durrell Stone: John F.
Kennedy Center, Washington, first model, 1964 (USIS).
119a Bruce Goff: Bavinger House, Norman, Oklahoma, 1957
(Timothy Street-Porter). **119b** Herbert Greene: Prairie House,
Norman, Oklahoma, 1961 (Timothy Street-Porter). **119c** Paolo
Soleri and Mills: Desert House, Cave Creek, Arizona, 1951
(Julius Schulman).

120 Minoru Yamasaki: Consolidated Gas Building, Detroit,
1964 (Balthazar Korab). **121** Eero Saarinen: TWA Building,
Jamaica, New York, 1956-62 (USIS). **122** Eero Saarinen: Dulles
Airport, Chantilly, Washington, DC, 1964 (USIS). **123** Harrison
& Abramovitz: Alcoa Building, Pittsburgh, 1955 (USIS).
124 SOM, Air Force Academy, Colorado Springs, 1957-62
(USIS). **125** John M. Johansen: Clark University Library,
Worcester, Massachusetts, 1966-9 (Louis Checkman and George
Cserna). **126** Philip Johnson: Glass House, New Canaan,
Connecticut (Roy Summers). **127** Philip Johnson: New Har-
mony Church, New Harmony, Indiana, 1960 (Ezra Stoller).
128 Andy Warhol: Campbell Soup Can, 1964. **129** Buckminster
Fuller: Wichita House, Kansas, 1946 (Buckminster Fuller).

130 Charles and Ray Eames: Eames House, Los Angeles, 1949
(Charles Eames). **131** Pierre Koenig: Case Study House 22,
Hollywood Hills, 1959 (Julius Schulman). **132** Vehicle Assembly
Building, Cape Kennedy, Florida, 1964, and SOM, Solar
Telescope, Kitts Peak, Arizona, 1965 (USIS and SOM). **133**
Robert Venturi: Chestnut Hill House, Pennsylvania, 1965
(Rollin R. La France). **134** Robert Venturi: Football Hall of
Fame, 1968 (George Pohl). **135** Robert Venturi: Lieb House,
Long Beach Island, New Jersey, 1966-9 (Stephen Hill).

136 Charles Moore and William Turnbull: Faculty Club interior, University of California, 1968 (Morley Baer). 137 Sert, Jackson, Gourley and Associates, Boston University Tower, 1965 (USIS). 138 Sert, Jackson, Gourley and Associates: Holyoke Center, Cambridge, Massachusetts, 1963 (Charles Jencks). 139 Kallmann, McKinnell & Knowles: Boston City Hall, 1964-9 (Charles Jencks).

140 Louis Kahn: Medical Research Building, Philadelphia, 1961-8 (USIS). 141 Louis Kahn: Trenton Bath House, Trenton, New Jersey, 1958 (John Ebstel). 142 Louis Kahn: Salk Institute, Laboratories, La Jolla, California, 1965 (USIS). 143 Louis Kahn: Axonometric of Servant and Served (Louis Kahn). 144 Louis Kahn: First Unitarian Church, Rochester, New York, 1964 (USIS). 145 Louis Kahn: Axonometric of light hoods (Louis Kahn). 146 Louis Kahn: Dacca Assembly Building, Bangla Desh, 1962- (Su King). 147a Reyner Banham and François Dallegret in their Un-house, 1965 (Reyner Banham). 147b Richard Hamilton: Hommage à Chrysler Corp., 1957 (Richard Hamilton). 148 Robert Matthew and others in the LCC Architects Department: Royal Festival Hall, London, 1951 (E. R. Jarrett). 149 Foster Associates: Computer Technology Ltd. Office, London, 1970 (John Donat).

150 LCC Architects Department: Alton East Housing, Roehampton, London, 1953-6 (Gregory Jones). 151 Chamberlin Powell & Bonn: New Hall, Cambridge, 1966 (Charles Jencks). 152 Alison and Peter Smithson: Hunstanton School, Hunstanton, 1949-54 (Robert Vickery). 153 Mies van der Rohe: Alumni Memorial Hall, Chicago, 1947 (Hedrich-Blessing). 154 John Weeks and Llewelyn-Davies: Northwick Park Hospital, London, 1961-70 (Weeks and Davies). 155 Leslie Martin, Colin St John Wilson and Patrick Hodgkinson: Hostel for Caius College, Cambridge, 1962 (John Donat). 156 Peter and Alison Smithson: Golden Lane Competition, 1952 (A. and P. Smithson). 157 Lynn, Smith and Nicklin under Wormersley: Park Hill, Sheffield, 1961 (Jane Beckett). 158 Stirling and Gowan: Leicester Engineering Building, Leicester, 1964 (Richard Einzig). 159 James Stirling: Four axonometrics and a Lunar spacecraft (James Stirling).

160 James Stirling: Cambridge University History Faculty, 1968 (Richard Einzig). 161 James Stirling: Florey Building, Oxford, 1966-71. 162 Alison and Peter Smithson: Sheffield Scheme, 1953 (A. and P. Smithson). 163 Peter and Alison Smithson: House of the Future, 1956 (A. and P. Smithson). 164 Richard Hamilton: This Is Tomorrow, 1956 (Sam Lambert). 165 Michael Webb: Furniture Manufacturers Building, 1959 (Archigram). 166 Michael Webb: Sin Centre, 1962 (Archigram). 167 Cedric Price with Lord Snowdon and Frank Newby: Bird Cage, London, 1961-2 (Sam Lambert). 168,169 Cedric Price: Potteries Thinkbelt, 1966 (Cedric Price).

170 Archigram: Living City Exhibition, 1963 (Archigram).
171 Archigram Projects (Archigram). 172 Archigram 7, 1966
(Archigram). 173 Peter Cook: Control and Choice, 1967
(Archigram). 174 Archigram: Instant City, 1969 (Archigram).
175 Archigram: Monte Carlo Entertainments Building, 1969–
(Archigram). 176 Ray Affleck and Partners: Place Bonaventure,
Montreal, 1962–6 (Chris Payne). 177 Lucio Costa: Brasilia,
1956, plan, and Oscar Niemeyer: Brasilia, Government Build-
ings, 1956–60 (Brazilian Embassy). 178 Van den Broek and
Bakema: Project for Kennemerland, 1959 (J. B. Bakema).
179 Van den Broek and Bakema: Marl Town Hall, Marl,
Germany, 1964–9 (Stadt Marl).

180 Alison and Peter Smithson: Berlin – Hauptstadt Scheme,
1958 (A. & P. Smithson). 181 Affonso Eduardo Reidy: Pedre-
gulho Estate, Rio de Janeiro, 1947–53 (Brazilian Embassy).
182 Maki and Ohtaka: Shinjuku Project (F. Maki). 183 Aldo van
Eyck: Children's Home, Amsterdam, 1958–60 (P. G. Goede).
184 Children's Home, pavilions (J. J. van der Meyden). 185
Children's Home, plan (KLM). 186 Aldo van Eyck: Arnheim
Pavilion, 1966 (Koen Wessing). 187 Herman Hertzberger:
Factory Extension, Amsterdam, 1964 (Jan Vershel). 188
Kiyonori Kikutake: Miyakonojo Civic Centre, Japan, 1965–6
(T. Oyama). 189 Kenzo Tange: Kurashiki City Hall, Japan,
1958–60 (Fumio Murasawa).

190 Arata Isozaki: Clusters in the air, 1962 (A. Isozaki).
191 Franco Albini and Franca Helg: Rinascente Department
Store, Rome, 1957–62 (Oscar Sario). 192 BBPR: Torre Velasca,
Milan, 1957 (Italian State Tourist Office). 193 Guy Debord:
Situationist Map of Paris, 1961 (Guy Debord). 194 Alison and
Peter Smithson: Soho Route Building and Road Net, 1959 (A.
and P. Smithson). 195 Louis Kahn: Existing and proposed
Philadelphia Movement patterns, 1952 (Louis I. Kahn).
196 Richards and Chalk: Interchange, 1966 (Sandra Lousada).
197 Brian Richards: Comparative Anatomy of Movement Sys-
tems, 1966 (Brian Richards). 198 Christopher Alexander: Ideal
type street pattern (C. Alexander). 199 Frank Lloyd Wright:
Broadacre City, 1934 (Roy E. Peterson).

200a Kenzo Tange and the Metabolist Team: Tokyo Bay
Plan, 1960 (Osamu Murai). 200b Kenzo Tange: Yamanashi
Press Centre, Konju, Japan, 1967 (Osamu Murai). 201 Kenzo
Tange: Tokyo Bay Plan (K. Tange). 202 Candilis, Josic and
Woods: Toulouse-le-Mirail, France, 1961 (Yan). 203 John
Andrews: Scarborough College, Toronto, 1964–6 (John
Andrews). 204 Candilis, Josic and Woods: Free University of
Berlin, 1963–   (Nina von Jaanson). 205 Colin Buchanan:
Directional Grid, 1966 (C. Buchanan). 206 Lionel March:
Parameters of Form, 1967 (L. March). 207 Le Ricolais: Trihex,
1968 (Le Ricolais). 208 Yona Friedman: Spatial City, 1961 (Y.

Friedman). **209** Wimmenauer, Szabo, Kasper & Meyer: City Superstructure above Dusseldorf, model, 1969 (K. Wimmenauer).

210 Christopher Alexander: Form Diagram for an Indian village, 1962 (C. Alexander). **211** Hugh Wilson and others: Cumbernauld New Town, Scotland, centre, 1956– (Cumbernauld Development Corporation). **212** Christopher Alexander: Semi-lattice and Tree (C. Alexander). **213** Christopher Alexander and Centre for Environmental Structure: Generic plans for a barriada house, Peru, 1969 (C. Alexander). **214** Consumer democracy (Charles Jencks). **215** Delphi Technique, 1967 (*Sunday Times*). **216** Gabriel Bouladon: Transfer System Network for the Future, 1967 (G. Bouladon). **217** Gabriel Bouladon: Car of the Future (G. Bouladon). **218** Systems analysis (*Scientific American*). **219** Archigram: Future Possibilities (Archigram).

220 Paul and Percival Goodman: A New Community, 1947–60 (P. and P. Goodman). **221** Vesnin Brothers: Project for the Pravda Building, 1923 (Arts Council). **222** Citizens for Local Democracy: 'What a Democratic New York would look like', 1970 (Citizens for Local Democracy). **223** Action Committee, Sorbonne, Paris, May 1968 (Jean Guyaux).

INDEX

References in **bold** type
indicate whole chapters or sections,
those in *italic* indicate
illustrations and/or captions thereto.

mutualism, 59, 92, 180
Mycenae, 236

Nairn, Ian (critic), 247
Narkomfim Communal House, Moscow (Ginzburg and Milinis, 1928–9), *44, 86, 87,* 373
national characteristics, 320
Nazi: architecture, 46; Villas, 208, *208*
Nazis and Nazism, 40, 47, 48, 106, 113, 119, 185, *185,* 206, 208, 333
Nebraska Art Gallery (Johnson), 208
Neo-Classicism, 186, 325
Neo-Expressionists, 153
Neo-Gothic work, 325
Neo-Liberty, 325, 326 *bis*
Neo-Marxists, 288
Neo-Platonism, 250
'Neos', various other, 328
Nervi, Pier Luigi (structural engineer), 63, 73, 74, 186, 384; *quoted,* 73; Palazzetto dello Sport, Rome (1958–9), *74,* 373
'Net, the', 336, 343
Neutra, Richard, 212, 214
New Academicism, 250
New Bauhaus, Ulm, Germany (*see also* Bauhaus), 75
New Brutalism (*see also* Brutalism), 42, 239, 250, 251, 256–9
New Brutalism, The, 392
New Canaan, Connecticut: Glass House (P. Johnson, c. 1949), 206–7, *207*
New Community, A (P. and P. Goodman): The Elimination of the Difference between Production and Consumption (1947–60), 369, *370*
New Criticism, 34
'New Empiricism, The', 239, 247, 250
New England (Eastern states of USA), *119*
New Hall for Girls at Cambridge, England (Chamberlain, Powell and Bonn, 1966), 249, *249*
New Harmony Church, New Harmony, Indiana (Johnson, 1960), *208*
New Haven, Connecticut: Art and Architecture Building (Rudolph, 1963), 153, 190–91, *191*
'New Humanism, The', 247

New Left, 75, 81, 361
New Palladianism and New Palladians, 249–52, 255, 256, 273
'New Style', the, 117
New Towns, 76, 242, 287, 300, 303, 355; in Britain, 77, 242, 243 *bis,* 245 *bis, 355*
'New Unity' (Gropius), 113 *bis,* 117, 118
New York City: Guggenheim Museum (Wright, 1943–59), 133, 136–7, *136, 137,* 372; Lever Building (House), Park Avenue (SOM, 1951/52), 41–2, *41,* 200; Lincoln Cultural Center (Johnson, Harrison and Ambrovitz), 184, 204, 206, 372; Pan-Am Building (Gropius with TAC, 1958), 120, *120;* paternalism inappropriate in, 181; Pepsi-Cola and Seagram Building (Mies van der Rohe, 1958), 42 *97,* 100, *100, 101, 102,* 102, 200; Park Avenue, 42 (view down, in 1970, *42);* World's Fair (1964), 58
New York State Theatre (Johson, 208
Niemeyer, Oscar, 20, 50; his cathedral in Brasilia, 21; Government Buildings, Brasilia, 153, *305*
Nietzsche (*The Birth of Tragedy*): *quoted, 141*
1984 (Orwell), 363
'No-place' (Utopia), 331–2
Non-Camp architecture (*see also* Camp), 198, *199,* 212, 218–37
Non-Place, Forward, to, **328–32**
Non-Pop architecture, **242–55**
Non-Pop to Pop, **255–70**
Norbury-Schultz, Christian, 319
Norman, Oklahoma: Bavinger House (Goff, 1957), *193,* 193–4; Prairie House (Greene, 1961), *194*
Northwick Park Hospital, London (Llewelyn-Davies and Weeks, 1961–70), 253–4, *253*
Notes on the Synthesis of Form (Alexander), 352–3
Nottingham School of Architecture, 282
Novembergruppe, 60
Nowicki, Matthew, 212
numerical taxonomy, 187
Nürnberg, Germany: Zeppelinfeld (Speer, 1934), *184*

Pei, I. M., 122, 190
'People's Detailing', *245*, 245, 264
Pepsi-Cola and Seagram Building, New York (Mies van der Rohe, 1958), 42, 97, 100, *100*, *101*, *102*, 200
Perpetual Savings and Loan Association, USA (Stone, Ed., 1961), 185
Perret, Auguste, 20, 46, *84*
'personal choice and impersonal science', 148
personality cult, 191
Perspecta 7 (Yale journal), 204
Peru: Barriada (outside Lima) squatter town, *91*; *barriadas*, 91–2
Pevsner, Nikolaus, 11–12, 49, 84, 153, 274, 328, 381, 383; *quoted*, 12, 49
Phalanstère (Fourier), 15
Philadelphia, USA: Medical Research Building (Kahn, 1961–68), 230, *230*, 231, 232, 233; Movement Patterns, existing and proposed (Kahn, 1952), *335*, 336
Philosophes, Les (in France), 380
Picasso, Pablo, 124
Pichler, Walter: *quoted*, 55
picturesque, 243, 246, 247
'Picturesque Theory', 247
Pioneers of Modern Design (Pevsner), 11, 12
Pirelli Building, Milan (Gio Ponti, 1961), *49*, 50
Pittsburgh, USA: Alcoa Building (Harrison and Abramovitz, 1955), 200, *201*
'place', 258, 284, 287, 311, 313, 316, 393
Place Bonaventure, Montreal (Ray Affleck and Partners, 1962–66), *303*
Place – Non-Place, 301–2, 332
Place to Space, From, 301–2; and Back to Place, **302–18**
planners' 'categories', 304–5
planning for the future (*see also* forecasting), 358
Plato, 'the old bore', 246, 252
Platonism and Platonists, 31, 44, 95–6 *passim*, 97, 100, *102*, 103, 105 *ter*, 146, 210, 232, 255 *bis*, 259, 263, 273, 280, 333; Academic, 252–5; Neo-, 250
Playboy: Architecture, 326; Club, 120
Plug-In-City (Peter Cook, 1965), 68, *280*, 291; Medium Pressure Area (Cook, 1964), *290*

pluralism, 13, 31, 204, 222, 298
Plurality of approaches, **11–27**
pneumatic architecture, 93–4, *93*, 185
'Pneumatic Logic Tube Train', 365
Poelzig, 62, 365
Poem to the Right Angle (Le Corbusier, 1955), 146, 158; *quoted*, 146
poetry, 34
political compromise, 48
politicians (*see also* politics and architecture), 72–3
politics and architecture (*see also* Traditions, the Six), 29, 30–31, 45, 67, 72–3, 75, 94, 204, 213, 243, 250, 272, 280, 292, 298, 309, 343, 367, 373, 375; radical, 361
'Politics of Architecture, The' (Anthony Jackson), 391
politics of the apolitical, 40
Pollock, 256
polycentralism, 334–9, 344
Ponti, Gio, 50, 58, 186, 383; Pirelli Building, Milan (1961), *49*, 50; *quoted*, 50
Pop Art, 218, 272–3
Pop movement in England, 13, 27, 247, 256, 270–99
Pop – Non-Pop architecture, 239–98
Pop paintings, 209, 273
Pop-theorists, 248
Popper, Karl, 106, 299, 362, 370, 385, 388, 391, 394
popular clubs and societies in France (1793 & 1848), 377
'Post-Industrial Society', 73
Potteries Thinkbelt (Price, 1966), *285*, *286*, 286–8
Poverty of Historicism, The (Popper), 333
pragmatism and pragmatists, 37, 40 *bis*, 47, 48, 50, 105, 113, 114, 118, 123, 151, 186, 187, 200 *bis*, 203, 212
Prairie House, Norman, Oklahoma (Greene, 1961), *194*
Pravda Building project, Russia (Vesnin brothers, 1923–4), 84, 373, *374*
'precedents (not principles)', 246
predicting future developments, 362–70; methods of, 363
pre-fabrication, Russian, 76–7
'preform', 228, 230, 234
'Presage of Roses' Dream Bed, Florence (Archizoom, 1968), 52, *54*

Rosselli, Alberto: Lightscraper Project (1965), *49*

Roth, Alfred, 147-8

Rousseau, Jean-Jacques, 375, 376

route buildings, 336

Route One, 79

Route One City, Florida, 349

Rowe, Colin (historian), 249, 250 *bis*, 254, 260 *ter*

Royal College of Art, 259-60

Royal Festival Hall, London (Matthew and others, 1951), *242*

Royal Institute of British Architects (RIBA), 243

Rudolph, Paul, 122, 189, 190-1, 194, 204, 222, 325; *quoted*, 108, 189-90, 190 *bis*; Art and Architecture Building, New Haven, Conn. (1963), 153, 190-1, *191*

Rudow-Buckow Housing, 120

Russia: Constructivism in, 32, 34, 35; Communal House in, 35; housing units, mass-produced large-scale (1965), 76-7, *77*; New Towns, 77-8; state capitalists in, 88; post-revolutionary, 269, 373; Marxist, 333; 1905 Soviet in, 378; symbolic rituals, 380; Cubo-Futurists, 380; Pravda Building project (Vesnin brothers, 1923-24), 84, 373, *374*; Palace of Labour (Vesnin brothers, 1923), 84 *bis*, *85*, 373

Russian Revolution (the 'October' Revolution, Nov. 1917), 81 *bis*, 83, 115, 379

Ruzhnikov, Evgeny, 384

Rykwert, Joseph, 391

SCSD (Schools Construction System Development), 75-6, 79; (Ehrenkrantz, 1964), *75*

SOM (Skidmore, Owings and Merrill): Air Force Academy, Colorado Springs (1957-62), 202, *202*; Solar Telescope, Kitts Park, Arizona (1965), *217*; Lever Brothers Building, New York (1951/52), 41-2, *41* 200

Saarinen, Eero, 197-8; *quoted*, 197; TWA Building, Jamaica, New York State (1956-62), 197, *197*, *198*; Dulles Airport, Chantilly, Washington,

DC (1964), 197-8, *199*; MIT work of, 322

St Andrews Residence, Scotland (Stirling, 1964-9), 44, *44*, *45*, *266*, 269

St Die, 15

St Paul's Cathedral, London, 261

St Peter's, Rome, 192

Saint-Simon's Parable (1832), 72

Salk Institute Laboratories, La Jolla, California (Kahn, 1965), 231-2, *232*, *233*, 233

San Rafael, California: Marin County Civic Center (Wright, 1959-63), 133, 138-9, *139*

Sandys, Duncan, 243, 244

Sant'Elia, 12, 367

'satisfice' and 'satisficing', 358-9

Saugnier (Ozenfant, *q.v.*), 143, 144

Säynätsalo Town Hall, Finland (Aalto, 1950), 172-5, *173 bis*, *174*, *175*, 181

scale, 226

Scandinavian countries: paternalism and social responsibility, 180-81

Scarborough College, Toronto (Andrews, 1964-66), *343*

'Scenario', 365

Scharoun, Hans, 64, 66; Berlin Philharmonic Hall (1956-63), 64, *64*, *65*; *quoted*, 64-5

Schawinsky, 118

Schinkel, 206

schizophrenia, 233

Schlemmer, Oskar, 118, 123; *letters quoted*, 116, 117

Schnaidt, Claude, 384

school building (*see also* SCSD), 76, 78

Schools Construction System Development, *see* SCSD

Schultze-Naumburg, Paul, 46, 47, 383; *quoted*, 46-7

'science fiction' and 'science fact', 278

Scotland: St Andrews Residence (Stirling, 1964-9), 44, *44*, *45*

Scully, Vincent (critic), 189, 390; *quoted*, 189

Seagram, 50

Seagram Building, New York (Mies van der Rohe, 1958), 42, *97*, 100, *100*, *101*, *102*, 102

Secular City, The (Harvey Cox, 1965), 328-9; characteristics of, 329

and Froebel blocks and Constructions, 125, *125*, 126; Unity Church (interior), Oak Road, Illinois (1906), 126, *127*; Midway Gardens, Chicago (1914-18), *127*; Hollyhock House, Los Angeles (1916-20), 128, *128*; St Mark's Tower, 128; Price Tower, Barlesville, Oklahoma (1953-5), 128, *129*, 130, *130* (angular furniture in, 130, *131*); Taliesin West (1938), 131; Unitarian Church (1949), 131; and the circle, 131, 133-4, 136-9; his low-cost houses, 131-2; Usonian Houses (1930s & 1940s), 132, *132*; Johnson Wax Building, Racine, Wisconsin (1936-9 & 1950), 133-5, *133*, *134*, *135*; Second Jacob's House, 133; Guggenheim Museum, New York (1943-59), 133, 136-7, *136*, *137*, 372; Huntington Hartford Play Resort (1947), 133; Marin County Civic Center, San Rafael, Cal. (1959), 133, 138-9, *139*; and rugged individualistic millionaires, 135-6; his later projects, 137-8; in his eighties, 138-9; summary, 140; attack on clichés, 248; and 'deflowered classicism', 248

Wright, Iovanna Lloyd, 387

Xanadu Calpe, Spain (Bofill and Partners, 1967), *57*

Yale University, USA, 189 *bis*, 191, 222; Stiles and Morse Dormitories (Saarnen), 198 Kline Center (Johnson), 208

Yamanashi Press Centre, Konju, Japan (Tange, 1967), *341*

Yamasaki, Minoru, 50, 325, 327; quoted, *196*; Consolidated Gas Building, Detroit (1964), 194, *196*

Yippies, 361

York, University of (Matthew, Johnson-Marshall, 1965), *78*

'Young Towns' (*barriadas*, *q.v.*) in Peru, 92

'*Zeitgeist*', 13, 32, 50, 51 *bis*, 106, 107, 113, 114, 120

Zeppelinfeld, Nürnberg, Germany (Speer, 1934), *184*

Zetkin, Klara, 384

Zevi, Bruno, 116, 325, 386

Zurich: Café Voltaire, 83